D0919218

God
in the Teachings of
Conservative Judaism

Edited by
SEYMOUR SIEGEL
and
ELLIOT GERTEL

JACK WALDMAN MEMORIAL LIBRARY
BETH EMETH SYNAGOGUE
DOWNSVIEW

4050

THE RABBINICAL ASSEMBLY
NEW YORK

אמת ואמונה
EMET VE'EMUNAH

STUDIES IN
CONSERVATIVE JEWISH THOUGHT

VOLUME III

God
in the Teachings of
Conservative Judaism

Edited by
SEYMOUR SIEGEL
and
ELLIOT GERTEL

JACK WALDMAN MEMORIAL LIBRARY
BETH EMETH SYNAGOGUE
DOWNSVIEW

THE RABBINICAL ASSEMBLY
NEW YORK

NEW MATTER
COPYRIGHT © 1985
THE RABBINICAL ASSEMBLY

Library of Congress Cataloging in Publication Data
Main entry under title:

God in the teachings of Conservative Judaism.

(Emet ve'emunah : studies in Conservative Jewish
thought ; v. 3)
Bibliography: p.
Includes index.
1. God (Judaism)—Addresses, essays, lectures.
2. Conservative Judaism—Addresses, essays, lectures.
I. Siegel, Seymour. II. Gertel, Elliot. III. Series:
Emmet ve'emunah ; v. 3.
BM610.G57   1985   296.3'11   84-26435
ISBN 0-88125-066-X

Distributed by
KTAV PUBLISHING HOUSE, INC.
900 JEFFERSON STREET
HOBOKEN, NEW JERSEY 07030
Manufactured in the United States of America

Contents

ACKNOWLEDGMENTS		vii
CONTRIBUTORS		ix
PREFACE		1
Elliot B. Gertel		
INTRODUCTION		3
Seymour Siegel		
I.	The Idea of God	10
	Jacob B. Agus	
II.	How Shall Modern Man Think About God?	22
	Ben Zion Bokser	
III.	Two Ways to Approach God	30
	Elliot N. Dorff	
IV.	Perceiving God's Providence	42
	Elliot B. Gertel	
V.	Evil in God's World	58
	Robert Gordis	
VI.	God and Man	86
	Simon Greenberg	
VII.	On Proving God's Existence	96
	Monford Harris	
VIII.	The "God-Idea" and the Living God	102
	Will Herberg	
IX.	The Divine Pathos	114
	Abraham J. Heschel	
X.	Faith and Trust	124
	Louis Jacobs	
XI.	How Man Comes to Know God	136
	Mordecai M. Kaplan	
XII.	God as the Whole	150
	Jacob Kohn	
XIII.	The Development of the God-Idea	160
	Israel H. Levinthal	
XIV.	God and the World: A Jewish View	170
	Yochanan Muffs	

XV. Are Philosophical Proofs of the Existence of God
    Theologically Meaningful?   188
    David Novak
XVI. The Concept of God in Jewish Education   202
    Fritz A. Rothschild
XVII. The Symbols of Judaism and the Death of God   222
    Richard L. Rubenstein
XVIII. From God to Godliness: Proposal for a Predicate
    Theology   236
    Harold M. Schulweis
XIX. Theological Reflections on the Destruction of
    European Jewry   250
    Seymour Siegel
XX. The Common Sense of Religious Faith   260
    Milton Steinberg

Acknowledgments

Agus, Jacob B., "The Idea of God." From *Guideposts in Modern Judaism* (New York: Bloch, 1954), pp. 228–254. The chapter, which actually begins on p. 10, was condensed. Reprinted by permission of the author.

Bokser, Ben Zion, "How Can Modern Man Think About God?" From *Jewish Heritage Reader*, ed. Morris Adler (New York: Taplinger–B'nai B'rith, 1965), pp. 97–102. Reprinted by permission of the author.

Dorff, Elliot, "Two Ways to Approach God." *Conservative Judaism*, 30:2 (Winter 1976), pp. 58–67. Reprinted by permission of the author and the Rabbinical Assembly.

Gertel, Elliot B., "Perceiving God's Providence," previously unpublished manuscript provided by the author.

Gordis, Robert, "Evil in God's World." From *A Faith For Moderns* (New York: Bloch, 1960), pp. 159–189. Reprinted by permission of the author.

Greenberg, Simon, "God and Man." From *Foundations of a Faith* (New York: Burning Bush Press, 1967), pp. 34–45. Reprinted by permission of the author.

Harris, Monford, "On Proving God's Existence." *Judaism*, 16:1 (Winter 1967), pp. 37–41. Reprinted by permission of the author and editors.

Herberg, Will, "The God-Idea and the Living God." From *Judaism and Modern Man* (Philadelphia: Jewish Publication Society, 1951), pp. 57–68. Reprinted by permission of the Will Herberg Estate.

Heschel, A. J., "The Divine Pathos." *Judaism* 2:1 (January 1953). Reprinted by permission of the editors.

Jacobs, Louis, "Faith and Trust." From *Faith* (London: Vallentine-Mitchell, 1968), pp. 149–160. Reprinted by permission of the author and Vallentine-Mitchell.

Kaplan, Mordecai M., "How Man Comes to Know God." From *Proceedings of the Rabbinical Assembly of America 1943–1944*, vol. 8, pp. 256–271. Reprinted by permission of the Rabbinical Assembly.

Kohn, Jacob, "God as the Whole." From *Evolution as Revelation* (New York: Philosophical Library, 1963), pp. 22–23. Reprinted by permission of Hannah Kohn Lipsky and Eliezer Lipsky.

Levinthal, Israel Herbert, "The Development of the God Idea." From *Judaism: An Analysis and an Interpretation* (New York: Funk and Wagnalls, 1935), pp. 53–66. Reprinted by permission of the author.

Muffs, Yochanan, "God and the World: A Jewish View." From *The Samuel Friedland Lectures* (New York: Jewish Theological Seminary, 1974), pp. 63–84. Reprinted by permission of the Jewish Theological Seminary and the author.

Novak, David, "Are Philosophical Proofs of the Existence of God Theologically Meaningful?" From *Conservative Judaism* 34:2 (November–December 1980), pp. 12–22. Reprinted by permission of the author and the Rabbinical Assembly.

Rothschild, Fritz, "The Concept of God in Jewish Education." From *Conservative Judaism*, 24:2 (Winter 1970), pp. 2–20. Reprinted by permission of the author and the Rabbinical Assembly.

Rubenstein, Richard L., "The Symbols of Judaism and the Death of God." From *After Auschwitz: Radical Theology and Contemporary Judaism* (Indianapolis: Bobbs-Merrill, 1966). Reprinted by permission of the author.

Schulweis, Harold M., "From God to Godliness: Proposal for a Predicate Theology," *The Reconstructionist* (February 1975). Reprinted by permission of the author and of Rabbi Ira Eisensrein, editor, *The Reconstructionist*.

Siegel, Seymour, "Theological Reflections on the Destruction of European Jewry." From *Conservative Judaism* 18:4 (Summer 1964). Reprinted by permission of the author and the Rabbinical Assembly.

Steinberg, Milton, "The Common Sense of Religious Faith." From *Anatomy of Faith*, ed. Arthur A. Cohen (New York: Harcourt, Brace and Co., 1960), pp. 80–108.

Contributors

JACOB B. AGUS is Rabbi Emeritus of Beth El Congregation, Baltimore, Maryland. He has served on the Committee on Jewish Law and Standards of the Rabbinical Assembly, and on the faculties of the Reconstructionist Rabbinical College and Temple University. Among his writings are *The Evolution of Jewish Thought, Guideposts in Modern Judaism,* and *Modern Philosophies of Judaism.*

BEN ZION BOKSER (1907–1984) was Rabbi of the Forest Hills Jewish Center, New York City, and served on the faculties of the Jewish Theological Seminary, Queens College, and other institutions of learning. Among his writings are *Judaism: Profile of a Faith, The Legacy of Maimonides,* and *The Wisdom of the Talmud.* He edited prayerbooks for use in Conservative congregations.

ELLIOT DORFF is Provost and Associate Professor of Philosophy at the University of Judaism in Los Angeles, California. He is the author of *Conservative Judaism.*

ELLIOT B. GERTEL is Rabbi of Congregation Beth El-Keser Israel, New Haven, Connecticut, and an editor of *Conservative Judaism and Jewish Law* and this volume.

ROBERT GORDIS is Rabbi Emeritus of Temple Beth-El of Rockaway Park, New York, and a past president of the Rabbinical Assembly. He has served on the faculties of the Jewish Theological Seminary, Columbia University, Temple University, Dropsie College, and other institutions of learning. He served as founding editor of *Conservative Judaism* and *Judaism* magazines, and is currently editor of the latter. Among his many books are *A Faith For Moderns, Judaism for the Modern Age,* and *Understanding Conservative Judaism.*

SIMON GREENBERG is Vice-Chancellor and Professor of Education and Homiletics at the Jewish Theological Seminary and a Rabbi Emeritus of Har Zion Temple, Philadelphia. His writings include *Foundations of a*

ix

Faith, *The Ethical in the Jewish and the American Heritage*, and *A Jewish Philosophy and Pattern of Life*.

MONFORD HARRIS is Professor of Jewish Texts and Institutions at the Spertus College of Judaica, Chicago.

WILL HERBERG (1902–1977) was Graduate Professor of Judaic Studies and Social Philosophy at Drew University. His books include *Judaism and Modern Man* and *Protestant-Catholic-Jew*.

ABRAHAM JOSHUA HESCHEL (1907–1972) was Ralph Simon Professor of Theology and Ethics at the Jewish Theological Seminary. His works include *God in Search of Man, The Insecurity of Freedom, Man Is Not Alone, The Prophets*, and *The Theology of Ancient Judaism* (Hebrew).

LOUIS JACOBS is Rabbi of the New West End Synagogue in London, England. He has authored, among other words, *We Have Reason to Believe* and *Principles of the Jewish Faith*.

MORDECAI M. KAPLAN (1881–1983) was Professor of Philosophies of Religion and Founding Dean of the Teachers Institute of the Jewish Theological Seminary of America. He was the founder of the Society for the Advancement of Judaism (1922), the Jewish Reconstructionist Foundation, and the Reconstructionist Rabbinical College (1967). Kaplan left the Seminary in 1963 to devote himself entirely to Reconstructionist Judaism, which he created. Among his many writings are *Judaism as a Civilization* (1934), the manifesto of Reconstructionist Judaism; *Questions Jews Ask; The Future of the American Jew; Judaism Without Supernaturalism;* and *The Religion of Ethical Nationhood*. Though he founded his own movement, he is included here because of his long involvement with Conservative Judaism and his influence on Conservative rabbis.

JACOB KOHN (1881–1968) was Rabbi of Sinai Temple, Los Angeles, and a founder, Dean of the Graduate School, and Associate Professor of Theology at the University of Judaism, Los Angeles. He was the author of *Evolution as Revelation, Modern Problems of Jewish Parents*, and *The Moral Life of Man*.

ISRAEL H. LEVINTHAL (1888–1982) was Rabbi of the Brooklyn Jewish Center, which he founded in 1919. He served on the faculties of the Jewish Theological Seminary and the Jewish Institute of Religion in New York City. One of the outstanding Jewish preachers of all time, he authored many classic sermonic works, including *Judaism: An Analysis and an Interpretation, Judaism Speaks to the Modern World, A New World Is Born*, and *Point of View: An Analysis of American Judaism.*

YOCHANAN MUFFS is Professor of Bible at the Jewish Theological Seminary of America.

DAVID NOVAK is spiritual leader of Congregation Darchay Noam—The Bayswater Jewish Center in Far Rockaway, New York, and teaches philosophy at the New School for Social Research in New York. His writings include two series of *Law and Theology in Judaism* (1974, 1976), *Suicide and Morality* (1975), and *The Image of the Non-Jew in Judaism* (1983).

FRITZ A. ROTHSCHILD is Associate Professor of Philosophies of Religion at the Jewish Theological Seminary, and the author of *Between God and Man: An Interpretation of Judaism from the Writings of Abraham J. Heschel.*

RICHARD L. RUBENSTEIN, Robert O. Lawton Distinguished Professor of Religion at Florida State University (Tallahassee), is author of *After Auschwitz, The Cunning of History, The Religious Imagination, Power Struggle*, and other works.

HAROLD M. SCHULWEIS is Rabbi of Valley Beth Shalom Congregation, Encino, California, and Adjunct Professor of Contemporary Jewish Civilization at the University of Judaism, Los Angeles. He is contributing editor to *Moment, Sh'ma*, and *The Reconstructionist.*

SEYMOUR SIEGEL is Ralph Simon Professor of Theology and Ethics at the Jewish Theological Seminary of America, former chairman of the Committee on Jewish Law and Standards of the Rabbinical Assembly, and editor of *Conservative Judaism and Jewish Law.*

MILTON STEINBERG (1903–1950) was Rabbi of the Park Avenue Synagogue, New York City, and author of *Basic Judaism, A Believing Jew, The Making of the Modern Jew, A Partisan Guide to the Jewish Problem*, and other works. His life and thought are reviewed in the biography *Milton Steinberg: Portrait of a Rabbi*, by Simon Noveck.

Preface

The present volume is the third in a series of anthologies intended to present the major writings of leading thinkers in Conservative Judaism. The essays collected in these pages represent the rich and varied approaches to God and the God-idea within the Conservative movement. The major essays presenting the Conservative view of revelation and the authority of Jewish Law (*halakhah*) were collected in *Conservative Judaism and Jewish Law* (Rabbinical Assembly, 1977). The pioneering work in this vein, which presented an overview of Conservative literature, was *Tradition and Change*, edited by Rabbi Mordecai Waxman (Burning Bush Press, 1959).

Since it was our purpose to offer only those essays that explore modern options in religious belief, we have had to exclude some important Conservative writings about God that describe the beliefs of the Biblical and Rabbinic periods without explicitly offering a theology for moderns. These include the works of Solomon Schechter, Louis Ginzberg, Louis Finkelstein, and Max Kadushin. Needless to say, the writings of these men are essential for the understanding and appreciation of Judaism, and hence offer much to anyone seeking a faith grounded in the normative beliefs of historical Judaism. The reader is strongly urged to seek out Schechter's *Some Aspects of Rabbinic Theology* and his important essay on "The Dogmas of Judaism" in the First Series of his *Studies in Judaism*. The wit and charm and wealth of knowledge of the father of American Conservative Judaism will gratify the reader. Max Kadushin's volume *Worship and Ethics* should also be sought out, for it is an exploration of the Rabbinic approach to prayer which offers much to Jews of our own time who want to learn to pray as Jews. These works are mentioned by some of the writers included in this volume, and are thus applied for the reader toward the development of modern approaches to God.

Whereas in *Conservative Judaism and Jewish Law* the present editors found that certain historical considerations had to be followed in the ordering of the contents, we have decided to list the essays here in alphabetical order, as they represent parallel and sometimes overlapping attempts to explore and to interpret perennial theological ques-

1

tions, concerns, and commitments. The guiding principle of our selection was to make it possible for the reader to gain an appreciation of the diverse and fruitful perspectives on the God-faith within Conservative Judaism, without being frustrated by the barriers of jargon or esoterics. We have therefore replaced Hebrew characters with transliterations and appropriate translations and explanations. In some instances we have incorporated into the text stylistic and other changes provided by the contributors themselves.

In order to accentuate the emphases of the selections, each reading has been provided with an introduction calling attention to its main points. The lengths of the introductions are determined by the structures of the contributors' argumentation, and are not, of course, to be taken as barometers of relative profundity. The sources of the selections, as well as biographical information on the contributors, are provided in the front of this book.

It is our hope that this book will be useful for college courses in Judaism as well as for adult education classes in Conservative synagogues and Jewish centers. We also hope that it will introduce the reader to the wealth of ideas and convictions that Conservative Judaism has brought to contemporary Jewish life.

Elliot B. Gertel

Introduction

SEYMOUR SIEGEL

Traditional Jews speak *to* God frequently. They even argue with Him. Only rarely do they agree *about* Him. (Indeed there is a contemporary dispute whether we can speak of God as Him.) Today, critical and skeptical people ask hard questions about God. They want to know, Can we know that He exists? How can we understand the phenomenon of evil in the world, especially in this age of Auschwitz? Of course, there are many for whom the traditional responses to the agonizing questions suffice. But rabbis and theologians are increasingly turning their attention to the task of explaining what the word "God" means.

This is especially true in Conservative Judaism. This branch of contemporary Jewish life is based on the twin notions of tradition and change. That means the old is revered and a synthesis is sought with the new. This is frequently a harder task than it looks to be. For the hard question is, Where does "tradition" end and "change" begin? To what extent can inherited ideas suffice and not be replaced by new ideas? The various answers to this question expressed in the classic organs of expression of the movement are gathered together in this volume.

All writers on God agree on the experience of the Divine as Power. We tend to identify that aspect of reality which is overwhelming and evokes awe and what the German theologian Rudolph Otto called the *mysterium tremendum* as God. We are aware at the deepest levels of our consciousness that our destiny and fate depend in large measure on forces greater than we can control and understand. It is that aspect of Reality which is best expressed in the verse from the Bible, included in our liturgy: "To You, O God, we ascribe greatness, strength, and majesty." If that was all we understood by the term "God" all would agree that there is a Divinity and His majesty extends throughout all the earth. However, this Power must be more than that—otherwise He would not be worthy of praying to and would in the last analysis be irrelevant to our plans and hopes: for sheer Power is there and cannot be changed.

3

Therefore, the writers included in this volume can be grouped into five different approaches to the special character of God and His powers. These can be grouped as the Helping God, the Dialogic God, the Feeling God, the Saving God, and the Hidden God. These five approaches are not mutually exclusive; rather they complement each other. Perhaps at a deeper level they are five ways of saying the same thing. One of the theologian-poets whose work is part of our prayerbook declares: "They have described You in many visions. Yet you remain One in spite of all imaginings."

THE HELPING GOD

This approach is identified with the late Professor Mordecai Kaplan, whose work is included in this volume. Following the school of philosophy known as pragmatism, Kaplan believes that we will never know just exactly what God is. All we can know is what effect He has in human life, or His function in existence. What difference does it make to believe in God?

In order to answer that question as we look at ourselves, we realize that every individual has hopes, aspirations, goals about himself or the rest of mankind. These can be summed up in the ancient word "salvation." God is to be understood as the sum total of forces within reality which assist us in achieving salvation. In Kaplan's famous phrase, "God is the Power Who makes for salvation." In this era of naturalism, when we believe that all reality is included in what we call nature, this Power is not some supernatural force which miraculously intervenes within our ordinary life. He is the sum total of the forces within reality which help us. Our salvation should be aimed at being achieved within natural dimensions. Those forces like sickness which frustrate our desires for salvation are the enemies of God. We have to help Him conquer these unfriendly forces. In sum, the belief in God is the assertion of optimism: Reality involves within it forces which are friendly to man. We can achieve salvation by cooperating with those friendly forces. This is how the God idea always functioned in the past—though the content has changed depending on our view of the world and all there is. We maintain a continuity of *function* with our past, though not necessarily a continuity of *content*. God saves us if we cooperate. Prayer does not mean influencing a supernatural force to help us, but rather a mobilization of our resources to help ourselves find salvation. In a sense we are praying to our better selves when we pray to God. Many Jews and others found this idea of God convincing and persuasive.

THE DIALOGIC GOD

The late Professor Martin Buber was known as the philosopher of Dialogue. He gave rise to a whole school of disciples. His famous phrase was, "Real life is meeting." He counsels that we enter into a relationship with our fellow beings and the world with our whole being, holding nothing back. In this kind of dialogue we will sense and hear the Thou, the other addressing us with a "summons and a sending." The Eternal Thou, that is, God, is ready to address individual I's and send them to do the right thing. It is a command to stand witness to love and to do. When we do not sense this address of our beings it is not God who is absent, it is we who are absent. Like Kaplan, Buberians are impatient with discussions about what God is. "God can be addressed, not expressed," was one of his favorite sayings. Just as another person is known only when we address him, so theories about God are useless unless we decide to enter into relations with Him.

Buber insists that God is personal, that is to say, He is not only a process or a sum total of forces, but a Being who can and does enter into personal relations with His creatures. He is not the sum total of Nature or some Potency within Nature, but the Eternal Thou who is always available for dialogue.

In times of great tragedy and unspeakable evil (the Holocaust, of course, is a prime example of such an occurrence), Buber and his disciples use the profound term "the Eclipse of God"; that is, the Presence is somehow not available for dialogue. He has hidden His face. "Man penetrates step by step into the dark which hangs over the meaninglessness of reality until the mystery is disclosed in a flash of light. He who suffers for the sake of God finds God in his suffering."

The Buberian approach is called dialogic. We learn about God, we sense His presence only by entering into relations with Him. And if, at first, we cannot hear His voice, we are bidden to persist, and we are assured that eventually He will be there.

THE FEELING GOD

This is an aspect of the experience of God which is stressed by the late great philosopher of the Jewish Theological Seminary, Abraham Joshua Heschel. Heschel, expressing the basic ideas of the mystical tradition, teaches that there are sparks of the divine throughout all of creation. With increased sensitivity we experience the grandeur of existence and the ineffable power of its Creator. Heschel likes to call this the experience of the Ineffable. This is how he describes it: "But then a moment comes like a thunderbolt in which a flash of the undisclosed rends our dark apathy asunder . . . The Ineffable has shuddered its self into the soul. It has entered our consciousness like a ray of light passing into a lake. A tremor seizes our limbs. Our nerves are struck, quiver like strings, our whole being bursts into shudders."

This experience is universal, not only Jewish. It has been interpreted in different ways. The ancient Greeks saw this Reality behind reality as basically impersonal and unconcerned with human beings. This gave rise to a sense of fatalism. Many moderns believe that this Ineffable is another name for that which is yet unknown. They believe that with the progress of the human mind, mystery will disappear. According to Heschel, the sense of the Ineffable gives rises to a question and a command. The Ineffable asks us to complete His work and to serve Him; to realize in creation that which was intended: justice and mercy. There is one aspect of the prophetic experience which is unique and superbly important. The Ineffable God is a demanding God. He is also a feeling God; the God of pathos who "suffers" when His children do not fulfill the demands put upon them. The prophets of Israel are primarily men and women who empathize with the God of pathos, they feel God's sadness at the backsliding of the children of men. Therefore, when humans promote the good they are not only helping themselves and their fellowmen, but in a real sense "helping God." The God of pathos is eminently the God of the Bible and the rabbinic sources. He can be called the "feeling God" because He is not an impersonal force, but a Deity directly involved in the affairs of creation, and seeks men to cooperate with Him.

THE SAVING GOD

This stream of thought is closely linked with the contemporary school of existentialism. Its most powerful presentation is found in the writings of such thinkers as Franz Rosenzweig, Will Herberg, and Emil Fackenheim. Existentialists begin by profoundly thinking about human ·existence. Their thinking is called participant thinking, not spectator thinking—that is, thinking that is existential, in which the person feels his own existence is at stake; not looking at it from the outside. The difference is vividly illustrated by two syllogisms which appear, on their face, formally identical. But they are vastly different. The two statements are: "All men are mortal. Socrates is a man. Therefore, Socrates is mortal." Another way of stating this logical assertion is: "All men are mortal. I am a man. I am going to die." For the student of cold logic, there is no difference between the two syllogisms. However, there is a world of difference. Franz Rosenzweig, perhaps the greatest of the

Jewish existentialists, begins his magnum opus, *The Star of Redemption*: "With death, with the fear of death, does all thought begin."

What is being said is that when life is taken seriously we find that existence is full of contradictions, failures, and incompleteness; symbolized by the universal experience of death. One way of relating to this phenomenon is the way of atheist existentialists such as Camus and Sartre. This is a recognition that life, taken in its own terms, is threatened with absurdity. The only option is to make a herculean attempt to create some meaning out of our own effort. However, religious existentialists, Jewish included, believe that we can overcome the threat to meaning by relating ourselves to a Being beyond our own limitations, i.e., God Who is available to us. This is what is usually meant by the famous phrase "a leap of faith." Beyond life there is God Who is available to us. This does not lead to smug security where all problems are solved. On the contrary, by profoundly relating ourselves to a God beyond all other beings, we are challenged in our false securities and bogus achievements. A life with God is a life full of challenge, judgment, and crisis. This is why the term "The Living God" appears so often. God is not a process or an impersonal force. Rather He is living, active in our lives. He is also the Reality in which the endemic brokenness of life is overcome. Rosenzweig's book, which began as we said, with the fear of death, ends with the words "into life." The relation to the Living God makes life possible and profound.

The existentialists' God can be called the Saving God because through our relationship with Him we can overcome absurdity and meaninglessness.

THE HIDDEN GOD

The literature created by the survivors of the Holocaust is filled with agonizing questioning of the concept of Deity. The literary figures who have chosen the Holocaust as their theme are perhaps the most profound of our theologians today. They experienced human cruelty and they have faced the demons of history face to face, and no easy answers will suffice. True, the problem of God's seeming silence in the face of evil is not a new problem—it is certainly as old as Job, but the writers of the Holocaust have expressed the depth of this experience with shattering power, a power born out of the crucible of their own suffering.

We cannot surrender God, they assert, in the face of the cruel forces that banish meaning as a result of the gas chambers. We must in some way bring God out of His hiding, by recreating the world so that He will want to return to it. Elie Wiesel, the most eloquent spokesman for the survivors, put this thought in an enigmatic tale he appends to the end of one of his books, *The Town Beyond the Wall*.

Legend tells us that one day man spoke to God in this wise: "Let us change about. You be man, and I will be God for only one second."

God smiled gently and asked him, "Aren't you afraid?"

"No, and you?"

"Yes I am," God said.

Nevertheless, he granted man's desire. He became man and the man took his place, and immediately availing himself of his omnipotence, he refused to revert to his previous state. So neither God nor man was ever again what he seemed to be.

Years passed, centuries, perhaps eternities and suddenly the drama quickened; the past for one and the present for the other were too heavy to be borne. As the liberation of the one was bound to the liberation of the other, they renewed the ancient dialogue whose echoes come to us in the night, charged with hatred, with remorse, and most of all, with infinite yearning.

God's fate is in our hands. With His help—and this is perhaps the ultimate irony—we will help Him redeem us.

In all of the five currents we have described, we start with man. We try to understand the type of being we are. We strive for perfection and God helps us. We find our true being in dialogue—with God the Eternal Thou, responding and calling to us. We sense the Ineffable—and God is the reality behind all reality, who is concerned with us and suffers with our failures and rejoices in our achievements. We are threatened with meaninglessness—and God relates to us, saving us from the dead-ends of life. We find men capable of the most unspeakable deeds—and therefore we must address the Hidden God so that we can help Him bring about the redemption.

Thus the idea of God is related to the idea of man. And the scholars in Conservative Judaism have struggled to find the essence of God's meaning so that we can learn more about our duties as men and women and above all as Jews.

JACOB AGUS traces developments in modern physics and mathematics which point to a "field" and "point" polar relationship: the "field" being the "pattern of infinite relationships to which every 'point' in space is subject." The tension between "field" and "point" is the tension between "the tendency to particularization and responsiveness to the total system of which it is a part." Like all the elements, human personality involves a tension between the poles of self-assertion and self-surrender. If there is an "infinite tendency in the rising scale of being" which proceeds from the electro-magnetic field of force to the human personality, then we can logically assume the existence of "an Infinite Personality, representing the ultimate pole of being." We are therefore justified in concluding "that in the space-time continuum, as it exists in itself, and the Deity, as the projection into the infinite of the field-making capacity, are the two poles of being."

Agus traces the importance of the field-point relationship, or the "capacity to build fields of relationship," to the thinking process. Since the "process of achieving logical clarity is endless in both extent and sub-tlety," the rational process must "lead us on to the Pole of Being that is God." In the harmony and beauty of objects, in the persistent imperatives of our moral faculties, we can perceive relationships projected by the Deity. Agus argues, then, that "God as the field-building pole of being is achieved through the highways of reason, aesthetics, and ethics."

I.

The Idea of God

JACOB B. AGUS

I

THE UNIVERSE IN which we live is hopelessly mysterious, in its outer reaches as in the unimaginable complexity of its minutest particles. Of the vastness of the infinite void we cannot ever expect to receive more than occasional glimpses. But the world that is open to our senses, how do we understand it? The merest acquaintance with the facts of science awakens us to the realization that the qualities which are apprehended by our senses are not really present in the world as it truly is. In the real world, there are no tastes, colors and sounds, only a hectic chaos of whirling particles and trembling waves. At one time, it was believed that atoms and molecules constituted the irreducible bricks of the universe. The world was a vast assemblage of these tiny particles, travelling through space like myriads of billiard balls, and all the complexities of its phenomena were nothing but reflections of the motions and gyrations of these simple particles.

At present, even the general public is aware that matters are not quite so simple. In the first place, there does not seem to be any limit to the divisibility of matter, with the most recently discovered particles being possibly subject to further breakdowns. We confront now the possibility that empty space may merely be an abstraction, representing a pole of existence, which is only reached asymptotically. In the second place, we now know that matter and energy are at bottom somehow one. In modern physics, it was realized long ago that electrons sometimes behaved as if they were not particles of matter, but multi-dimensional waves of energy. The emergence of the quantum theory, insisting that

10

energy comes in spurts, like particles, and the Einstein relativity theory, erasing the absolute line of distinction between space and matter, made the old vision of the universe as a mass of moving particles completely out of date. Finally, the rapid progress of atomic science in the last decade demonstrated in world-shaking experiments the possibility of converting matter into energy. We know now that matter in all its forms is but a coagulation, as it were, of energy, which is the basic reality in the world about us—the energy of radiation, gravitation, nuclear attraction, electromagnetism, and heat. But with the exception of heat, none of these forms of energy can be understood in the mechanistic terms of whirling particles.

What then is energy? The term has meaning for us in that it is derived from a number of situations in which it is always associated with matter. In physics, energy is defined and measured in terms of the capacity to set matter into motion. But if matter is itself a form of energy, how shall we think of energy?

For a long time, science clung to the notion that the waves of light and electromagnetism were undulations in a quasi-material substance called ether, for motion could be understood only as the motion of something, and the conception of light as waves could be taken to make sense only if there were really something in which the waves could take place. Then the theory of an ether was given up, and the waves of energy were left waving while yet there was nothing to wave. Finally, the relativity theory gave the *coup de grace* to the conception of space as the vast inert container of moving particles, proving that there was no absolute boundary between space and matter, since space was itself quasi-material, "bending" and "contracting" round masses of matter. Thus, the mechanistic theory of the universe is now as dead as a door-nail.

More and more, we are driven to the realization that the physical universe must be viewed in terms of the "field" and "point" polar relationship. The "field" is the pattern of infinite relations to which every "point" in space is subject. As in every polar relationship, each pole represents a direction of being, rather than a definite state or quality. Neither the "point" nor the "field" exist as such, but every existent is a combination of both in varying degrees. The final, irreducible element of existence is as the trembling of a chord, withdrawing into a definite point in space, yet issuing out of itself, in response to the "field" in which it is found. Things are not spatial entities alone, but "events," in Whitehead's terminology, units of space-time, reflecting the tension and the rhythm of the polar relationship.

How profoundly revolutionary is this point-field polar concept! We are accustomed to think of true reality as motionless, massive stability, but now the realization dawns upon us that in reality things are tensions and rhythms. Nothing exists that is wholly self-enclosed, but things are real insofar as they partake of the two opposites—particularity reaching down to a point in space, and responsiveness to the total field of relations. Behold this paradox: if it were possible to take a still shot of the universe at any one point in time, eliminating all incipient relations, the universe would be absolute nothingness! For it is in the tension between the two poles of existence that events endure.

Yet difficult as is the point-field polar concept for the layman, modern mathematics long ago constructed the logical framework for its understanding. It was through the logic inherent in mathematical formulae that Einstein's theories were developed. The groundwork was laid in the seventeenth century by Descartes' theory of analytic geometry, which solved complicated problems of curvature by translating them unto a field of relations, based on two coordinates. The essential congruence of this theory with fundamental reality is demonstrated in the circumstance that by means of it the actual curves of motion in the physical universe could be calculated. Related to the field-concept is the theory of the differential, dy/dx, which expresses in mathematical language the asymptotic character of incipient motion or change. A differential is defined as the ratio of two rates of change when the amount of change approximates zero. With this paradoxical method of "approaching zero," modern mathematics was able to unlock and plot all forms of change, opening up new vast fields of calculation, while the earlier concepts of pre-modern algebra and geometry could only describe an abstract, static world. The differential, as contrasted with the conception of a static point, and the integral, as contrasted with the elementary notion of a class of objects or group of points, reflect together the polar concepts of this dynamic universe, the restless quality of its being, matter and energy "approaching" the two poles of being in itself and in relation respectively, without quite reaching either pole. In the mechanistic view of the universe, the process of explanation consists in the equating of each effect as the arithmetical summation of the forces that impinge upon it, as in Newton's laws of motion. But the question remains unanswered as to the manner in which influence proceeds from part to part—the influence of gravitation, for instance, or the force of nuclear attraction. In the organismic view, each part is explained by the whole, but the differentiation into parts remains unexplained. The principle of polarity offers us a synthesis of both mechanism and organism.

The essence of the polar relationship is seen in the circumstance that when the attempt is made to apprehend either pole as an existent, the result is incomprehensible absurdity. Thus, the attempt to envisage matter is led, through the channels of analysis, to energy, while the corresponding attempt to conceive of energy leads to the description of it as a quality of matter. This paradox is carried over into the ultimate units of the universe whatever they may be. As we have noted, reality in its ultimate shape cannot but bear a point-to-point correspondence with the fundamental character of the phenomena that science describes to us.

We thus arrive at the conception of a universe, in which all parts exist in a state of tension—tension between the tendency to particularization and responsiveness to the total system of which it is a part. If human terms could be used to express this two-way quality of every existent, we could speak of the tension between the poles of self-assertion and self-surrender. In the history of thought, quasi-human expressions were indeed employed to characterize that which must remain inexpressible, since all forms of expression derive from the phenomenal world while fundamental reality reposes behind the veil of phenomena. Suffice it for us at this stage to note the polar character of existence, the tension between point and field which constitutes the ineluctable mold of reality.

II

We have said that the fundamental character of all existents is given in the tension between "point" and "field." The meaning of the polar quality of "point" is clear enough, but what do we mean by the term "field"? Is not the limit of the field of force in which every existent is found rather vague and indefinite? To be sure, in the inanimate universe, there is no definite limit to the field of relations of each point. Fields of force are superimposed upon each other in concentric circles, declining in relevance and shading off into the infinite. While we can envision the end result of the tendency toward absolute rest in an absolute point, we do not see the "field," as a terminal goal, but as the first link in a chain. If the second law of thermodynamics, which foresees the ultimate running down of the energy in the universe and the achievement of a perfectly stable equilibrium, were to be fully realized, we should require only a "general theory of space" to describe the unvarying stillness of sameness and death.

However, there appears to be a contrary tendency in the universe, running counter to the law of entropy—a tendency for "fields" to assert themselves as particularizations or "points" over against their environment. A field of force is a way of reacting to change at any one moment of time. But when the field is itself individualized to the point of maintaining a unitary pattern of action, in spite of continuous change, we have in fact an achievement of individuality—that is, the establishment of a permanent pattern of energy relations. Thus, when radiation suffusing space condenses into an atom, establishing a powerful and complex field of force in a tiny area of space, we recognize in the process the emergence of an individuated field. The emergence of a living cell, constituting a unitary pattern of action, in spite of continuous change, is another great milestone on the ladder of the individuation of fields of force. Jan Smuts' emphasis on "wholes" in nature, imposing their patterns upon their constituent parts, so that these parts function in a manner that is measurably different from the way they function when they are separated, is of interest in demonstrating additional links in this chain of individuation. Every step consists in the achievement of a pattern representing a measure of freedom from the sway of the outside environment. Atoms, cells, multicellular plants, animal cells, animals, mankind: all these stages of creation represent a continuous ascent upon the infinite ladder of individuation and freedom.

The manner whereby energy condenses into matter or atoms coalesce into cells, as well as all the other steps in the vertical ascent of creation, is properly the subject for scientific research and investigation. Suffice it to note that the universe can only be understood in terms of a polar relationship, between point and field—a relationship which is steadily compounded, the "fields" becoming "points" as against other "fields," the whole picture presenting a continuous state of tension, not only along the horizontal plane of space-time, but also on the vertical plane of individuation and freedom.

In this scale of being, the human personality presents the highest, observable field of individuation. Speaking objectively, the human personality represents the greatest measure of freedom attained in the scale of creation: the capacity to reflect on the experiences stored in memory, to envision alternative procedures, to reason and to evaluate, to imagine and to create are but so many expressions of the field-building capacity or the power of freedom that is stored in the human personality. In turn, freedom must be understood not as a break in the chain of cause and effect, or as the injection of a "non-materialistic" factor in the economy of nature, but as the causation and self-maintenance of a "field" or an individualized pattern of action as against the rest of existence.

If now we have learned to recognize an infinite tendency in the rising scale of being, proceeding from the electromagnetic field of force that is space to the human personality, we must next inquire whether we can logically escape the assumption of an Infinite Personality, representing the ultimate pole of being, on the vertical coordinate of freedom. We have seen that the understanding of the universe requires the application of two polar principles that are set over against each other, and we have learned that the same polarity of field and point, whole and part, freedom and mechanism, pervades the whole range of creation. In the human personality, freedom attains its highest manifestation, but it is still far from perfect. Applying the principle of polarity, we conclude that an Absolute Personality representing the highest measure of the field-building capacity, constitutes a pole of being, standing in continual opposition to and tension with the mechanistic universe. God and the physical universe are the two polar concepts of thought, and since logical thought is in correspondence with reality, we are justified in concluding that the space-time continuum, as it exists in itself, and the Deity, as the projection into the infinite of the field-making capacity, are the two poles of being.

We have spoken of freedom in the human personality as the power of field-building and field-maintaining. This equation is not apparent at first glance. However, bearing in mind the point-field relationship as the most fundamental generalization of reality, we recall that the emergence of life was a leap unto a higher level of the relationship that obtains throughout existence. In a living cell, each part is manifestly in a functioning relation to the whole, with the result that the field or pattern of force is maintained, while the parts continue to change. In the emergence of consciousness, we see another level of this field-building capacity, the data of the senses being set in relation to each other, with the sensations of the present moment viewed against the experience of the past. So immediate is the field of consciousness, in the simplest experience, as for example, in the apprehension of color or sound, that we are not aware of the operation by which the mind relates the new experience to the accumulated data in it, identifying the new sensation as a definite color or a meaningful sound. Yet we know that colors and sounds are meaningful to us only because they are so related to the ever-growing field of memory. The process of relating each datum to the apperceptive mass of consciousness is incomprehensible on any mechanical basis. Several decades ago, in the heyday of materialism, much was made of Pavlov's conditioned reflex experiments on a dog whose brain had been severed from the spine. The extreme care that had to be taken in order to establish a selective reaction of the dog's saliva to the sound of the bell amounted in fact to the establishment of an artificial field of relations in the dog's nervous system by the experimenter. In a similar manner, it is possible for the hypnotist to affect and distort the consciousness of the person subjected to his influence. But in consciousness, many sensations are automatically related to the field of experience, each falling into its own groove. And precisely this selective capacity is the distinctive quality of consciousness. While in nature, fields of force operate in only one pattern, in the field of consciousness, many different possibilities are viewed in relation to each sensation, until an identity is established. Treating of the different manner in which events are arranged in nature and in consciousness, William James wrote of the "hard" order that prevails in nature as contrasted with the "soft" order of arrangements that is characteristic of consciousness. He was right in calling attention to the flexibility of consciousness, but wrong in his choice of terms. For the distinction is not one of "hardness" and "softness," but of the unitary field of force versus the capacity in consciousness of setting many events in relation to each other and thereby establishing new fields. As life implies the power of the self-maintenance of a field, consciousness implies the capacity of setting data into relation with each other, thereby setting up new fields. Neither life nor mind is explained by these powers, but the progressive advance in terms of the point-field polar relationship is nevertheless apparent.

This polarity is manifested especially in the operation of logical thought. Aristotle it was who first reflected on the nature of logic and formulated the principles of what came to be known as deductive logic. There is the major premise affirming a proposition concerning a class of objects, as when it is said, "All men are two-legged." There is the minor premise, declaring of one individual that he belongs to the above class, such as the statement, "Socrates is a man." Inevitably, the conclusion follows, "Socrates is two-legged." In this syllogistic process, we have first the vision of a class or a field, followed by the recognition of an individual, leading to the inclusion of that individual within the class. In other words, the process of logical reasoning consists in the setting up of a field of relations between an infinite group of objects, or a class, and an individual object.

Francis Bacon is generally credited with the popularization of the inductive process of reasoning, which advances from a series of particulars to the formulation of a general law, instead of proceeding in the reverse way from the general to the particular. In inductive logic, too, a number of particular facts are classed together and used for the formulation of a law, which describes a field-point relationship. This type of reasoning first lifts a number of particular events out of one field of relations, then recognizes them as forming a new field, in which each event is related to a class or field of consequences. Bacon was interested not so much in the formulation of known facts as in the discovery of new truths. Hence, not logic, but the creative thinking process was his main concern. Now in the process of thinking, observations of particular events form the starting point, but when the universal law leaps out of the multitude of particulars, the achievement is again made possible only by the setting up of a field or class which embraces all the particulars. Thus, whether you begin at the one end or the other, reasoning consists in the setting up of fields of relations and in studying the identities thus discovered.

Hermann Cohen, who founded the new-Kantian school of "critical" philosophy, sought to discover the manner in which "pure" thought operates—that is, thought which is abstracted from any data that are provided by the senses. The net result of his investigation was the suggestion already referred to that the differential, dy/dx, and the corresponding mathematical process of integration, constitute the twin poles of thought. Here, too, we see the projection of point-field relationships, or the capacity to build fields of relationship, as the essential distinction of the thinking process.

III

Logical thinking is the most perfect form of the field-building capacity that is available to us. Exemplified in the building up of the hypothetical constructs of mathematics, human logic is manifestly not a body of knowledge and procedures, complete in itself, but a continuously expanding circle, certain to transcend all its presently visible boundaries in both scope and refinement. Did Euclid in all his brilliance foresee the possibility of a non-Euclidean geometry of space? Did Newton, in all the exactitude of his calculations, sense the possibility of a "curvature" of space? Even so, we may be certain that the "general field-theory" of Einstein will one day be further refined through the emergence of new concepts—that is, new vistas of fields. Mathematical thought, which is logic in action, is an endless quest for the comprehension of the possibilities of the field-building capacity, and its end is not in sight. It is an advance toward the Deity, the Eternally Present, the Field-Builder of the universe in which we live.

We know that logical thinking is not the only form of activity of the human mind. There is the vast extent of "prelogical" thought, characteristic of the mind of primitive man, to which Lévy-Bruhl pointed, and there are also the profound depths of the unconscious that Freud and his associates have begun to plumb. While we cannot at this point enter into an analysis of these insights, we invite the reader to examine for himself whether all these forms of thinking are not due to the formation in the mind of incomplete fields. In the unconscious, as well as in primitive thought, we have associations formed on the basis of similarities that we, in our clearest moments of reflection, consider "irrelevant" because they do not take the whole of the relevant fields into consideration. By the same token, it will appear upon analysis, that the cures effected by psychiatry are achieved by opening up the vista of a larger field. The impulse that was side-tracked and allowed to fester in a blind-alley is brought into the total pattern of values and ideals of the human personality, so that a rational "adjustment" is achieved. In Otto Rank's writings, particularly, it is made clear that it is the self, as a field-making entity, that is cured through its own assertion and through the encouragement of the analyst.

The process of achieving logical clarity is endless in both extent and subtlety, and if humility succeeds in dissuading us from stopping at any one point, the rational process leads on to the Pole of Being that is God. But the way of reason is not the only road to Deity. Is not our experience of beauty the recognition of the rightness of a pattern of events that enters into our ken? As reason differs from imagination in that the fields built up by the latter are arbitrary while those of the former are "right" and "true," so the beautiful differs from the ugly in that its fields are automatically "approved" by us. There is an element of universality and personal distinterestedness in the awareness of beauty. Things *are* beautiful; they are not made thus by the vagaries of our taste. The fields of relationship, in color or in sound, that constitute beauty and harmony are manifestations of God's fields. In cognizing them, we join in approving His handiwork, even as it said: "And the Lord saw all that He had made, and behold, it was very good."

If the aesthetic appearance is the silent symbol of the relationships projected by Deity, our moral faculties bring home to us the imperative quality of the Divine Field. For the essence of morality is expressed in the double command: to integrate our own self to the fullest, so as to accord every element of our being its rightful place within our personality, and to place our own self within the larger wholes of the family, the state, and the emergent society of mankind. The nature of the first command has been frequently neglected in European thought, owing partly to the formalistic methods of philosophy and partly to the pervasiveness of the neo-platonic contempt for the flesh that has entered into the mainstream of our thinking. Yet it is basic, a modern depth-psychology has demonstrated. The social implications of the progressive awareness of ever larger wholes in society are obvious.

Thus, God as the field-building pole of being is approached through the highways of reason, aesthetics and ethics. We think of Him as the Self of the Universe, related to our self, in its field-building capacity, as our self is related to the material world. Yet these ways of cognizing are only formal, belonging more to philosophy than to religion. Basic as these avenues are, they constitute only the substructure of religion. For it is in attachment to God and His will that religion is born, and once this attachment is discovered, a new level of aspirations and feelings is opened up for the human personality.

It is in prayer that religion is born. In the beginning is the self's immediate reverence before the Master of the universe, its abasement before the Majesty of its source. It is not the believer in God who prays, but it is the worshipper who believes. The polarity of being has its correspondence and reflection in the life of the soul, which moves rhythmically from aggressive self-assertion in the world of reality to passive self-surrender to the Maker of this world.

After reviewing classical "proofs" for the existence of God, BEN ZION BOKSER concludes that there must be a supreme intelligence behind the world as we experience it. The existence of evil merely suggests that the universe is still growing, for God deliberately made life imperfect in order to allow for such growth in the world. While we cannot know God in His essence, we know what He is not (for He is greater than all our conceptions and tangible representations), and we have an idea of what He is like from His creation.

II.

How Shall Modern Man Think About God?

BEN ZION BOKSER

HOW SHALL MODERN man think about God? Belief in God is essentially an interpretation of the universe and of life within it. It is the antithesis of atheism, which is an interpretation of the world based on the conviction that this whole vast existence—the entire cosmos and not only our own tiny earth—is nothing more than an elaborate, precise machine affected by the laws of cause and effect, but without any purpose of its own.

The religious interpretation of life, on the contrary, insists that God is the sole creator and ruler of the universe, and that everything in the world, despite its complexity and apparent contradiction, exists according to His plan. Since it is obvious that there is ugliness in life as well as beauty, pain as well as joy, good as well as evil, there would seem, on the surface, to be a measure of chaos in the world. According to the believer, however, what appears chaotic and contradictory is nevertheless an integral part of God's plan, representing the creative achievement of a beneficent intelligence proceeding toward some great and noble purpose.

Various arguments and proofs are found in religious literature to justify this conviction. A classic example, stemming back to Aristotle and repeated by Maimonides, is the "argument from motion." We are all familiar with the phenomenon of inertia that governs every object in nature. We know that all matter must remain at rest in a fixed position unless made to move by some outside force. Aristotle and Maimonides both pointed out that since the universe is constantly in motion there must be a force responsible for initiating and sustaining this motion. In the religious view, this force is God.

Another approach which tries to prove the existence of a creator is the "cosmological argument" advanced, among others, by the Jewish sage Saadia Gaon, who lived in Babylonia in the tenth century. Simple observation demonstrates conclusively that there is no spontaneous creation in nature, that objects cannot form themselves. Since there is a world, the world could not have sprung into existence by itself. Therefore, there must have been a primal cause, a powerful generating agent—God—who fashioned the universe and brought it into being.

Still another proof that is often advanced is the "argument from design." If one walks into a house and finds that the furnishings are placed in good order, one knows that this cannot be the result of mere chance, that some human being must have arranged the furniture, the books and the pictures on the wall to reflect his own sensibilities and taste.

Similarly, a modern building is the product—good or bad—of some architect's design. Certainly, chance could not have brought together the bricks, beams, girders, pipes, and all the countless elements of construction in such a way as to form an edifice fit for human use. Much more wondrous certainly is the design revealed by the universe, and it argues for a being working with design and purpose to create and sustain the various enterprises of existence.

We may use a more striking analogy to demonstrate this point—the creation of a poem. Suppose one threw a bottle of ink into the air. Of course, it would come down with a crash, and if it fell on a sheet of paper, the ink would spatter. Here and there, it is theoretically possible that the spots of ink might accidentally form a letter, perhaps even two or three letters in combination to make a word. But to think even for one instant that these spots could arrange themselves into even a simple poem would be absurd. To imagine that these drops of ink could ever be shaped accidentally, without the assistance of a human intellect, into a masterpiece like Shakespeare's *Hamlet* would be preposterous.

If we are willing to accept the fact that an intellect, some reasoning power, must lie behind the furnishing and décor of a house, the construction and design of a building, or the dramatic artistry of a Shakespeare, it follows, as a matter of common sense, that the universe, with its design of infinite complexity, was shaped and is guided by a supreme intelligence that puts man's accomplishments into the shade. The vastness and variety of the universe—the thirty billion stars that have been so far accounted for; the fantastic number of animal, insect and microbic species; the multitude of human beings, not two of whom are exactly alike; even snow, every flake of which has a different crystal pattern—lead only to one conclusion: the universe cannot possibly be the result of chance, but obviously represents the work of an all-knowing, all-powerful intelligence.

In addition to the above "proofs" of God's existence, there is the wonder and majesty of the universe, which, to many, is a manifestation of God. A. J. Cronin in his autobiography, *Adventures in Two Worlds,* states that God cannot be proved like a mathematical equation. Nevertheless, he says, there are certain simple arguments that may help us to discover Him. If we consider the physical universe in its mystery and wonder, its order and intricacy, we cannot escape the notion of a primary cause.

Who, on a still summer night, dare gaze upward at the constellations, glittering in infinity, without the overpowering conviction that such a cosmos came into being through something more than blind, indeterminate chance? And our own world, whirling through space, is surely more than a meaningless ball of matter, thrown off by the merest accident from the sun. Although primarily a novelist in his later years, Cronin began his career as a scientist. For some years he was a practicing physician. Cronin's view of the workings of the universe is not far from that of many of the greatest scientists of our day. In reading of their lives and their intellectual growth as scientists, we are constantly struck by their sense of the mystery, majesty and wonder of the universe, and, above all, of the breathtaking intelligence which they see embodied in it, evoking in them an appreciative awe. As Maimonides said, the sense of wonder is the very heart of a truly religious spirit; religion begins with a sense of awe—not at nature as such, but at what is behind nature. And the highest reality to which nature points is God.

When we look at our children, how often do we pause to consider what is involved in their birth—the wonder of the creation of new life? In Thornton Wilder's play *Our Town,* when Emily, who has died, returns for one day to live among the living, she cries out against their blindness. They are surrounded by the wonders of life. But they are so insensitive that they take them for granted. Similarly, many of us tend to forget that there is a giver of life, who is the source of the beauty, the wonder and the very love that lives in the heart of the parent when he reaches to embrace his child.

If it is true that the universe represents the creation and materialization of a plan or purpose, supervised by a God who is all-powerful, wise and good, then why is there so much evil and suffering in the world? Why does life contain so much imperfection? Many people, without examining the matter deeply, take the fact that there is corruption and evil in the world as proof that there is no God.

The Jewish conception is that God deliberately made life imperfect in order to give the world a chance to grow toward perfection. No plan is complete at its inception; the perfection of any plan is visible only at its final development. Thus, much of the evil we see about us derives from the fact that God's plan remains unfinished. We are still living in the infancy, so to speak, not only of man but of the universe itself.

Science has shown us that even physically the universe is growing. It is in a constant state of expansion, of movement and change. To put it perhaps too simply, there is a "disturbing element" in the cosmic system that induces this change, just as there is a "disturbing element" in the world of men. The Biblical verse—often quoted but usually misinterpreted—states: "The nature of man is evil from his youth." While some take this to mean that man's nature is corrupt from his very childhood, our interpretation is that man as a creature, a product of this cosmic growth, is still in the infancy of his development and is therefore an imperfect being.

Many Jewish thinkers are convinced that while the world is moving toward greater perfection, toward the kingdom of God, some imperfections would have to remain in it because a world without imperfection would lack the force to give incentive to life. The elimination of the so-called "disturbing element" from life would leave man with nothing to keep him moving, nothing to make him aspire toward his own improvement and a higher plane of existence.

Jewish theology has made the profound observation that man can never know the nature of God; he cannot give any positive definition of Him. In order to define an object, we must, in some respects, master it or transcend it. To define literally means to draw a boundary of words around an object so that it can be recognized. But God has been called illimitable, and is often referred to as the "boundless."

Abraham Heschel uses a term popular in Kabbalistic and Hasidic literature: "God is the ineffable," defying description. Just as words fail to convey the grandeur of most natural wonders, so too are God's attributes inexpressible, remaining greater than our power to characterize them except by resorting to indirect techniques drawn from our own limited observation and knowledge. That is why Jews say that it is daring and almost frightening to hope to encompass our praise of God in words.

There is a parable in the Talmud concerning a pious man who was overheard by a rabbi as he sang the praises of God. After he finished, the rabbi said to him: "Did you list all the praises there are? Have you exhausted the subject?" "No," the man replied. The rabbi then said: "When you kept adding adjective after adjective and finally stopped, the implication was that you had exhausted them. Isn't it better, therefore, not to use any adjectives at all?" Recognizing that silence is at times the greatest form of eloquence, our sages also sensed the hopelessness of attempting to define God's omnipotence and greatness by resorting to mere words.

When we say that God cannot be defined, we also admit that we cannot know what God is. God is a reality, a being, an intelligence. Sometimes we use the phrase, "God is a spirit." But what is spirit? In the Bible, when Moses addresses God and asks: "Tell me Your name, How will I be able to identify You?" God answers: "I am that I am." This means, simply, that God is pure existence.

Why then *do* we talk about God? How can we fill the prayer book and the Bible with so many characterizations of God?

This is not a contradiction. Although we cannot know God as an essence, there are two possible ways in which we can gain knowledge about Him. One is the negative: we know what God is not. No matter what we know in our experience concerning tangible representations of greatness and perfection, God is not like that. God is not a person; He is not a body; He has no concrete shape or form.

The second way in which we can know God is through the qualities of His work. To draw a parallel, it is true that without having met or heard anything about the personal life of a serious creative writer, it is possible to know a great deal about him by reading his books. God is the great unseen author of the universe. We cannot look into His face, but we can see what He, as author, has brought into being. From these observations, we can generalize and use certain adjectives to describe Him.

We know, for example, that in the universe there is order, beauty and a ceaseless urge to create life and perfect it. That means that order and beauty, creation and the search for perfection are apparently part of God's plan. We say that God is just, that He is merciful, compassionate and gracious. Certainly, this is applying the limited vocabulary of man to describe God. But again, knowing God's works—His incorruptibility, His concern with all of life from the highest to the lowest, the bounty of His natural treasure bestowed equally upon the good and wicked alike—it is possible to use adjectives drawn from human experience to describe Hm.

It must be noted that the various human attributes used to describe God are not to be taken literally. They are figures of speech used to express God's grandeur and power. In Isaiah, for example, we find the expression: "The mouth of the Lord hath spoken." This does not mean that God has a mouth and speaks as human beings speak. When Isaiah used the phrase, he meant that the words that had come out of his own mouth were inspired by God, that he was merely the instrument of God's message to the people of Israel. What Isaiah intended to convey was that God is the source of all inspiration, the author of all wisdom.

Isaiah's passionate call for moral reformation, his flowing affirmation of hope in a good world that was yet to be born out of the chaos of his time, was not a figment of his own imagination but came to him from God. Thus, graphically and vividly, he asserted: "The mouth of the Lord hath spoken." In this poetic statement he paid tribute to God's presence, which had imbued him with the strength of heart and mind to speak words that will endure for all time.

One other term applied to God merits special discussion. God is sometimes described as the judge of the universe. This implies that there is law in the world, and when that law is violated punishment is meted out. That is the essence of judgment. When a catastrophe occurs—war or famine or flood or plague—we say that it is God's judgment. Certainly a scientist can trace the catastrophe to the violation of certain principles, principles of human relations or of hygiene. But these principles are part of the structure of life, they are part of God's plan, of the law by which He wants life to be governed.

The commission of moral evil, the pursuit of vanity, of wealth or bodily pleasures as the supreme goal in life lead to an inner distress, to a sense of guilt or futility and emptiness. Thus God visits judgment upon those who live in violation of principles by which He wants man to govern his life. Man has of course the privilege to change his life and return to obedience of God's law, and God will forgive him. We, therefore, say that God is a merciful judge, who waits like a loving father for His children's return.

The Jewish conception of God is noble and exalted. It is free from the weaknesses and limitations characteristic of man, while giving us a vocabulary than enables us to speak of God in terms that are vivid and stirring to the human heart. It is a doctrine of God equal to the intellectual needs of our time—and of all time.

After citing Judah Halevi's proposition that the God of the philosophers is opposed to the God of the patriarchs, ELLIOT N. DORFF protests that the two God-concepts should in fact be mixed.

"*All* our experiences," Dorff observes, "including revelations from God, must be interpreted by us according to our own lights in order to become part of our knowledge." God may be different from the "conception which emerges from our experience," but we must still understand Him that way. Our experience teaches us that the concept of the "divine" points both to what is beyond human understanding and to the finest qualities in human beings, such as love, care, and concern. Our experience is not limited to observation of the world but includes interaction in it. Social, emotional, and aesthetic forces also affect our worship of God. Intellectually, we find it difficult to pray to a personal God, though, emotionally, a personal God is needed.

Dorff concludes that there are good reasons for belief in a personal God, and equally good reasons to deny such belief. Yet the idea of a personal God has strong support—historically, from tradition; and philosophically, because there must be a God that can be *addressed* if prayer is to make sense. Since *interaction* with God is as necessary as *description* of Him, Dorff affirms that it is possible to speak of the Personal God in the former context and of a philosophical concept in the latter. Both are "legitimate and complementary conceptions of God, and we need both to be true to the totality of our experience as human beings and as Jews."

III

*Two Ways to Approach God**

ELLIOT N. DORFF

THE GOD OF the philosophers is not the God of Abraham, Isaac, and Jacob. Yehudah Halevi made this distinction in order to disparage all philosophic attempts to come to know the God of religious faith—who, he claimed, can only be known through revelation and history.[1]

Halevi's distinction is an important and fruitful one, but the conclusion we ought to draw from it is quite different from the one he intended. The crucial point is not that the God of the philosophers is totally irrelevant to the God of religious faith, but that human beings can experience God in different ways, and their image of Him will vary accordingly. When we think about God as rational beings, what emerges from our philosophizing about Him is usually an abstract, and often deistic, Creative Force or Moral Principle. On the other hand, when we try to relate to God with our conative and emotional powers, we encounter a personal God, who interacts with us in a very intimate way. These disparate conceptions of God are functions of the different ways in which we approach Him in the first place.

Realizing this, several possibilities emerge. We can, as Halevi suggests, simply dissociate the two concepts, rescuing God from all rational attack. That option is objectionable, however, on two counts: it reduces

*I would like to express my sincere thanks to my friends and teachers Rabbis Sheldon Dorph, Neil Gillman, David Gordis, David Lieber and Harold Schulweis, and Professor James McClendon, Jr., with all of whom I have had the privilege of having an ongoing dialogue in recent months regarding many of the issues treated in this paper. None of them agrees with me fully, and that has made our conversations all the more lively and enlightening. They certainly are not responsible for any of the faults of this paper, but whatever insights it contains have been generated or refined in large measure by them.

our religious commitment, since it excludes the rational side of our being; and it removes religion from the sphere of intellectual analysis and criticism, encouraging superstition.

On the other hand, we can mix the two concepts, which is precisely what Jews did historically: they grafted their original notion of God, conceived individually as a superhuman Person, onto the Greek notion of God, conceived generically as the concept of Godhood, in an attempt to show that Jewish theology was in no way inferior to the best that philosophy had to offer; that, indeed, the Jewish concept of God included all that the philosophers had to say about Him long before they articulated their positions. This sort of grafting, however, results in hopelessly confused theology, plagued by many difficulties and outright contradictions: an abstract and infinite God is simply not the same as the personal, particular God of the Bible.

In order to arrive at a coherent Jewish theology, where religious faith can truly be a matter of "all your heart, all your soul, and all your might," it is necessary to integrate the knowledge we have gleaned from the two different approaches to God—the God of the philosophers that Halevi had in mind, whom we experience as passive observers; and the God whom we find in personal interaction with the world around us.

My reliance on reason and experience is based on the assumption that we have no alternative, because God does not reveal His nature to us directly in a clear, unambiguous way. In this I am simply echoing the Jewish tradition which recognized long ago that the meaning of revelation is crucially dependent upon the ability of the receiver to understand it,[1a] and I am also reflecting what we know from our encounters with people and objects in our daily lives. *All* of our experiences, including revelations from God, must be interpreted by us according to our own lights in order to become part of our knowledge. That does not mean that we can understand the workings of the world in whatever way we want; we human beings have developed shared criteria by which we judge the adequacy and truth of competing interpretations. But it does mean that our conclusions must be restricted to how we *conceive* of God. God may be very different from the conception which emerges from our experience, but we human beings can never know that because our knowledge is confined to what we learn from our reason and experience.

THE GOD OF DETACHED REFLECTION

Before discussing this approach to God, it will be helpful to analyze the way we experience day-to-day objects. When we experience an object directly, we have the best proof possible that it exists and the most straightforward indication of its properties.[2] When we do not have such direct experience, however, we must seek evidence. What constitutes convincing evidence varies with the circumstances, but in all cases contradictory evidence poses major problems. Under these conditions careful investigators will adhere to a quasi-agnosticism in which they describe and interpret the phenomena, but stress that their interpretations are hypotheses, not conclusions based upon direct evidence. A good example of this is the case of light. Since light manifests characteristics of both waves and particles, physicists sometimes use the wave and sometimes the particle to describe the behavior of light, while pointing out that these are only *analogies* from common experience to assist our understanding of light. They are not claiming that light *is* a wave or a series of particles; the phenomena of light simply do not lend themselves to neat categorization.

The same methodology can be applied to our experience of God. We do not see God directly, and we have serious doubts about the accounts of those who say they do. We seek evidence, but it remains ambiguous. There are a variety of phenomena which could lead one to belief in a traditional God, such as the starry heavens and the existence of order in the world. On the other hand, there are phenomena, especially the existence of evil, which lead us to question that belief. As a result, there is no one metaphysical system which irrefutably suggests itself. We can choose to emphasize the aspects of our experience which lend themselves to a religious interpretation of the world, or we can choose to stress those phenomena which would mitigate against such an interpretation. The facts do not compel us either way; whichever alternative we choose, we are going to have to account for contrary phenomena.[3]

In this situation, I would choose the method of the careful physicist described above: that is, I affirm that there are certain phenomena in my experience which I call "divine" (a term which I shall define momentarily), without asserting the existence of a Being underlying those phenomena, both because I have not experienced such a Being apart from the phenomena, and also because the phenomena I do experience do not lend themselves indisputably to a theological interpretation. (On the contrary, parts of my experience make that interpretation very difficult to maintain.) I may therefore use the model of a Being called "God" to describe and explain certain aspects of my experience, while refusing to use it in other contexts.

DIVINITY

There are at least two different ways in which the term "divine" refers to phenomena which we experience. One is the sense of "divine" as the word which describes "an act of God." Here "divine" means "superhuman" or "beyond human knowledge and control." In asserting the existence of divine phenomena in this sense I am stressing that we human beings are not all-powerful or all-knowing, but rather that we are vastly limited in our knowledge and control of the most fundamental conditions of human existence and welfare, and that we should therefore have the humility to give thanks for the good things in life and tremble before the bad. As Schleiermacher[4] saw, it is this realization of our creatureliness, our limitations, that lies at the heart of the religious experience generally. Judaism is no exception: it tries to show us— through *berakhot* and many other *mitzvot*[5]—that even the most mundane aspects of life involve forces beyond our control and reveal our dependence. Of course, this is not to deny the more spectacular manifestations of the divine, those events which are more easily recognized as being beyond our ability to produce or control. The starry heavens and the order in the world, which impressed Kant so much, as well as more subtle experiences, like Heschel's perceptions of the sublime, the mysterious, and the glorious aspects of experience, all make us very much aware of the limits of human knowledge and power. No less wondrous are the birth of a baby and the workings of the human psyche. These certainly qualify as manifestations of the divine in our experience.

But there is a second sense of "divine," reflected in slang when we call something "utterly divine." Here "divine" means "good," and is used to express extreme approval of certain qualities or acts which are *not* "superhuman." On the contrary, when we talk about divine qualities in human beings, such as love, care and concern, we mean that those qualities are very good, that they make people Godly in contradistinction to bringing out their animal nature.

Which of these is the true conception of God? Both, and neither. Both are, because we have ample experience of both. We are clearly subject to powers beyond our control, and we also experience benign forces, people, and objects in our lives. On the other hand, neither is true, since each excludes an aspect of our experience. Moreover, the two meanings that we give to "God" are often incompatible, because power does not always act for the good, and the good is not always powerful. On the contrary, we encounter many examples of apparently unjustified evil; the problem of evil is a serious threat to any theistic philosophy.[6] Whichever way that problem is resolved, the God of detached reflection in the Western world combines elements of power and goodness.

THE GOD OF PERSONAL INVOLVEMENT

Our experience is not, however, limited to what we gain in our function as observers of the world. We also interact with the world. Then, all of our rational, physical, emotional, moral, aesthetic and conative powers come into play, and we become personally involved with other segments of reality. It is essential to recognize that our personal experiences are just as true and objectively verifiable as our detached, cognitive experiences. We can and should learn from the latter, and our theology should reflect that learning.

If it were only that our intellect says one thing and our emotions and will another, we could conclude that the latter represent what we wish were the case, but that we should act on the hard facts we learn in the careful deliberation of the former. But our intellect, emotions and will do not exist separately within us: they interpenetrate. Consequently, we learn objective facts about ourselves and the world in which we live at least as much when we relate to people and objects outside us as when we stand back to examine them in a detached way.

This consideration becomes especially important in the matter of prayer, for there the personal side of God is most in evidence. The traditional God hears our praises and appeals. People as simple as Tevye the milkman can talk with Him. In contrast, the detached God of power and goodness does not hear prayer, which is a major drawback to this concept, for the warmth generated by one-to-one contact with a personal God is lost. Prayer is a format by which the community is brought together for purposes of comradeship, education, celebration, mourning, sensitivity training and moral stimulation, as Doctor Kaplan and others have stressed, but if there is no personal Being to interact with us in prayer, then all the noble functions I have just listed are not enough to sustain our interest. Without a personal God, prayer loses its soul.

Those of us who formulate this dilemma in theory often resolve it in practice. Even we who construe God in untraditional ways generally *pray* to the traditional God, because it is easier to picture a Being in our mind's eye than to conjure up the image of a Force, a series of attributes, etc. It may be our intellectual laziness, but we come to services hoping to activate the emotional and conative parts of our nature, which usually means allowing the intellect to recede into the background.[7] Consequently we pray to a personal, largely anthropomorphic God.[8]

We are left, however, with a certain sense of discomfort about this apparent dishonesty, or at least schizophrenia. All our conclusions about the nature of God that we reach through an effort of intellect suddenly appear null and void in the context of prayer—or seem to.

A PERSONAL GOD

To resolve this dilemma it is important that we analzye what led us to it: specifically, why do we hesitate to affirm a personal God, and why do we think it is nevertheless important to do so?

Our problems are not those of the medieval Jewish rationalists, who were embarrassed by the depiction of God's personal traits in the Bible and Talmud because they thought that attributing elements of personality to the Deity compromises His infinity and eternity. Heschel and others have shown us that a Greek notion of perfection was behind their dilemma. We aver that real divine perfection requires personal involvement, even if God has to contract His being and His powers in order to enable that to happen.

And yet many of the characteristics that we usually associate with personality do not apply to God in any direct way. For example, we normally expect that a being with personality will speak to us, answer our questions, and communicate love, concern and anger, but when we try to apply those attributes to God, we have great difficulty. Does God speak to us? Our ancestors thought that He did, although they restricted such communication to the biblical period, substituting in its stead the process of midrash.[9] Does God answer prayers? If so, how? Clearly, people become strengthened and relieved through prayer, but not by a direct, verbal response from God. To conclude that God replies through action rather than speech raises the problem of how to recognize an act that is meant to answer a prayer—especially since God can presumably say "No!" And how does God show concern for us? We are clearly the beneficiaries of miracles each day, as the traditional prayerbook reminds us, but we are also the victims of suffering, disease, crime, natural disaster and other evils of all sorts. Are these signs of His anger? But then we could expect a *quid pro quo* relationship between our actions and God's responses, as the Deuteronomist envisaged, and this is obviously not the case.[10]

There are, then, a number of intellectual problems in applying the attributes of personality to God.[11] On the other hand, there are three reasons why we persist in the effort. One is historical: God's personal characteristics are so central to a Jewish conception of Him that one wonders if any theology that drops them can deservedly be called Jewish.

The second reason is moral: God has always functioned within Judaism as a model for human behavior.[12] Consequently, if we deny personality to God in our conception of Him, we are in effect denying the importance of our own personality and our concern and involvement with others; and Judaism has always been and must continue to be centrally concerned with those aspects of life—especially in our largely depersonalized modern world.[13]

The third reason is epistemological: our interpersonal experiences give intersubjective evidence of the reality of human personality, and our attempts to relate to God seem to follow the same pattern. Although these attempts may be a manifestation of our tendency to anthropomorphize God, many thinkers in Western tradition find that their relationship with God is best expressed in personal terms. Halevi was certainly correct in affirming that the religious experience is not abstract and cerebral but rather concrete and total, involving the whole of a person's personality as an individual and as a member of a group. Buber expanded on this description by pointing out that the religious person forms a bipolar relationship with God, such that God is no longer a distant, absolute Being but our partner.[14] Again, this view may be a misinterpretation or even a total delusion, but the number of people involved and the commonality of their descriptions make the religious experience of a personal God the basis for a serious knowledge claim.[15]

In sum, there are some good reasons to support belief in a personal God and some good reasons to deny it.

DIVINE ATTRIBUTES WITHOUT A DIVINE BEING

In this situation we could simply affirm the divinity of attributes of personality without claiming that there is a personal Being whom we call "God," an approach Rabbi Harold Schulweis has suggested.[16] Prayer is then understood as being directed to ourselves, with the Shema as the classic example.

There are two difficulties in that suggestion. The first is historical. There are, of course, prayers which are addressed to ourselves; indeed, the etymological meaning of "hitpallel" is "self-judgment," and Samson Raphael Hirsch interpreted every *berakhah* as a call to ourselves to act.[17] But that self-judgment and call to action were always understood as emanating from a relationship to a personal Being, and eliminating that reference represents a radical departure from traditional theology and liturgy. Rabbi Schulweis is prepared for a major rewriting of the prayer book, but I am wary of such a step, if only because one important function of prayer is to establish ties with our past.

But second, and more important, this step is unwarranted philosophically, because our experience in trying to relate to God in prayer and other contexts virtually demands a personal Being as a respondent, despite all of the problems involved in identifying and describing the response. At the very least, we must say that prayer would become difficult and rather strange if it were not addressed to a personal Being— which leads me to wonder whether we have given due regard to what we learn about God from the prayer experience in the first place.

It is precisely in this question that the considerations I developed earlier come to the fore. For Halevi, the God of the philosophers and the God of Abraham, Isaac and Jacob were radically distinct, because philosophy was understood to include only the knowledge gained in trying to *describe* experience in as detached a manner as possible. But since we learn objective facts about the world when we *interact* with it as well, it is thus *intellectually justifiable* to include that element of our experience in our concept of God. Moreover, it is *intellectually necessary* to do so, because otherwise our image of God neglects a major part of our experience. Indeed, it may be the case that experiences of love, anger, hope, fidelity and the like are logical prerequisites to an adequate understanding of God; it is certainly true that sensitive souls have told us as much about the nature of God as great minds have.

INTEGRATING THE TWO APPROACHES

As a result, I find myself in the same position as that of the physicist I described above: some elements of my experience lead me to believe in a personal God, and some lead me to doubt such a God. In this situation I would adopt the physicist's approach: i.e., use the concept of a personal Being in the context of prayer and other forms of relating to God, but assert unequivocally only the phenomena of matter, motion and personality in the context of a detached, intellectual discussion about God. In such a discussion I would then add that we do experience personal qualities when we relate to God, but that there are serious questions concerning the nature and operation of those attributes. It therefore follows that the evidence forces us to be agnostic about the existence of a personal Being, rather than atheistic.[18]

Under these circumstances, the personal God of prayer is not a contradiction, but an expression of one element of my agnostic position—that part of my experience which supports belief in such a God. To refuse to respond to that part of my experience because of others would be to deny the validity of the personal part, even though there is intersubjective testimony to confirm it. On the other hand, to assert the existence of the personal God of the Bible and Talmud unequivocally is to ignore crucial questions concerning His existence and is, paradoxically, to be deficient in that very faith of which adherents of this position usually boast. For what need is there of faith if the existence of such a Deity is beyond question and clear to all? Thus, it seems to me to be most honest and most adequate both intellectually and religiously to express myself in personal terms in prayer and other contexts of relating to God, while admitting openly that this personal expression represents an extension of the detached, critical point of view: here, as elsewhere, we have simply not been able to fit all of our various experiences into a neat, systematic whole.

The import of recent philosophy of religion is that different activities may well call for different rules of language usage and different procedures of justification,[19] and this approach is another example: what we are willing to express in prayer we are not willing to assert in detached intellectual discussions; and what we maintain unequivocally in such discussions proves inadequate for prayer. We have different *purposes* when we engage in those disparate activities, and therefore *use language differently* in those pursuits—even to the extent of intending different meanings by the same words when we use them in both contexts. The intellect, the emotions and the will interpenetrate in different proportions in many areas of life. In theology that difference means that the God of the philosophers is not identical with the God of Abraham, Isaac and Jacob—which disparages neither the one nor the other. On the contrary, as I have tried to show, both are legitimate and complementary conceptions of God, and we need both to be true to the totality of our experience as human beings and as Jews.

NOTES

1. Yehudah Halevi, *Kuzari*, Books IV, V.

1a. Cf., for example, *Lev. R.* 1:14, and *Pesikta de Rav Kahana*, ed. Buber, 109b-110a, ed. Mandelbaum, pp. 223-4.

2. J. L. Austin, *Sense and Sensibilia* (New York: Oxford University Press, 1962), chapters IX and X, esp. pp. 100-2 and 115-117.

3. Cf. John Hick, ed., *The Existence of God* (New York: The MacMillan Co., 1964), pp. 9-12. Cf. also note 18 below.

4. Friedrich Schleiermacher, *The Christian Faith*, I, sec. 4; cf. also his earlier work, *On Religion: Addresses in Response to Its Cultured Critics*. Emil Fackenheim has pointed out (*God's Presence in History*, p. 15 ff.; *Quest for Past and Future*, pp. 32, 39) that Schleiermacher's stress on man's dependence was so great that he ultimately advocated that we strive to annihilate our own personalities and live in the One and the All. That goes beyond normative Christianity and certainly beyond Judaism: in Christianity man must retain enough individuality to be saved by God; and in Judaism man must retain enough worth and power to meet God, make a covenant with Him, and even argue with Him. Nevertheless, Schleiermacher's insight into the core experience of religion is, I think, correct, even if he took it too far.

5. Cf. Kadushin, *The Rabbinic Mind*, pp. 203-4, 210-15, 307-8.

6. My own suggestion on that issue is contained in a paper, "God and the Holocaust," *Judaism*, Vol. 26, No. 4 (Winter, 1977), pp. 27-34. In many ways that paper is an extension of this one. Cf. also note #18 below.

7. Jewish prayer *does* include more intellectually stimulating material, but it is a *separate* part of the service, centering around the Torah-reading and the attendant lesson or sermon. Even here we expect to learn about our emotional or moral life, and come away somewhat disappointed if we have been given an academic treatise—not that the lesson or sermon should be intellectually sloppy, but that we have very different expectations of teaching in the context of services than we do in a college lecture, or even a synagogue adult education course.

8. I say this despite the traditional doctrine that "He is not a body and has no body," for even though that is what tradition expresses intellectually, in prayer it employs anthropomorphic symbolism—e.g., "Open Your hand and satisfy every living thing with favor" (Ps. 145:16, used in the early part of the morning service); or "Exalt the Lord, and worship at His footstool," which is said when we take out the Torah.

9. *Sanhedrin* 11a; *Baba Metzia* 59b; *Baba Batra* 12a.

10. It seems to me that these considerations effectively answer Emil Fackenheim's claims against British empiricism in his recent book, *Encounters Between Judaism and Modern Philosophy* (Philadelphia: Jewish Publication Society of America, 1973, chap. 1). Obviously the Jewish tradition records and encourages encounters with God, but these encounters lack some of the crucial features I have mentioned, and hence the empiricist's question is still very much in order: are we experiencing a Divine presence or only inferring its existence from the phenomena we experience? I would agree with William E. Kaufman's assessment (*Jewish Spectator*, vol. 40, no. 1, Spring 1975, pp. 71-3) that Fackenheim has not really confronted modern philosophy and has thus not allowed for a total and authentic encounter with God, much like Halevi in his day.

11. The solution of claiming that God has a personality which expresses itself in ways that are radically different from human personality is a pyrrhic victory, because we are then talking about something very different from what we normally mean by "personality." That term in regard to God is then a misuse of the word, and misleading besides.

12. Cf., for example, Lev. 19:2 and the Sifra on that verse; *Sotah* 14; *Sifre, Ekeb*, 85a; *Mekhilta Shirah* 3; etc.

13. A point Buber has stressed, especially in *I and Thou*. Cf. also John Macmurray, *The Structure of Religious Experience* (New Haven: Yale University Press, 1936), pp. 1-38, and Will Herberg, *Judaism for Modern Man* (Cleveland and New York: World Publishing).

14. Martin Buber, *I and Thou* (New York: Charles Scribner's Sons, 1958), especially pp. 81-83; *Eclipse of God* (New York: Harper and Brothers, 1952, 1957 [Harper Torchbook]), pp. 42-6.

15. I should note that experiencing God as a person is a feature of Western religious experience; Eastern attitudes are very different, especially in Hinduism and Hinayana Buddhism. I suggest that the difference is due to the fact that personality (especially our concept of free will) is viewed as an illusion and an entrapment in the East, while it is a reality and a blessing (indeed an imprint of the Divine) in the West. This opposition results in totally different kinds of religious experience and worship: in the East religious training and practice is designed to rid us of our sense of individuality as much as possible, while in the West we are taught to relate to God in an active and intensely personal way in both word and deed. Thus, the metaphysical outlook of each tradition has influenced the religious experience and its interpretation in each—understandably, since metaphysics similarly affects our comprehension of all other kinds of experience as well.

16. Harold Schulweis, "From God to Godliness: Proposal for a Predicate Theology," *Reconstructionist*, vol. 40, no. 1 (February 1975).

17. Samson Raphael Hirsch, *Horeb*, I. Grunfeld, trans. (London: The Soncino Press, 1981), p. 479.

18. There are those who would deny a personal God altogether. Cf., for example, Michael Scriven, *Primary Philosophy* (New York: McGraw-Hill Book Company, 1966), Chapter IV, esp. pp. 158-164. As Scriven shows, the problem

of evil *does* make belief in a totally omnipotent, benevolent God impossible, but the Jewish tradition thinks that God purposely limits His omnipotence to allow for human free will. Dr. Lieber has pointed out to me that here the kabbalistic doctrine of *tzimtzum* is right to the point: the God of Abraham, Isaac and Jacob represents a contraction from the *Ein Sof* of the philosophers. As a result, the problem of evil does not make it a *contradiction* to speak of a personal, benevolent and powerful (but not all-powerful) God: it merely presents a major difficulty in this position, as the starry heavens are a major support. We are then in the situation well described by Hick (cf. note 3), in which we must weigh contrary evidence—and individuals weigh the various factors differently. For that reason we should remain agnostic about such a God in our intellectual discussions.

19. Cf., for example, Ian Ramsey, *Religious Language* (London: Student Christian Movement Press, 1957); Frederick Ferre, *Language, Logic and God* (New York: Harper and Row, 1961); Wm. T. Blackstone, *The Problem of Religious Language* (Englewood Cliffs, N.J.: Prentice-Hall, 1963); and James A. Martin, *The New Dialogue Between Philosophy and Theology* (New York: The Seabury Press, 1966).

Perceiving God's providence is, according to ELLIOT B. GERTEL, a matter of viewing history as a human domain which can be *influenced* by God, but is "normal" to the extent that it is "made" by man. If one studies the Bible in the light of modern understanding of its meaning and development, one can see that, in the Bible itself, the interpretation of events as "providential" depends upon human effort to understand God's Word to the prophets, which was directed to human history. One must develop a sensitivity to the teachings of Scripture regarding God, as well as to the divine order of the world. Then one can attempt to bring to one's studies and experiences a sense of God's providence.

IV.

Perceiving God's Providence

ELLIOT B. GERTEL

HISTORICAL NORMALCY, or "normal history," as I would call it, implies human struggle in life-situations, struggle that further implies *human* freedom to interact with the forces, human and natural (and Divine), whch confront people and nations.[1] Normal history is the domain of man, addressed by God Whose creation makes history possible—Who wills history, but Whose will is not contained in it; Who is committed to history,[2] but has committed it into the hands of man, His precious experiment.

The Bible expresses God's hope and direction for history, or, rather, for man, who is the subject of history. Normal history must therefore be understood, in the words of Michael Oakeshott, as "an unpredictable course of events, the connexions in which are not necessarily logical, but merely temporal or accidental. Consequently, nothing can be known of this course of events except by considering it in detail. And historical truth can be nothing save the correspondence of the historian's ideas with this essentially 'empirical' course of events."[3]

The domains of normal history are the domains of human value: spiritual, political, economic, etc.[4] Yet the religious domain of history claims to guide and to influence history, and even to interpret history in the light of God's Word. Michael Oakeshott, whose definition of historical truth we accepted in the previous paragraph, observes: "Whatever God is, he is not in history, for if he were there would no longer be any history."[5]

How shall we affirm Divine providence, given our legitimate zeal to affirm, at the same time, that the human domain is not invaded?

In speaking of "Divine providence," I refer not only to God's "pre-seeing" of human events (the literal meaning of the term, "providence"), but to His guidance of the world. Yet it would seem, at first blush, that a concept of normal history would eliminate any affirmation of Divine intervention in history.

In affirming God's providence, we assent to belief in His guidance of *all* His creatures, both individually and generally, according to His supernal concerns. This God exercises through laws and considerations which must, if He is truly God, operate beyond our finite human postulations of His "limitation" or "self-limitation" by the "natural order." In sum, affirmation of providence is our way of confessing that God transcends even the human postulates of "natural laws" which "should" regulate Divine behavior. After all, as Will Herberg observed: "Saying that 'science knows nothing of miracles,' is, at bottom, merely saying that, *on the level of existence,* every event must be taken (assumed) to be part of the causal continuum (order of nature). To convert this *methodological postulate,* which defines the enterprise of science, into a *metaphysical principle,* revelatory of the structure of reality, is utterly illegitimate."[6]

HISTORY, NATURE, AND MIRACLES

The normal history that we so zealously guard as the human domain (as indeed we must and should as human beings anxious to retain our dignity as free agents), is not so radically "human" as we may think. Normal history, as such, has no meaning, no "revelation" for us, except that which we read into it. The error of some religious thinkers is to assume that there is a process of Divine revelation *through* history. Such a view violates both normal history and Divine omnipotence. To believe that human beings are taught by God through history is to regard history as a kind of classroom, in which man is guided. How is history to be the free domain of human activity if it is to be regarded as a vehicle of Divine revelation? And, furthermore, what kind of God depends upon such a fickle and unpredictable medium as human history to communicate His will? "If we posit a mutual relationship between God and history," Rotenstreich appropriately replies, "we imply a historical god, a developing god, a god that is not eternally present, whose reality is not absolute and distinct from the world."[7]

In affirming God's providence, then, we must also assent to His revelation of His concern through a vehicle other than human history, lest we do violence to both normal history and to Divine uniqueness.

Though we cannot claim that history is a Divine lesson to be experienced and read by man, it may prove constructive and meaningful to regard normal history as a transcript that *God* can read. Man's activity in normal history, and God's "reading" of it, may be compared to some works of modern art which are conceived as the moment dictates, and are left to the purchaser to interpret. God can occasionally "annotate" the transcript of normal history, without ending its spontaneous composition, by performing certain acts in *nature*.

It is significant that biblical miracles are related to natural phenomena: the sea, the sun, the pillar of fire. When the sun stands still for Joshua (Joshua 10:13-14), it is light in nature, and not hours in history, which is prolonged. Normal history remains in tact, even though the walls of Jericho may fall. One can escape from a lion's den (Daniel 6), but not from hours and years. In the early chapters of Genesis, where the "days" of God's creation and the life-spans of antedeluvian heroes are related in abnormal time-tables, what is being depicted is not normal history, but God's pre-historic guidance of man in "abnormal history," history dominated by the Divine presence rather than determined by human choice. These accounts persist until the Covenant with Noah (Genesis 9:9 ff.), when God promises, as it were, never to dominate normal history, never to punish human folly with direct and overwhelming natural phenomena, such as the flood. Nature would be used to chasten men, to pique his wonderment, but never to invade the domain of normal history.

In patriarchal history, the motif of late births for Isaac and Jacob, paralleled in the patriarchal myths of other peoples of the ancient Near East, are to be regarded more as miracles of *nature* than as miracles of *history*. This distinction is crucial. Although historical laws include natural laws, they are different sets of laws. In a particular situation, for instance, the laws of history may be proceeding normally, while the laws of nature do not coincide in an expected manner. A freak fall of meteorites could kill a human king as he rules his empire efficiently.

The laws of human history, which we formulate in order to enable us to gain an understanding of events, are conceived as we search for motivations. Yet nature has no "motives." A meteorite will fall, it is true, for a specific reason, which may be called a rule. But there is no motive or act of will to cause it to fall at one time, and not at another. Even when man acts irrationally, however, he still acts with motivation. Irrational human behavior is not at all like the quirks of natural occurrences. Man acts with motivations and intentions even when he cannot control them. (That is why psychology is so concerned with understanding even subconscious intentions.) We ought, therefore, to be able to conceive of God as working in nature, as employing it for His own purposes over and beyond the "rules" that we discover in it, in order to influence human motivations, without destroying the essential freedom of men and women in normal history.

PROVIDENCE

Affirmation of providence is perception of God's gracious concern for us, just as prayer and sacrifice are man's means of offering to God the "pleasing odor"[8] of submission to His will by pursuing the holy way of living. But what if man affirms as providential that which is not? When does man have the right to articulate the extent of God's Providence? How determine when Divine graciousness ends and the course of nature begins? How measure His benignity? And how can man be sure that such Providence operates in history without destroying its normalcy?

Before responding to these questions, I had better point out that in affirming that *God* determines the laws of nature which may not correspond exactly to our conception of them, I do not feel that I open the floodgates to fundamentalism. Whether the natural miracles of Balaam's talking ass (see Numbers 22) or of the parting of the Red Sea (better, the "Sea of Reeds") occurred as Cecil B. DeMille would cinemascope them, or whether they were the people's experience of natural phenomena during the course of Revelation, or whether they are legends elaborating on God's Providence in preserving Israel is not an issue with which I care to deal. Enough has been said for each argument; any further discussion would be a bore. God's miracles cannot be verified, but believed or rationalized; only His Word and the Prophet's claim to have received it can be read and judged.

God does not force us to recognize Him because of His miracles. We do not really possess "knowledge of God" until we perceive that He cares for us and for our history. But His miracles, as Jewish philosophers have recognized, are ephemeral events that are meaningful only because the people have testified to them. Each of us can attempt to comprehend His Word; in this sense, as the Sages taught, all the generations of Israel stood at Sinai. Yet we did not all stand at the Sea of Reeds.

We shall never know the exact nature of His miracles, either in their objective sense, or in the perception of those who experienced them. By the same token, the Prophetic experience remains a private matter between the prophet and God. That He can perform miracles we affirm because He is God; that He is God we can affirm only if we have sought Him enough, only if we were reared to seek Him in the Torah where He surely can be found.

The first sustained theological approach to the problem of God's Providence is to be found in the fifth Biblical book, Deuteronomy, which is actually a collection of ancient Israelite traditions, probably dating back to Mosaic times, and collated by scribes in the form of Moses' final discourse to his people. This book probably was composed as the constitution for Israel under King Josiah's Reform (621/2 B.C.E.) to eliminate paganism and to centralize the worship of the One God.[9] The so-called "Deuteronomic" books are those that follow the style and theology of the Fifth Book of the Bible, and include, among others, the Books of Jeremiah, Samuel and Kings. Particularly important in Deuteronomic historiography is the prophetic oration. Von Rad, in *Studies in Deuteronomy*, observes that the Deuteronomist "demands the keenest attentiveness on the part of his readers: they are to discern [an] . . . all-pervading correspondence between the divine word spoken by the prophets and the historical events even in those cases where notice is not expressly drawn to it. . . . This Deuteronomic theology of history, the theology of the word finding certain fulfillment in history, and on that account the creative word in history, may be described, in respect of its origin, as pertaining to old prophecy."[10]

Moshe Weinfeld elaborates that the "deuteronomic word of God relates to all periods and generations and blends with the long-range divine historical scheme."[11] He adds that the prophetic orations are almost invariably ascribed to popular prophets, whose word "relates to the personal fate and future of the kings." Following the theology of the Book of Deuteronomy, the later composers of the books of Kings append a second Word to that of the earlier tradition, which "deals, not with the individual and personal fate of the king, but with the fate of his 'house,' i.e., his dynasty; in other words, it concerns his historical destiny—his place in the divine historical scheme."[12] Thus, in the case of Ahab, Elijah, the popular prophet, announces as his punishment the dogs' licking of his blood (I Kings 21:17ff.) for the crime of killing Naboth in order to seize a vineyard for Jezebel. Yet the deuteronomic editor of this story adds another crime: Ahab's failure to eliminate pagan shrines, which is not specifically mentioned by Elijah. As Weinfeld explains:

> The punishment . . . according to the Deuteronomist, was . . . not to be merely personal (i.e. the shedding of his blood), but was to include his house and dynasty. He therefore added to Elijah's original prophecy a programmatic prophetic speech [vv. 2b-6]* which largely consists of stereotyped maledictions already encountered in connection with Jeroboam [14:10ff] and Baasha [16:3-4]. Its conclusion is drawn up in indirect speech and is the editor's own summary remarks on the religious policy of Ahab [vv. 25-6]. . . .
>
> The deuteronomic editor altered the prophecy concerning the transference of Ahab's punishment to his son in accordance with the purpose which he intended these prophecies to serve. [Punishment

transferred to the son was not due to Naboth] . . . but . . .[resulted] from Ahab's historical sin, whereas Naboth's blood and the curse of Elijah were to devolve on Ahab himself.[13]

According to Weinfeld, the concept of the prophetic *dabar* (Word) as an active force "begetting future events" is already found in the earliest Biblical literature, which predicts the fulfillment of God's Word to grant the Land of Canaan to the descendants of the Patriarchs after sojourn in Egypt. Yet the Deuteronomist made the prophetic Word of God the "focal point of history. Every event of religio-national significance must occur as the result of the word of God which foreordained that event and to which historical reality must exactly conform."[14] The oft-repeated phrase of Deuteronomic theology, which serves as its credo, is: "Not a Word failed among all the good Prophetic Word which God spoke unto the house of Israel. Everything came to pass."[15] According to the ancient, pre-deuteronomic Word of God, the Israelites were to have all the lands of the Canaanites, from Egypt to the Euphrates (Gen. 15:18, Ex. 23:31), a promise reaffirmed in a Deuteronomic account of a *dabar* given to Joshua (Joshua 1:1-9; 13:1-6a). According to the Deuteronomic account, these remained territory to be conquered after Joshua's death (23), but this was never carried out. The Deuteronomic editor therefore added a second Word which replaced the first (Judges 2:20-1), and attributes the unconquered territory to Israel's sins.[16] When the Deuteronomic editor could not attribute his second Word to a particular prophet, he ascribed the oracle to God Himself.[17]

INTERPRETING PROVIDENCE

One finds in Deuteronomic theology the basis for a dialectic between God's revealed Word and the subsequent revelation that derives not *from history*, but from the history of the Word: from study of its effect or lack of effect in history. No Divine communication, inscribed in sacred literature by the prophet, can be understood without sages pouring over it, without its historical effectiveness being tested and applied. Within the Bible itself, and particularly within Deuteronomic literature, the concept of Providence emerges in a dialectic between the revealed Word and the normal history that follows it. The dialectic is canonized in Biblical literature to remind us of its sacredness, so encouraging us to be continually aware of how God's Word actualizes itself, and how we might aid it to be actualized, in normal history.

Let us return to the questions we have already posed about our perceptions of God's providence. Our queries now seem more urgent because of our conclusion that God's providence can only be understood through man's attempt to comprehend and even to help along God's Word. Is providence therefore to be determined by subjective human assessments of events which may really mean nothing? Is our understanding of providence to be left to a consensus between priests and sages as to which happenings are "divine"? Could this not lead to attribution of crude and evil events to "providence"?

It is not surprising that Deuteronomic theology, which was the first to interpret God's providence, was also the first to discuss in some detail the problem of false prophecy, of perverse ascription to phenomena of Divine providence (see Deut. 13:2-6). The solution offered by the biblical text is in full consonance with our modern commitment to normal history, even though the Deuteronomist chooses to study history only from the perspective of the actualization of God's Word in the course of human events. The validity of prophecy is not determined by what comes to pass, as much as by the *content* of what is claimed to be revealed. Biblical law must be honored. The Deuteronomic editors felt no guilt in "helping along" the prophetic Word, because that Word was legitimated by its very content. The Word as revealed through a true prophet reinforces the way of Torah as concretized in the life of the people. The Deuteronomic Word, which is the product of such conditioning and sensitivity to Divine communication in prophecy and in nature, is an interpretation of the prophetic Word through appreciation of the meaning of providence.

The Deuteronomic Word which is added to that of the prophet is but an extension into history of the original prophecy. If in the latter God shares His thoughts about man, in the former, a perceptive Word-watcher, as it were, projects the implications of those thoughts for normal history, as it has and will be shaped by mankind. Yet the Deuteronomic Word does not proceed from the mouth of a prophet! It emerges from the mind of a biblical redactor who is profoundly concerned with the problem of Divine providence.

But the Deuteronomic Word is as holy as the original, prophetic Word because *both* words make up *our* Scripture: they form the poles between which we must struggle with questions of providence. The Torah, as modern, critical scholarship helps us to understand it, leaves us with a creative tension between prophetic predictions, and subsequent conclusions as to why those predictions did not happen in just the way the prophet said. And this very tension is the perfect model for our own humble investigations into Divine providence. *The only way for us to perceive God's providence is by attempting to pinpoint it in our own experience within the guidelines set by Torah.* In order to do this, it is necessary for us to have an understanding of biblical law and thought, to consult tradition so as to engender Jewish sensibilities concerning the nature of God, His attributes, and His relationship to man.

BUILT-IN PROVIDENCE

According to the Bible, the prophet is called against his will to relate God's revelational Word. The call is entirely a matter of Divine choice, a mystery, and is not induced by the prophet or contingent upon his talents or desires.[18] Man cannot perceive God's revelational Word as an inner inspiration, as an insight implanted somewhere within the human psyche or biology. Yet he can perceive within himself, as within nature, God's constant concern. Man can feel God's providence in his natural functions, in his very being, in his psyche and physique—both so frail, so brittle and yet so strong and recuperative; so easily shattered yet so steadily and so soundly healed. Man, like all of God's creatures, is *providentially formed*, made to stand up again when he falls down, to nurse himself when he is bruised, to regain healthy perspective when the mind is dazed. His mechanisms of self-preservation and self-defense bare in each individual a unique manifestation of the human pursuit of meaning and justice.

The awareness of the providence in human physiognomy is articulated with dignity and simplicity in the old Hebrew prayer, found in the traditional morning liturgy:

> Blessed art Thou, O Lord our God, Sovereign of the universe, Who hast formed man in wisdom, and created in him varied orifices and vessels. It is revealed and known before the throne of Thy glory, that if one of these be opened, or if another be closed, it would be impossible to exist and to stand before Thee. Blessed art Thou, O Lord, Who healest all flesh and doest wondrously.

The world of nature, like man, is providentially governed in the sense that the same mechanisms of self-defense and individual survival and growth propel each creature and plant through the web of life. Each preditor is, in this sense, "providentially" guided by his instinct of self-preservation, as is his prey, who is sometimes spared by the very ineptitude of the preditor's manner of attack. Nothing happens by chance in God's world, if we mean that chance itself is part of His design in nature. He allows "chance" to operate in nature in order that normal history not be confronted with an oppressive Nature. He sustains every living thing by His design. "His tender mercies are above all His Works." (Psalm 145:9). Pain and starvation may be the price of being netted in the web of life.

WHAT THEOLOGY CAN DO

I am afraid that I shall disappoint the reader who expects me to offer some "mechanism" of providence, who anticipates a scientific or at least a definitive statement on how God "operates" or "keeps tabs" on His world. Both the earnest seeker of deeper faith and the sober critic of theological ecclecticism would relish such an attempt on my part. I am afraid that I can only add another dimension to the problem, raising old difficulties in the process. For the interpretation of God's providence entails attention to His omnipresence (itself a difficult theological problem if human freedom and natural law are to be affirmed), which in turn causes us to consider His omnipotence, as well as His *omniscience.* The Sages affirmed that before a human being is formed in his mother's womb, his thought is revealed to God.[19] "From the beginning of creation," we are taught, "the Holy One, blessed be He, foresaw the deeds of the righteous and of the wicked."[20] "If one proceeds so as to defile himself, openings are made for him; if one proceeds so as to purify himself, aid is vouchsafed him."[21] Each human being is unique and precious; none is perfect. God realizes our chances and our capacities to deal with our imperfections. We must affirm such omniscience, for without it we could not declare His compassion. If indeed we imitate God by being compassionate, and if the prerequisite for compassion is understanding, we must believe that He Who shows infinite compassion possesses infinite understanding.

We must at this point recall Rabbi Akiba's famous dictum which is the formulization of the classical Rabbinic view that God's omniscience does not destroy human freedom: "Everything is foreseen, yet freedom of choice is given."[22] The Sages never really elaborated on the paradox here offered; they merely accepted it. We moderns will ultimately have to accept the paradox, as well, for we shall never draw closer to understanding the "mechanics" of how God knows and deals with each individual human being. The "solutions" offered to this problem constitute medieval scholasticism; the ability to accept enduring problems as eternal paradoxes is the necessary skill of a scientific age. Affirmation of God's providence should not be as simple as an existential leap. Once God is found and given, the attributes that testify to His Godhood follow logically.

Yet, like the proverbial "spoon full of sugar," theology can help us to digest what living faith forces us to swallow. One theological suggestion that I particularly like, and that the reader may find somewhat palpable, is that offered by Rabbi Jacob Kohn:

What we really mean by God's omniscience is that God knows eternally both today and tomorrow but not that his knowledge of today includes that of tomorrow. They remain two items in his eternal wisdom. God's knowledge of all time is due to the fact that all time is in God, not God in time. If then we cannot truly say that God knows what is going to happen tomorrow, the element of determination does not enter.[23]

Some will object that we cannot assert that God's knowledge is so "compartmentalized." Of course, Kohn here writes somewhat figuratively, referring to God's self-limitation to allow for human freedom, which parallels the Kabbalistic concept of His withdrawal into Himself in order to allow for creation. All theological attempts at rectifying God's omniscience with human freedom must in the end affirm that God both grants and defines human freedom. He creates man as human being, and therefore sets limits upon freedom and responsibility for our species. Yet one great responsibility He *does* set upon man—that of recognizing Him as the One God, for "all is in the hands of Heaven, save fear of heaven."[24] God defines man's physical freedom before nature by imposing biological limitations upon him. He also allows for certain spiritual weaknesses in man, promising to aid us in the task of redemption. Even human freedom to act wickedly testifies to His omnipotence, for, to cite Kohn again, ". . . even the wicked who defy God express God's will to freedom in their defiance."[25]

WAYS TO SENSE PROVIDENCE

Gratitude enables us to perceive God's everyday gifts as manifestations of His providence. Each day, the pious Jew rises and declares, before doing anything else, "I am grateful to Thee, O Living and Eternal God, Who, in mercy, have restored my soul. Great is Thy faithfulness." The humble acknowledgment of the miracle of life is echoed in many Hebrew prayers, such as that cited above which praises God for the vessels of the human body. Perhaps the most basic and yet the most all-encompassing of these prayers is that found among the *Shemoneh Esrei*, the "Eighteen Benedictions," which constitute *the* Jewish prayer, *par excellence*:

> We render thanks unto Thee, for Thou art the Lord our God and the God of our fathers forever. Thou art the Rock of our lives, the Shield of our salvation throughout every generation. We will give thanks unto Thee and will recount Thy praise for our lives, committed into Thy hand, and for our souls, which are in Thy charge, as for Thy miracles, which are daily with us, and for Thy wonders and benefits, which occur at all times: morning, evening and noon. O Thou Who art All-good, whose mercies fail not; Thou, O Merciful One, Whose lovingkindnesses never cease—we have ever hoped in Thee.

The prayer of praise, which originates in many of the Psalms, best expresses our acknowledgment of God's providence. George Eliot once described well the majesty of such prayer:

> The most powerful movement of feeling within a liturgy is the prayer which seeks for nothing special, but is a yearning to escape from the limitations of our own weakness and an invocation of all Good to enter and abide with us; or else a self-oblivious lifting-up of gladness, a *Gloria in excelsis* that such Good exists; both the yearning and the exultation gathering their utmost force from the sense of communion in a form which has expressed them both for long generations of suffering men. *(Daniel Deronda)*

By sensing God's providence, we affirm His beneficence, that even in our affliction is He afflicted (see Isaiah 63:9), for He guides the world in goodness and mercy and not by compulsion or by indifference. We cannot comprehend how God sustains us individually at all seasons, perceives our joy and affliction at all times, and yet is not in the private service of any one of us.

History is in the hands of people, who must find humility and direction through God's Word and through gratitude for His gifts in nature. If we do not engender the sense of gratitude that comes with searching for God's providence, then we can destroy in history the wonderful creation in nature that God has promised to preserve in the realm of nature (see Genesis 8:21-2).

There are two ways to interpret God's providence. The first is that of the dialectic of God's Word, through which we turn to those who study Torah in order to learn what we can expect from God and what we must expect of ourselves. "The unlettered cannot be pious."[26]

If we are not all scholars enough to master Torah, then we can all perceive God's work in creation. Hegel insisted that God created history to distinguish Himself from nature. I think it is more the thrust of Biblical and Rabbinic thinking that God created nature for man to understand what He expects of human history. For nature is the second way that *all* of us can interpret God's providence. In nature we perceive infinite possible situations governed by certain laws and limitations. Can we not therefore conclude that normal history has its saturation points? There is only so much that man can tolerate from himself. However free man is to make any decision, to act in a variety of ways, he can never decide or do more than his being human allows.

Some of the Rabbis observed that even a bird is not caught in a fowler's snare without a decree of Heaven.[27] Some went so far as to preach de-normalized history, declaring that whatever man does below (including injury of a finger!) is already decreed above.[28] While we must reject the literal implications of the latter assertion (which was never accepted as dogma), we can sympathize with those Rabbis' perception that, despite his peculiar human freedom, man can be a most predictable creature. Because history is bound by its humanness, it requires God. The "Divine cunning" (Heschel)[29] of history is that it is human. Man errs against himself, and there is a Divine economy in his very propensity to error. Thus, man can perform a good deed even when he does not intend to do so:

> Rabbi Eleazar ben Azariah said: In Deuteronomy (24:19) the *Torah* states, "When you reap the harvest in your field, and have forgotten a sheaf in the field, you shall not return to collect it up; it shall be for the stranger, the fatherless. . . . [etc.]," note that it says immediately afterwards, "that the Lord your God may bless you. . . ." God thus gives the assurance of a blessing to one through whom a meritorious deed came about without himself knowing about it [for he *forgot* to remove the sheaf from the field]. You must now admit that if a *sela** was tied up in one's pocket and fell from it, and if a poor man finds it and sustains himself by it, the Holy One, blessed be He, gives the assurance of a blessing to the man who lost it.[30]

So, too, according to the Rabbis, the murderer who escapes with impunity may be punished, if not by the court, then by the "hands of God" acting through his own clumsiness or the clumsiness of others.[31]

Nature itself limits human actions. The Sages observed that although man and woman, created last, were the crown of creation, arrogant human beings ought to be reminded that the tiny and filthy fly preceded them in the order of creation.[32] Indeed, the Rabbis suggest that God punished the scoffing of the Roman Emperor, Titus, by sending a mere fly to bore through his brain.[33] Man can be vexed and chastened by the slimy insect as well as by the shattering earthquake. Nature constantly testifies that man is not omnipotent, suggesting at all times that there is Someone Who controls things with *His* Providence.

Judaism affirms unapologetically that "God created and He provides; He made and He sustains."[34] God maintains the world "in His goodness each day, renewing the work of creation," as the Prayer Book puts it. In man's everyday situations, he can experience God's Providence through what Kadushin describes as "normal mysticism." The Rabbis provided terminology for value-concepts derived from aspects of the Divine that they experienced. And these value-concepts

---

*The reference is still to First Kings.

. . . not only give the group as a whole a special character, but integrate the personality of every individual within the group. In reacting merely to the normal events or demands of the environment, therefore, . . . every individual is bound to have, at least in some degree, experience of God. Of course, individuals who are particularly sensitive, or who possess other advantages of temperament, will apprehend more than those who are less gifted or perhaps less well trained. But every member of the group, by being given the value-concepts, is thereby already given training and sensitivity [to perceive Divine love, Divine justice, etc.—in sum, Divine Providence]. In this kind of mysticism, normal mysticism, the ordinary man closely approaches the gifted man.[35]

As Max Kadushin affirms in the passage cited immediately above, every person possesses the ability to interpret Divine Providence in everyday existence.

God's providence, then, can be perceived by each of us when we concentrate on our relationship with God, when we rest within the Covenant, searching for the ways in which God keeps His side of the bargain. By praying to Him and awaiting response, by arguing with Him and attempting to read His stance within the cosmos, we integrate our personalities with Covenantal community and so learn what it means to stand before God as individual selves and as members of the Jewish people. We perceive that to stand in an "I-Thou" relationship with God is to be constantly searching for His providence, to be consistently seeking His guidance. To stand before God is, quite simply, to know how to pray. It is to be able to ask for His mercy while enduring His decrees.

NOTES

1. On the Divine commitment to history, see Eliezer Berkovits, "God and History," in *God, Man and History* (N.Y.: Jonathan-David, 1959). This chapter is one of the finest treatments of the subject to be found, and contains a significant analysis of the problem of evil in history.

2. See Melvin Granatstein, "Theodicy and Belief," *Tradition* (Winter 1973), and the sources he offers in evidence on p. 46, note 6. See, also, Elliot B. Gertel, "On History and Revelation," *Journal of Reform Judaism* (Summer 1980).

3. Michael Oakeshott, *Experience and its Modes* (Cambridge: Cambridge University Press, 1933), p. 107.

4. See Nathan Rotenstreich, *Between Past and Present: An Essay on History* (New Haven: Yale University Press, 1958), pp. 303 ff.

5. Oakeshott, pp. 126-7.

6. Will Herberg, "On Petitionary Prayer," *Conservative Judaism*, vol. 5, nos. 1-2, pp. 48, 49.

7. Nathan Rotenstreich, *Tradition and Reality* (N.Y.: Random House, 1972), p. 39.

8. See Exodus 29: 18, 25 and Levit. 1:9, and the classic Rabbinic interpretation of the expression "pleasing odor" (*reah nihoah*), where God is envisioned as saying: The odor "causes satisfaction to Me by the knowledge that I gave commandments and My will was carried out."

9. On Josiah's reform, see Yehezkel Kaufmann, *The Religion of Israel*, tr. Moshe Greenberg (N.Y.: Schocken, 1972), pp. 287 ff.

10. Gerhard von Rad, *Studies in Deuteronomy* (Oxford: S.C.M. Press, 1953), pp. 81, 83.

11. Moshe Weinfeld, *Deuteronomy and the Deuteronomic School* (Oxford: Clarendon Press, 1972), p. 15. Weinfeld (p. 16) reiterates several of von Rad's examples of how the Word was ultimately regarded as fulfilled (see von Rad, pp. 78 ff.).

12. Weinfeld, p. 16.

13. *Ibid.*, p. 19. James Montgomery notes this in his commentary on the *Book of Kings*, International Critical Commentary series (New York: Charles Scribner's, 1951), p. 341.

14. Weinfeld, p. 22.

15. See Joshua 21:43, 23:14; I Samuel 3:19; I Kings 8:56; II Kings 10:10. These sources are provided by Weinfeld, p. 22.

16. Weinfeld offers several other examples, including the Book of Jeremiah. See pp. 23 ff.

17. See Judges 2:20, I Kings 11:11, and Weinfeld, p. 26.

18. See Yehezkel Kaufmann, p. 96.

19. *Genesis Rabbah*, 9:3.

20. *Ibid.*, 2:5.

21. B. *Shabbat* 104a.

22. *Avot* 3:19. Some scholars, like E. E. Urbach, translate this passage as referring to all being "seen" rather than "foreseen." Nevertheless, this passage has been regarded by post-Rabbinic philosophers as raising the problem of divine omniscience versus human will.

23. Jacob Kohn, *The Moral Life of Man* (N.Y.: Philosophical Library, 1956), p. 78.

24. B. *Berakhot* 33b.

25. See note 20.

26. *Avot* 2:6.

27. See *Pesikta*, ed. Buber, 89a, and George F. Moore, *Judaism in the First Centuries of the Common Era* (Cambridge, Mass.: Harvard University Press, 1962), Notes, p. 120, I, 385.

28. On the Rabbinic view of providence, see Ephraim E. Urbach, *The Sages: Their Concepts and Beliefs*, tr. Israel Abrahams (Jerusalem: Magnes Press—Hebrew University, 1975), vol. I, chapter II.

29. See Heschel, *Man Is Not Alone* (N.Y.: Farrar, Straus, and Cudahy, 1951), p. 225.

30. See Rashi on Leviticus 5:17.

31. See Rashi on Exodus 21:13 and the *Mekhilta* on that verse.

32. Indeed, the Sages observed that flies cannot harm the pious! See Louis Ginzberg, *Legends of the Jews*, vol. III, p. 472.

33. See *ibid.*, vol. V, n. 191.

34. See *Midrash Tanhuma*, ed. Buber, *Vayera* #24.

35. Max Kadushin, *The Rabbinic Mind* (N.Y.: Bloch, 1963), p. 204.

Though many would grant "convincing evidence" of God's presence in nature, in history, and in man, and though modern man may even yearn for God, his faith is shattered when suffering is encountered in personal ordeals. So maintains ROBERT GORDIS, who argues that the "problem of evil" rather than the "existence of God" has "always been the basic issue in Western religion." Some respond to the problem of evil by concluding that God is not all-powerful, but these thinkers actually raise the "problem of the existence of good," since it would be difficult to account for the goodness and harmony that can be seen universally if a malevolent or impotent being formed the world.

Taking the biblical Book of Job as a point of departure, Gordis reviews the various explanations for the suffering of the righteous—"sins of the fathers," ultimate triumph of the righteous, secret sins, moral discipline, etc.—that do not satisfy Job. Gordis finds direction in Job's conclusion that evil will remain a mystery whose pain is significantly tempered by the majesty of God's world. Though many evils are man-made, the question remains why man was so made as to cause evil. Religion answers that man's freedom to do good or evil is an essential facet of his being human. Also, the very interdependence of mankind, which entails benefits and pain from the actions of others, is a partial explanation of social evils that we must suffer in order to be part of the human family. As for personal suffering—disease, pain, etc.—these have served to strengthen people. In history, too, it is often the victim of tyranny or of other adversity who rises to greatness and advances mankind. Even so, Gordis argues, there are many tragedies which can never be understood, and it is best to recall that "what cannot be transformed can be transcended, through the vision of a world which is the handiwork of God."

V

Evil in God's World

ROBERT GORDIS

ACCORDING TO an ancient rabbinic legend, Alexander the Great, after he had made himself master of the world, was shown a pair of scales. In one cup all the gold and silver which he had amassed was placed, but it was outweighed by the other, which contained a single human skull with the socket of an eye, the symbol of man's limitless desires. When Alexander asked whether there was anything in the world more powerful than either man's achievements or man's desires, he was shown a handful of dust, the sign of death.

Similarly, if we were to place the impressive weight of evidence testifying to the existence of God in one scale, it would be outweighed for many by one hydra-headed fact, the existential tragedy of suffering, the burden of human misery, from which none are free. For untold sensitive men and women, the frail bark of faith has crashed on the hard rock of the persistence of evil in a world allegedly created by a good God.

Many will grant, without pretending to offer a mathematical "proof" of God's existence, that there is convincing evidence of His presence in nature, in history, and in man. The harmony and order of the universe point to a great creative Intelligence, and the processes of history reveal a God of righteousness, governing the destiny of men and nations. Finally, man, for all his imperfections, bears the stamp of his Divine Creator, whose attributes find a pale reflection in His creature.

That so many modern men feel themselves nevertheless unable to believe in God is not due to any innate contrariness of spirit. On the contrary, they yearn for God, and would gladly believe in Him if they could. With all their hearts they wish that they could feel the presence in the world of a Supreme Being, all-powerful and all-good, but they encounter a great stumbling block on the pathway to God—the widespread existence of evil, the limitless suffering among men, that blots out the glories of nature and turns life into a horror, or at best a trial, instead of a blessing and a joy. The forms of human misery are boundless, penetrating all the relations of men as individuals and as members of society, affecting the lives of nations and races. Evil is manifest in all the protean forms of poverty, oppression, and tyranny. It appears, without the apparent instrumentality of men, in disease, pain, and untimely death. Perhaps its most agonizing form is the spectacle of the suffering and death of children, who are surely too young to deserve such a fate, by any standard that has meaning for men.

When men encounter suffering in their personal experience, their reaction is immediate and powerful, and disbelief is often the result. Because of the strength of their feelings, they imagine that the problem arose with them or their contemporaries. Nothing could be farther from the truth. It is the problem of evil rather than the existence of God that has always been the basic issue in Western religion. This is the fundamental concern of the Bible, with which lawgiver and prophet, psalmist and sage, wrestled. With an honesty that has never been surpassed, the book of *Job*, which Carlyle described as "the grandest book ever written with pen," is devoted to this dark riddle at the heart of existence. The dilemma was put with crystal clarity by Saint Augustine: "Either God cannot abolish evil, or He will not. If he cannot, He is not all-powerful; if He will not, He is not all-good." It is, however, not human suffering as such that creates the full dimensions of the problem, but *undeserved* suffering, what the Talmud calls the question of "Why do the righteous suffer and the wicked prosper?"

The all-pervasive presence of evil in the world provides the basis for the position of the atheist, who denies the existence of God, and of the agnostic, who cannot affirm it. Some thinkers, conscious of all the drawbacks inherent in atheism or agnosticism, have sought to solve the problem of evil by seizing one horn or the other of the dilemma posed by Augustine. Thus some men have surrendered the belief in the goodness of God. Like Hardy, they see the universe as evil, or, like Bertrand Russell, they describe it as totally unconcerned with man's hopes and ideals. Housman expresses his reaction unforgettably in his lines:

> We for a certainty are not the first,
> Have sat in taverns while the tempest hurled
> Their hopeful plans to emptiness, and cursed
> Whatever brute and blackguard made the world.

Others, unwilling to conceive of God in such terms, have preferred the other alternative—God wills the good, but He is not all-powerful. This is the essence of the humanist position, upon which countless changes have been rung, as in the world-views of such varied thinkers as S. Alexander, H. G. Wells, C. E. M. Joad, and Mordecai M. Kaplan. And William James rejected both horns of the dilemma, when he declared: "God is finite, either in power or in knowledge, or in both."

Undoubtedly, these solutions offer a solution to the problem of evil in the world, to be sure, but at a very high price, *for they create the problem of the existence of good*. If the universe is the result of a malevolent or even of a morally neutral being, what is the origin of all the goodness, truth, and beauty that we do see everywhere in the world? How could a Being lacking these attributes create a life so richly endowed with them? Water cannot rise higher than its source, and man, who is assuredly a creature, points, by the qualities with which he is endowed, to a Being in whom they must inhere in more abundant measure.

On the other hand, if we assume that God is limited in power, how explain the harmony and order pervading the entire universe, the unmistakable signs of a single cosmos? Who created the plus in the world, the regions of reality that lie beyond the bounds of His allegedly limited sovereignty? If God is the sum total only of the forces of good in the universe, or even their source, what power originated the elements in the universe that are not-good? Nor can we meet the problem by the assumption of a Satan who disputes the rule of God, or of an evil Deity like the Persian Ahriman, who struggles for mastery with Ahura Mazda, the god of light, because the world is unitary, not dual, in character, and the same principles operate everywhere. Conscious of these unanswerable objections to a God of limited power, one humanist thinker has argued that it is not the function of religion to offer an explanation of the cosmos. But few men would agree to such a limitation on the role of religion or regard such a concept of God as satisfying.

Thus both alternatives offer no tenable solution to the existence of evil; the original problem in all its urgency remains. Let it be noted at the outset that Hebrew thought, though agonizingly conscious of the existence of evil, steadfastly refused to surrender its faith either in the power or in the goodness of God. Clinging passionately to their God, the Biblical writers succeeded in finding a way in the dark caverns of life. Their most profound contribution to the subject is to be found in the book of *Job*, which will amply repay lifelong study and meditation, far more than can be attempted here.

It is perhaps not astonishing that, like the Bible as a whole, *Job* is more celebrated than known. Because of the complexity of this masterpiece, its basic theme has not been generally recognized. Thus no phrase is less applicable to this manifesto of revolt than "the patience of Job." The understanding of the book has been further complicated because, like other great masterpieces, such as the *Oresteia, Hamlet,* and *Faust,* the basic theme of *Job* had undergone extensive development over centuries, before reaching its present form. The latest stage of the Job tale was utilized by a great poet as a framework within which he could insert his immortal dialogue on man's suffering in God's world.

The outlines of the story are, of course, familiar:

In the land of Uz, there lives a righteous and highly respected patriarch named Job, blessed with all the gifts of God. When the Lord, who is holding court in Heaven, refers with legitimate pride to this loyal servant Job on earth, Satan, the prosecuting attorney in the heavenly assizes, insists that Job's fear of God is motivated by the ample rewards which he has been receiving from God. A wager is struck in Heaven to test Job, and the patriarch is visited by a series of calamities on earth, which rob him of all his possessions and even of his children. Throughout all his afflictions, Job remains steadfast, and no complaint crosses his lips. Instead, he accepts the will of God: "Naked have I come forth from my mother's womb, and naked shall I return. God hath given, God hath taken away. Blessed be the name of God." Then his own person is smitten with leprosy, and his wife, unable to see his agony, tempts him to curse God and die, and thus win release from his torment. Job, however, shows himself as superior to her temptation as to Satan's trials. He rejects his wife's counsel: "Shall we receive the good from God and not the evil?" Job remains silent in his affliction and does not sin. When the news of his suffering reaches three of his friends, princes from nearby districts, they come to comfort him. Stunned by the sight of his misery, they remain silent for seven days. Then Job opens with a soliloquy, a deeply moving lament on his tragic fate, and begs for death to release him from his agony.

Distressing as is Job's situation to his Friends, they find nothing in it to trouble men's faith, for the accepted religious teaching of the day has a ready answer: In a world created and governed by a just God, suffering is the result, and consequently the sign, of sin. Hence, if suffering comes to a man, it behooves him to scrutinize his actions to discover his transgressions. Should he find that he is free from sin, he should wait patiently for vindication, remaining serene in the faith that God's justice will be done. The process of retribution may at times be delayed, but ultimately it will become manifest.

This approach was the distillation of centuries of Hebrew thought which had achieved the faith that a just God rules the world, and then had proceeded to apply it to the destiny of individuals and nations.

In the words of the Biblical psalmists:

For His anger is but for a moment,
His favour is for a lifetime;
Weeping may tarry for the night,
But joy comes in the morning.

(Ps. 30:6)

The Lord is good unto them that wait for Him,
To the soul that seeks Him.
It is good that a man should quietly wait
For the salvation of the Lord.
(Lam. 3:25-26)

A few months previously, Job himself would have had the same reaction. Had it been reported to him during the earlier period of his well-being that some individual had been visited by such devastating blows, the God-fearing Job would have proffered to the victim the same recipe of spiritual self-examination, resignation to God's will, and patient hope for restoration to His favor.

At the outset, therefore, the discussion between Job and his Friends is not a debate. When the Friends come to comfort Job in his affliction, they naturally take it for granted that his faith is unshaken. For even his tragic lament on the day of his birth (chap. 3) is couched in general terms; it is not yet directed against God. Eliphaz, the oldest of the Friends, is certain that all that is required is to remind Job of the basic religious truth that has been momentarily beclouded for him by his suffering:

If one ventures a word with you, will you be offended?
Yet who can keep from speaking?
Behold, you have instructed many
And you have strengthened weak hands.
But now it has come to *you*, and you cannot bear it.
It touches *you* and you are dismayed!
Think, now, who that was innocent ever perished,
Or where were the upright cut off?

(Job 4:2-3, 5, 7)

Soon enough, however, Eliphaz and his colleagues discover that it is a vastly changed Job that confronts them. Job has undergone a shattering personal experience, but he knows, with the knowledge that defies all the logic of theology, that he is innocent. Thus the simple cause-and-effect relation—sin causes suffering and suffering is the sign of sin—has broken down.

We who have read the tale of the wager between God and Satan in the

Prologue know that Job's misery and degradation are part of a cosmic experiment to discover whether man is capable of serving the ideal for its own sake, without the hope of reward. Job has no such inkling. For him, *the accepted religious convictions of a lifetime are now contradicted by his personal experience,* by his unshakable knowledge that he is no sinner, certainly not sinful enough to deserve such a succession of blows as have fallen upon his defenseless head.

Of Job's inner travail the Friends are unaware. Eliphaz, the oldest and the wisest of the three, proceeds to remind Job of the truths by which he has lived all his years. It is noteworthy that the author, whose sympathies are clearly on Job's side, nonetheless puts into Eliphaz' first speech the fullest and fairest presentation of the conventional theodicy on suffering. Divine justice does prevail in the world, the apparent contradictions in the world of reality notwithstanding. In the first instance, the process of Divine retribution takes time, and so Job must have patience. Besides, the righteous are never destroyed, while the wicked, or at least their children, are ultimately punished. Eliphaz then describes a vision from on high which disclosed to him the truth that all men are imperfect, so that not even a righteous man may justly complain if he suffers. Moreover, not God, but man, is responsible for sin and suffering, both of which, be it noted, are expressed by the identical Hebrew terms (*'aven* and *'amal*):

> Not from the earth does evil sprout,
> Nor from the dust does trouble arise;
> It is man who begets evil,
> As surely as sparks fly upward.
>
> (*Job* 5:6-7)

That man, and not the universe, is the source of evil is emphasized in the later pseudepigraphic *Book of Enoch,* which is more consciously theological in character. "Sin has not been sent upon the earth, but men have produced it out of themselves. Therefore they who commit sin are condemned" (98:4). Finally, Eliphaz adds, suffering is a discipline, warning men against sin, and hence it is a mark of God's love. Ultimately, the righteous are saved and attain to peace and contentment.

That is not all. In the succeeding cycles of speeches, Eliphaz adds that there is more to the punishment of the sinner than his final catastrophe, whether in his own person or in that of his offspring. During the long period of his ostensible prosperity, the evildoer lives in perpetual trepidation, never knowing when the blow will fall. His punishment is as long as his life.

In his later speeches, Eliphaz will also emphasize the familiar traditional doctrine that God visits the sin of the fathers upon the children, since all the generations constitute a unity. Hence, justice does prevail, though not necessarily within a single lifetime.

Job has scarcely heard, let alone been persuaded, by Eliphaz' arguments or by the considerably more heated and less illuminating speeches of the other Friends who follow Eliphaz. He has no theory of his own to propose as a substitute for their doctrine, merely his consciousness that he is suffering without cause. He does not claim to be perfect, but insists that he is not a wilful sinner. Against their conventional ideas he sets the testimony of his own experience, which he will not deny, whatever the consequence. As the round of debate continues, Job's fury mounts, as does the helpless wrath of his Friends. His attacks upon their disloyalty, his pathetic description of his physical pain and mental anguish, his indignant rejection of their deeply held faith, serve all the more to convince them that he is a sinner. For what greater impiety is there than for man to lay claim to innocence; what worse arrogance than for him to assume the right and capacity to pass judgment on God?

Bildad, the second of the Friends, paints a picture of the destruction of the wicked, and of the ultimate restoration of the righteous, while he hymns the power of God. Job dismisses this as irrelevant, for he does not deny God's power; it is His justice that he calls into question. Zophar, the youngest and least discreet of the Friends, bluntly summons Job to repent of his secret sins.

Three cycles of speeches are delivered by the Friends, in which the same ideas are reiterated, but with ever greater vehemence. The conventional theodicy, maintained by the Friends, has exhausted itself. As the debate continues, Job is fortified in his conviction that he is right. What he experiences existentially cannot be refuted theoretically; it must be taken into account in any conception of reality.

Job is aware of the contention that morality depends upon faith in Divine justice. If he denies God's justice, how can he maintain moral standards? Job is driven to a desperate expedient, which is to prove one of the great liberating ideas in religion—he cuts the nexus between virtue and reward: righteousness does not necessarily bring prosperity, nor does sin always lead to punishment, as his own tragic experience demonstrates. Hence honest men will tremble at his undeserved suffering, but they will not on that account be deterred from righteousness:

> Upright men are astounded at this,
> Yet the innocent will rise up against the godless,
> And the righteous will cleave to his way,
> And he that has clean hands will grow stronger and stronger.
>
> (Job 17:8-9)

The Mishnah is accordingly justified in concluding that Job's righteousness stems from the disinterested love of God and not from fear. Job cannot see how God's ways are justified, but he never wavers in the conviction that in the interim men's ways must be just.

We cannot here trace in detail the poignant crescendo of Job's faith. He turns first to His righteous God and pleads for an "arbiter" (*mokhiah*), to judge the suit between him and God (9:32-35). As the argument continues, Job's plea becomes a conviction that there is, there must be, a "witness" (*edh*) to testify on his behalf. Finally, he reaches the peak of faith. In a moment of mystic ecstasy, he sees his vindication through a Redeemer, who will act to avenge his suffering. The term he uses, *go'el*, means a kinsman, a blood-avenger, who, in earlier Hebrew law, was duty-bound to see that justice was done to an aggrieved brother. In all these appeals, Job is calling to the invisible God of righteousness in whom he passionately believes, to justify him against the visible God of power at whose hands he has suffered. The God in whom Job has faith is more than an impartial judge, or even a witness on his behalf—He is the Redeemer of the righteous:

> As for me, I know that my Redeemer liveth,
> Though He be the last to arise upon earth!
> For from within my skin, this has been marked,
> And from my flesh do I see God,
> Whom I see for myself,
> My own eyes behold, not another's!

But the momentary vision of God arising to redeem him fades; Job cannot permanently hold the ecstasy—

> My reins are consumed with longing within me.
>
> (19:25-27)

As the mystics have taught us, Job's exaltation is followed by a mood of depression, but the impact of his vision is never completely lost. Job's final speech, which contains his lament on his tragic decline, is a soliloquy, spoken to himself rather than to the Friends.

There now appears a brash young character named Elihu, of whom, we are to assume, the dignified elders have previously taken no notice. He has overheard the debate and feels impelled to inject himself into the discussion.

The authenticity of the Elihu speeches has evoked scholarly debate. Without entering here into this discussion, we may point out that these chapters occupy a vital position in the architecture of our book. It is noteworthy that young Elihu is at least as antagonistic to the Friends as he is to Job. Actually, he denies the truth of both positions. The Friends have maintained that God is just and that, therefore, suffering is both the penalty for and the proof of sin. Job has countered by insisting that his suffering is not the result of sin, and, therefore, he charges God with injustice. Elihu accepts the premises, but denies the conclusions of both sides! He agrees with the Friends that God is just, and with Job that suffering may come to the innocent.

How is that possible? Because suffering may come to men as a discipline, chastening them in the face of arrogance, and warning them before they commit sin. That suffering can serve the moral education of man had been indicated in one verse by Eliphaz (5:17), but had been left undeveloped thereafter. Moreover, the great Unknown Prophet of the Exile, Deutero-Isaiah, had utilized it to explain the mystery of Israel's suffering in a pagan world. It is Elihu who makes it central to this thought.

In addition, Job has contended that God is indifferent to man's suffering and therefore is inaccessible to His creatures. This charge Elihu denies. On the contrary, God does communicate with man through dreams and visions, and when these fail, through illness and suffering. This recognition of the uses of pain is the kind of mature insight that would come to a man after years of experience. We therefore believe that the Elihu speeches were added to the book by the author later in his career. But whoever the author, the theme is significant. At every hand, life teaches how frequently smugness and callousness characterize those who are always successful. No wonder it is not easy to tolerate the "self-made man" who worships his maker. If youth is often brash and self-centered, while age is more mellow, it is because frustration and sorrow lead men to a sense of fellowship and sympathy with their brothers.

Elihu's words end as a storm is seen rising in the east. The Lord himself appears in the whirlwind and speaks to Job. The argumentation of the Friends that Job must be a sinner is treated with the silence which it deserves. Nowhere does God refer to Job's alleged misdoings. Instead, the entire problem is raised to another dimension. Can Job comprehend, let alone govern, the universe that he has weighed and found wanting? Earth and sea, cloud and darkness and dawn, snow and hail, rain and thunder and ice, and the stars above—all these wonders are beyond Job.

Nor do these exhaust God's power. With a vividness born of deep love and careful observation, the poet goes on to picture the beasts, remote from man, yet precious to their Maker. The lion and the mountain goat, the wild ass, and the buffalo, the ostrich, the horse, and the hawk, all testify to the glory of God. For all their variety, these creatures have one element in common—they are not under the sway of man, nor are they intended for his use. Even the ponderous hippopotamus and the fearsome crocodile, far from conventionally beautiful, reveal the creative power of God and His joy in the world. Moreover, God declares, were Job able to destroy evil in the world, even He would be prepared to relinquish His throne to him—a moving acknowledgment by God that the world-order is not totally perfect!

The import of the God-speeches in *Job* has been generally misunderstood, because, in accordance with a characteristic feature of Semitic poetry, the theme is not explicitly set forth, but is suggested and left to be inferred by the reader. Commentators usually maintain that Job is finally overwhelmed by the evidence of God's physical power. But that fact Job has conceded time and again during the earlier debate with the Friends, and he has not been cowed into silence on that account. What impels Job to submit now is the essential truth of God's position, which, however, needs to be properly understood. The standpoint of the author emerges under two aspects. The first and minor theme has been expressed by Elihu, as we have seen—suffering frequently serves as a source of moral discipline and is thus a spur to higher ethical attainment. The second and major idea is reserved for the speech of the Lord out of the whirlwind, with the implications being as important as the explicit content.

The vivid and joyous descriptions of the universe in the God-speeches are not mere nature-poetry. They testify that nature is more than a mystery; it is a cosmos, a thing of beauty. The force of the analogy is not lost upon Job. Just as there are order and harmony in the natural world, so there must be order and meaning in the moral sphere. Man cannot fully fathom the meaning of the natural order, yet he is aware of its beauty and harmony. Similarly, though he cannot expect fully to comprehend the moral order, he can believe that there are rationality and justice within it. As Kant pointed out, if it is arrogant to defend God, it is even more arrogant to assail Him. Any view of the universe that completely explains it is by that very token untrue. The analogy of the natural order gives the believer in God rational grounds for facing the mystery of evil with a courage born of faith in the essential rightness of things. What cannot be comprehended through reason must be embraced in love. For the author of *Job*, God is one and indivisible, governing nature and human life. If there is pattern anywhere in the universe, there must be pattern everywhere. As nature is instinct with morality, so the moral order is rooted in the natural world.

One other significant contribution to religion emerges from the Book of *Job*. For the poet who exults in the beauty of the world, the harmony of the universe is important not only as an idea but as an experience, not only logically but esthetically. When man steeps himself in the beauty of the world, his own troubles grow petty, not because they are unreal, but because they dissolve within the larger plan, like the tiny dabs of oil in a masterpiece of painting. The beauty of the world becomes an anodyne to man's suffering.

We may apply Havelock Ellis' description of the function of the artist in general to the achievement of the author of *Job:* "Instead of imitating those philosophers who with analyses and syntheses worry over the goal of life and the justification of the world, and the meaning of the strange and painful phenomenon called Existence, the artist takes up some fragment of that existence, transfigures it, shows it: There! And therewith the spectator is filled with enthusiastic joy, and the transcendent Adventure of Existence is justified. . . . All the pain and the madness, even the ugliness and the commonplace of the world, he converts into shining jewels. By revealing the spectacular character of reality he restores the serenity of its innocence. We see the face of the world as of a lovely woman smiling through her tears."

It is before the breath-taking description of nature, the beauty and mystery of which are the counterpart of the law and mystery of the moral order, that Job yields up his rebelliousness. His surrender, however, is still a victory, for his wish has been granted:

> I had heard of thee by the hearing of the ear,
> But now mine eye has seen thee.
> Wherefore I abhor my words, and repent,
> Seeing I am dust and ashes.
>
> (*Job* 42:5-6)

To use the language of our day, Job's protest is existential, but it contributes to a deeper essential religion. Incidentally, the author of *Job* does not reject the conventional theology of the Friends out of hand; he merely regards it as inadequate. What he has added to religious thought is of central importance—after all legitimate explanations of suffering are taken into account, a residue of mystery still remains.

We have presented the ideas of the book of *Job* at some length because no deeper insight into the issue may be found elsewhere. With the book of *Job* as a background, we may now seek to grapple with the problem of evil on our own terms.

At the outset it should be recalled that not all suffering poses a difficulty, because in large areas of experience it is justified, since it is the penalty for wrongdoing. We may not be able to share completely the optimistic faith of some Biblical writers that virtue is always rewarded and vice invariably punished. But in a very substantial measure, the principle does operate in life. It may be true that success is not measured out in exact proportion to one's deserts, but in general the qualities of reliability, truthfulness, and diligence win their rewards in the practical world; and, conversely, the man who cannot be trusted or lacks a sense of responsibility may enjoy temporary success, but ultimately fails. Even in our imperfect world there is generally a rough kind of correspondence between an individual's actions and his destiny. Though we may be tempted to deny it in an hour of bitterness and trial, by and large justice does prevail, both positively and negatively.

When we say that "evil is punished," we are, of course, using human vocabulary to describe a cosmic process. What we mean is that in a world based on the moral law, the consequence of a wrong act is inherent and inevitable. This truth the Talmudic sage Rabbi Eleazar finds in the Biblical verse, "Not out of the mouth of the Most High do good and evil proceed" (*Lam.* 3:38), which he interprets to mean, "Of itself, the punishment comes upon the evildoers and the blessing upon the doers of good" (*Midrash Debarim Rabba*, chap. 4).

Job's Friends also underscore another aspect of retribution, its long-range character. All through the years during which the successful malefactor is apparently enjoying well-being, punishment is at work in the perpetual fear and worry which he experiences, the gnawing uncertainty as to whether the blow will descend upon him, and when and how and through whom.

The suffering of the wicked, however painful to behold, does not do violence to our sense of justice and therefore poses no problem for faith in a God of righteousness. Even a long delay in retribution, *so long as it finally comes*, would not prove a stumbling block, great as would be the strain upon men's patience. That such patience, born of faith, will ultimately be justified by events is a basic theme in the Psalms:

> God's anger is but for a moment,
> His favour is for a life-time;
> Weeping may tarry for the night,
> But joy cometh in the morning.
>
> (Ps. 30:6)

> Resign thyself unto the Lord, and wait patiently for Him;
> Fret not thyself because of him who prospereth in his way,
> Because of the man who bringeth wicked devices to pass.
> For evil-doers shall be cut off;
> But those that wait for the Lord, they shall inherit the land.
>
> (Ps. 37:7-9)

It is not the prosperity of the wicked so much as the suffering of the righteous that challenges the faith in a righteous God, who rules the universe in justice and truth.

Some religious philosophers, from St. Augustine onward, have sought to evade the issue by describing evil as being the absence of good, as darkness is the absence of light. Evil therefore has no existential reality, and God can therefore not be held responsible for what does not exist.

As an exercise in metaphysical logic, the attempt may command respect, but it fails utterly to come to grips with the burning urgency of the problem. A child who falls over a chair in the dark is bruised, even though darkness may be described by the physicist as the absence of light. Whether evil exists positively or negatively, war, poverty, and disease inflict a massive burden of agony upon millions of human beings. A youngster left forever crippled by poverty, a paraplegic tied in a hospital bed for life, a woman dying of cancer—their unheard cry pierces the walls of any ivory tower in which a philosopher may take refuge. The reality of evil is a basic conviction of vital religion. Even Job's Friends do not dare fly in the face of the facts and nowhere try to comfort Job by suggesting that his suffering is an illusion.

It is undoubtedly one of the functions of religion to teach men how to transcend the evils that they cannot transform, to endure the ills that they cannot cure, but the path does not lie in pretending that the evil does not exist. Those modern cults that offer this panacea to their devotees are directed to those whose troubles are self-induced or imaginary. To deny that men's suffering is real, that it is massive in its proportions and heart-rending in its intensity, is no service to the God of truth.

A vital faith must reckon honestly with the evils of the world, and particularly with the suffering of the innocent. How can the existence of these ills of life be reconciled with a good God? It is significant that while the basic thesis of *Job* is that evil is a mystery, the book recognizes that our limited intelligence is not altogether helpless before the mystery. To approach the problem, we must recognize that evil is a generic term covering many phenomena. If the problem is to prove tractable, it must be broken down into its various categories.

What are the major evils of the world? They are fundamentally three: disease, poverty, and war. As far as disease is concerned, many of its forms are the result of human acts both of commission and of omission. Malnutrition, squalor, overcrowding, the failure to apply preventive medicine or curative drugs—these major causes of disease are to be laid at the door of mankind. Thus even disease cannot be stigmatized as completely "an act of God." As for the other two evils, poverty and war, they are in their entirety manmade. God surely cannot be reproached with making poverty a "natural" and inevitable condition of human existence. We do not live in a world where the heavens above us are bronze and the earth beneath us iron, so that no green thing grows. Ours is not an earth where sunshine, rain, and dew are lacking and life must therefore grow pale and spectre-thin and die. The all-too-typical modern phenomenon of men destroying "surplus" food-stocks is tragic evidence that there is enough food in the world, so that hunger and nakedness are unnecessary. Human poverty is an evil that cannot fairly be charged against God.

As for war, no proof is needed that it is a human invention. Man is virtually the only creature that preys upon his own kind—and that from no real need but because of greed, ambition and—the supreme irony—for the sake of "honor." To describe war as the human counterpart of the struggle for existence in nature is totally false.

As Donald Culrose Peattie has reminded us: "To be sentimental would, in Nature, be suicidal; if there is no compassion in it, neither is there any persecution. You cannot find in nature anything evil, save as you misread it by human standards. Anger blazes in a fight between two bull moose; anger then is a plain preservative measure, as is fear, which is the safeguard of all living. Together, these primary emotions bare the fang, they tense the muscles in the crouching haunch. You may call that hate, if you will, but it is brief and honest, not nursed in the dark like ours. In all of Nature, which fights for life because it loves life, there is nothing like human war.

"We alone are responsible for the existence of cruelty, in the sense of maliciously inflicted pain. This is one of man's inventions—of which so many are already obsolete. . . . In this present agony of mankind, men talk, shuddering, of 'going back to the ways of the beasts.' Let them consider the beasts' way, which is cleanly and reasonable, free of dogmas, creeds, political or religious intolerances. Let no one think he will find in Nature justification for human evil, or precedent for it. Or, even among our natural enemies, any but fair fighting."

In sum, the massive evils in the world, war, poverty, and disease, are, in largest degree, man-made.

However, even if this be granted, we are far from solving our problem; we have merely moved it one step further along. For now a more basic question obtrudes itself: "Why was man created with a capacity to do evil?" Religion finds the answer in the nature of men, to which we shall return later. But some aspects of the theme must be taken into account here.

As we have seen, we do not know why God willed the act of creation. The medieval philosopher who declares that God's full nature includes the creative capacity, the Hindu thinker who insists that God is an artist who needed self-fulfillment, the mystic who suggests that He wanted to express and receive love, the pious believer who maintains that He created everything for His glory in what would otherwise be an empty universe—all are seeking to cast a little light on what remains a mystery. Whatever the motive, God called into being an untold number of creatures, who emerged on this planet, as we now believe, through the evolutionary process. In all this vast creation, God's will prevailed unchallenged. Every living creature obeyed unswervingly the laws of its nature, being governed entirely by its instincts and being totally determined by its environment. Yet in all this universe, the Creator still remained lonely, for He craved fellowship with a being who would possess, if only in part, some of His attributes, so that there could be a sense of true communion, a free relationship between them. Hence God fashioned one creature, man, "in His image, according to His likeness," whom He endowed with Divine reason and creative capacity, including the ability to control and re-create the world.

Now intelligence, the application of reason to a given problem, means the capacity of weighing alternatives and making a decision. But there can be no intelligence in any effective sense, without the freedom of choice among various alternatives, and freedom of choice necessarily includes the freedom to choose unwisely. But since man is morally free, he is by that token responsible for his decisions, be they good, bad, or indifferent. In sum, reason, freedom, and responsibility represent three facets of human nature. Possessing reason, man is free; being free, he is responsible. With few and partial exceptions, the lower animals lack the gift of reason; hence they possess no freedom of choice and are not morally accountable for their actions.

Even in the case of man, the degree of responsibility varies with the level of intelligence and the extent of freedom which he possesses. An infant may cause some damage, like smashing a vase, but he is not regarded as a sinner. Only as he begins to grow physically do we assume a parallel growth in intelligence and consequently demand an ever greater measure of responsibility.

Why did God create man with the capacity to do evil? The answer is that if man was to be human, no other course was open—if he was to possess intelligence, he necessarily had to be endowed with freedom of choice, and this implies the capacity to choose evil. Because of this ever-present peril, the Bible issues the call again and again:

> Behold, I place before you this day the blessing and the curse, life and death. Thou shalt choose life!

When man, nevertheless, prefers the wrong, as is so often the case, he invites the penalty inherent in his act, the inevitable consequence of sin. There is a profound truth in the semantic fact that in Biblical Hebrew, which is rich in the vocabulary of moral connotation, the same terms (such as *'aven, 'amal, 'avon, het,* and *hattat*) mean both "sin" and "suffering," both "wrong-doing" and "punishment." The same word represents the act and the consequence, because they are inseparable. The wrong-doing of man, rooted in his nature, is the source of most of man's misery. Not God, but man, is guilty of these evils.

Yet the issue is still not disposed of. If the sinner himself bore his punishment, our sense of justice would not be troubled. Unfortunately, however, experience demonstrates a tragic bifurcation between the evildoer and the sufferer—one man sins and another suffers. Hence, the agonizing cry still remains, "Why do the innocent suffer, while the guilty prosper?" Some men die of hunger because other men are gorging themselves. A powerful state covets additional territory belonging to a weak neighbor, and innocent people are bombed to death. Children grow up in squalid surroundings, surrounded by misery, cruelty, and crime, because other men grow rich from the rents of slums. Millions perish through starvation, while "surplus" food is destroyed to maintain profits.

Particularly if we consider the vast underdeveloped areas of the earth, rather than such advanced countries like the United States, it is still true, even at the midpoint of the twentieth century, that those who do most of the back-breaking toil of the world barely can keep body and soul together and live without a ray of hope for security and ease in the future. Contrasting the lot of the prosperous malefactor and the suffering poor, Job cried out:

> One man dies in his full strength,
> Being wholly at ease and quiet;
> His pails are full of milk,
> And the marrow of his bones is moistened.
> And another dies in bitterness of soul,
> And has never tasted any joy.

> (*Job* 21:23-25)

Job's passionate protest will continue to re-echo in men's hearts because it is so deeply human.

Yet we are not altogether helpless in facing even the problem of the suffering of the innocent. It is necessary to recall here a principle which is generally regarded as a beautiful ideal or a pleasant conceit. Actually, it is a basic reality of existence, indeed, a grim truth which we cannot elude. Religious teachers have called it "the brotherhood of man." Its full implications are better expressed, stripped of sentimentality, in the concept of the interdependence of mankind. The positive aspect of this principle was expressed by an ancient sage, Ben Zoma. Standing on the Temple mountain in Jerusalem, he saw masses of people streaming up the slopes and said, "Blessed is God, the source of all mystery, who has created all these for my service. How many labors did not Adam have to undergo until he had a piece of bread to eat! He had to plow the ground, sow the seed, harvest the grain, and then thresh, winnow, grind, and bake it, and then only could he eat bread. But when I arise in the morning, I find everything prepared for me!" (*Berakhot* 58a).

This interdependence of mankind, however, is not merely a source of strength to each member of the human race; it is a poignant source of tragedy as well, expressed in John Donne's famous utterance: "No man is an island entire of itself. Each man is a piece of the continent, a part of the main. If a clod be washed away, Europe is the less, as well as if a Promontory were, as well as if a manor of thy friends or these own were. Any man's death diminishes me, because I am involved in Mankind. And therefore never seek to ask for whom the bell tolls. It tolls for thee." Bereft of all poetic embellishments, the same truth is implicit in Benjamin Franklin's dry reminder to his fellow rebels in the American Revolution: "We had all better hang together, or we'll hang separately."

John Donne's admonition notwithstanding, each human being does develop an insular pride. He equates his personality with the limits of his physique; whatever falls within the territory bounded by his head at one end and his feet at the other is part of "himself," whatever lies outside these boundaries is alien. However flattering to our conceit this conception may be, the truth is that there is no disparate individuality in the world. All the members of a given generation are inextricably bound up with one another. They are heirs in common of all the contributions of the past, and share the benefits of the positive elements and achievements of the civilization in which they live. By the same token, they are responsible for all its shortcomings and failures, all its errors and sins.

The great Confession of Sin in the traditional Jewish liturgy is invariably couched in the plural rather than the singular: "For the sin which *we* have committed before Thee." It thus emphasizes the truth that each human being is accountable not only for his own personal acts of commission and of omission, but also for the sins of permission as well, the failings of the society of which he is a member, the collective transgressions of which he has acquiesced in by his inactivity, his indifference, or his silence. Biblical teaching rightly regards the commandment, "Thou shalt not stand idly by the blood of thy neighbor," as on a par with the imperative, "Thou shalt not kill." Each individual, in greater or lesser degree, can mold the weal or the woe of his generation and is therefore responsible for its shortcomings.

This conception, which may be described as "horizontal responsibility," the interdependence of mankind *across space,* uniting all men in a given generation, has both negative and positive aspects, as the Bible recognizes. Thus, according to the Book of *Samuel,* the entire people is visited by a plague because of King David's sin (*II Sam.* 24:11 ff.). On the other hand, it is this interdependence of mankind which makes it possible for the saint, by his presence, to redeem his sinful contemporaries, as when Abraham sought to save Sodom for the sake of a righteous minority. Similarly, Eliphaz promises Job that if he repents and makes his peace with God, he will be able to intercede with Him for sinners and save them:

> Thou wilt then issue a decree, and it will be fulfilled for thee,
> And upon thy ways, light will shine.
> When men are brought low, thou wilt say, "Rise up!"
> And the humble will be saved.
> Even the guilty will escape punishment,
> Escaping though the cleanness of thy hands.
>
> (*Job* 22:28-30)

Nor is this all. Men are linked together also through "vertical responsibility" *in time,* being united in the family-line across the generations of past, present, and future. However humbling it may be to our personal pride, the truth is that each of us is simply a link in a long chain. In completely amoral terms, this is the standpoint of biology. As Weissmann taught, each being is simply a temporary instrument for the transmission of the family genes. Viewed, therefore, *sub specie aeternitatis,* we are not sharply demarcated individualities, but closely interlinked cells of a single organism.

Because most of the Bible antedates the rise of individualism, Biblical thought expresses with clarity and vigor this perception of the interdependence of men, and the doctrine of group retribution that follows from it. Generally it is applied to the nation viewed as a unit, as in the famous passage, which is couched in the plural, in *Deut.* 11:13-17:

> And it shall come to pass, if ye shall hearken diligently unto My commandments which I command you this day, to love the Lord your God, and to serve Him with all your heart and with all your soul, that I will give the rain of your land in its season, the former rain and the latter rain, that thou mayest gather in thy corn, and thy wine, and

thine oil. And I will give grass in thy fields for thy cattle, and thou shalt eat and be satisfied. Take heed to yourselves, lest your heart be deceived, and ye turn aside, and serve other gods, and worship them; and the anger of the Lord be kindled against you, and He shut up the heaven, so that there shall be no rain, and the ground shall not yield her fruit; and ye perish quickly from off the good land which the Lord giveth you.

The doctrine of retribution could be held with total conviction, because it arose early in Hebrew history, when man's personal destiny had no existence apart from the clan and the nation to which he belonged.

The Biblical historians, the authors of *Joshua, Judges, Samuel,* and *Kings,* made the doctrine of national retribution the cornerstone of their philosophy of history, explaining the ebb and flow of Hebrew prosperity and disaster in terms of the people's fluctuating obedience or resistance to the word of God. The prophet Hosea, as we have seen, emphasized that the law of consequence was rooted in the universe, by expressing it in metaphors drawn from nature (*Hosea* 8:7; 10:12-13). Hosea's older contemporary, Amos, had applied the same principle of justice as the law of history to contemporary world affairs, and found in it the key to the destiny of all the neighboring nations, and not only of Israel (*Amos,* chaps. 1 and 2).

This conception became embodied in the folk-proverb cited both by Jeremiah (31:29) and Ezekiel (18:2): "The fathers have eaten sour grapes, and the children's teeth are set on edge." The idea received its most powerful religious expression in the famous affirmation that "the Lord visits the sins of the fathers upon the children" (*Ex.* 20:5). It is noteworthy that human agencies are specifically forbidden to act on this doctrine: "The fathers shall not be put to death for the children, neither shall the children be put to death for the fathers; every man shall be put to death for his own sin" (*Deut.* 24:16). It is not a principle of human jurisprudence, to be employed by men of limited life span and vision; it is a Divine law of life functioning in a world created by an eternal God.

We seem to have wandered far from our theme of inquiry, yet actually we have not strayed at all. The interdependence of mankind, for ill as well as for good, which links men through time as well as through space, is the key to much of the suffering of the innocent. From our limited view of disparate individuals, there is sense as well as agony in our cry, "If A sins, why is B punished?" But from the standpoint of God, the question may be meaningless, because A and B are part of the same larger organism. A naive parable may clarify the point. Let us imagine a youngster who is very fond of sweets, who helps himself to four or five servings of his favorite dessert and naturally develops a stomach-ache.

If his organs could speak, the stomach might well complain, "Why should I suffer pain, when it was the palate that committed the offense?" From the stomach's limited point of view, the situation is completely unfair. The answer is self-evident to the point of banality. The mouth and the stomach are not independent entities, but are part of a single organism, involved in a common destiny. So, too, all men are involved in one another, sharing each other's sin and bearing each other's penalty.

That human beings suffer for one another is an objective reality, rooted in the world, beyond men's power to change. The interdependence of mankind is, however, more than an impersonal law of man's being. It frequently becomes a voluntary act of his will. Wherever there is love, there is vicarious suffering, freely and gladly borne. As a man increases the number of human beings for whom he feels love and concern—his wife and children, his parents and kinsmen, his neighbors and fellow citizens—he increases correspondingly his vulnerability to pain, because he shares the suffering of those he loves. Nor would he have it otherwise, if only because enlarging the boundaries of loving means deepening the experience of living. No normal father or mother would be willing to be spared the pain, the fear, and the anxiety that flow from the love which he feels for his child. What is true within the family holds true in the larger household of mankind. The crucial distinction is that men are conscious of the link binding them together in the home, whereas they are not yet adequately aware of the larger unit of which they are a part in the world. Yet conscious of it or not, men encounter everywhere the reality of vicarious suffering.

A murderer who pays the supreme penalty visits punishment upon his innocent mother, upon his young children, upon all who are stained by the shame of his wrongdoing. Virtually no man is so thoroughly alone in the world that he can suffer without involving others with him. This law of human existence constitutes part of the existential tragedy of man. To be sure, the doctrine of interdependence of mankind is often professed, but all too rarely taken seriously, but that is the measure of the sin of our age and of its consequences. The physical and moral peril of modern man flows from the fact that he is a citizen of the world and does not know it.

To recapitulate, we have thus far dealt only with suffering which is the consequence of men's wrongdoing. This type of human suffering, as we have seen, falls into two categories. In one, the same individual is responsible both for the act and for its results. In the other, the consequences of the act, be they good or ill, do not necessarily fall upon the individual himself, but upon other members of society, who share an ineluctable unity of life and destiny with him. That vicarious suffering, which is a law of life, includes God himself, is one of the deepest insights of the Judeo-Christian tradition. It is expressed in the Rabbinic interpretation of a passage in *Isaiah:* "In all their troubles, He shares their pain"; and in the Talmudic utterance: "When Israel suffered exile, the Divine Presence went forth into exile with them." In Christianity, it was extended to the doctrine of vicarious atonement. Thus from their individual vantage points, both traditions underscored the truth of the interdependence of mankind, as well as the cosmic interrelationship of God and man.

Suffering is the consequence of sin—that is the heart of the position adopted by Job's Friends in the Dialogue. The great poet who is the author of *Job* expresses their standpoint with all the skill and power at his command *because he believes that it is true. But the Friends' error,* for which they must ultimately seek forgiveness, *is their insistence that it is the whole truth.*

Other facets of the theme, which call attention to the functions of suffering in advancing the quality of human existence, are expressed by other participants in the great Debate in *Job.* Thus Elihu, as we have seen, stresses the educative role of suffering in the formation of character and its preservation. Let it be noted that Elihu does not propose the sentimental argument that suffering ennobles men. It is a highly dubious proposition that suffering makes men better; what it does is reveal them as they really are, stripped of the layers of pretence, convention, and position which ordinarily swathe their lives. Hence, trials often disclose unsuspected sources of greatness in ordinary men and unplumbed depths of weakness in the great and mighty. What Elihu contends is that suffering often acts as a discipline, helping to overcome the fatal human tendency to complacency and arrogance. The Greeks regarded *hybris* ("pride") as the unforgivable crime against the gods. It is the same sin which is punished in the Biblical narrative of the Tower of Babel, and from which the Biblical sage asks to be protected:

> Give me not poverty or riches,
> Feed me mine allotted bread,
> Lest I be full, and deny, and say: 'Who is the Lord?'
> Or lest I be poor, and steal,
> And profane the name of my God.
>
> (*Prov.* 30:8-9)

Those who have never suffered are all too often insufferable. In Goethe's words:

> Who ne'er with tears his bread has eaten
> Knows you not, ye heavenly spirits.

It is this disciplinary function which is expressed by the Hebrew term for suffering, *yissurim,* which literally means both "chastisement" and "instruction." It is expressed in the familiar passage, "Whom the Lord loveth He chastiseth, and He speaks like a father with his child" (*Prov.* 3:12). Precisely because of man's reasoning faculty, which permits him to rationalize his basest desires and defend his most indefensible actions, suffering is an indispensable instrument for advancing the moral maturation of men.

To develop humility before God and sympathy with men is theoretically possible to all, but in practice, these virtues generally flower in the soil of suffering. *Non ignara mali miseris succurrere disco,* Dido declares, "Not unknowing of sorrow have I learnt to succor the distressed." To cite one example out of thousands, before Franklin D. Roosevelt was afflicted with poliomyelitis, he gave little evidence of greatness, or even of sympathy for the ill and underprivileged. Viewed from the aspect of history, his affliction, however painful for him, may seem a small price to pay for the emergence of a dedicated leader in the hour of world crisis.

In his masterly biography of Sigmund Freud, Ernest Jones points out: "It was just in the years when the neurosis was at its height (1897-1900) that Freud did his most original work. There is an unmistakable connection between these two facts. The neurotic symptoms must have been one of the ways in which the unconscious material was indirectly trying to emerge, and without this pressure it is doubtful if Freud would have made the progress he did. It is a costly way of reaching that hidden realm, but it is still the only way. That Freud dimly perceived this connection even at the time, is shown by several allusions to his mode of working. He did not work well when he felt fit and happy, nor when he was too depressed and inhibited; he needed something in between. He expressed this neatly in a letter of April 16, 1896: 'I have come back with a lordly feeling of independence and feel too well; since returning I have been very lazy, because the moderate misery necessary for intensive work refuses to appear' " (*The Life and Work of Sigmund Freud,* vol. I, p. 305).

Illustrations might easily be multiplied of how privation and disability have proved to be men's steppingstones to greatness. The phenomenon which modern psychology calls "compensation" is the method by which suffering becomes an instrumentality for achievement.

That suffering is a discipline is true of nations as well as of individuals. The American nation has matured far more in the four last decades than in all the century and a quarter preceding. The casualties of two World Wars, the suffering of the Great Depression, the bloody stalemate of the Korean conflict, and the horrible threat of atomic destruction have brought to increasing numbers of Americans a maturity of outlook which is finding expression in the growing recognition of America's responsibility to help the undeveloped nations of the world and advance the cause of world peace and well-being. It is the trials of the twentieth century that have made it clear to Americans that isolationism, racialism, and xenophobia constitute the cardinal sins. The process is far from complete, but the trend is unmistakable.

When startling advances made by Soviet science caught America off-guard, a reporter as hardheaded as Arthur Krock was prompted to write a column in the *New York Times*, October 29, 1957, entitled, "The Spur That Has Won Our Race." His thesis was that throughout its history, America registered progress only when it sustained defeat. That suffering is a spur to achievement is a lesson of human history as a whole. Most human progress is not the result of disinterested inquiry or idle curiosity, but the response to a basic lack or a felt need. Necessity is the mother of invention. Man's primitive ancestors were driven by hunger and cold to discover the arts of agriculture and cattle-herding. Pain was the great incentive to man's first faltering steps in the study of anatomy, and the practical needs of society led to the beginnings of astronomy and mathematics. Geometry still bears in its etymology the meaning of "land measurement."

The cults that treat suffering as an illusion, and evil as non-existent, may succeed at times in desensitizing their devotees against pain, but they pay a high price. It is fortunate that their success is on the most limited and superficial of levels. Otherwise they would be anesthetizing men against the lacks and failings of the world and, to that degree, would be hindering progress and perpetuating misery. There is deep insight in the Hebrew phrase, "the birthpangs of the Messiah." Not only the advent of the Messianic age, but every act of birth, is accompanied by pain. Every true artist and scientist has experienced within himself the throes of creation. Suffering in all its myriad forms is an indispensable spur to human aspiration and achievement.

Perhaps the most significant aspect of this function of suffering remains to be mentioned. Suffering is an essential element in man's unending struggle against injustice in all its protean forms. It is part of the divine dialectic of history that men refuse to tolerate tyranny only when tyranny becomes intolerable. They do not rebel against evil, so long as it remains within limits that can be borne, and men's threshold of toleration in this respect is notoriously high. That each tyrant refuses to be "reasonable" in his rapacity, that each oppressor learns nothing and forgets nothing, is the saving grace of history, and, by that token, an essential element in the process of human liberation. This truth, be it noted, bears witness to the operation of the law of righteousness in the world.

A few illustrations from history may be adduced. In 1776, when the American colonies were chafing under British misrule, their slogan was, "No taxation without representation." Had King George III been sufficiently enlightened to follow the reasonable counsel of Edmund Burke and conciliate the colonies by permitting them to send a few representatives to Parliament, the bulk of the colonists would have been satisfied, and there would have been no American Revolution. The United States might today still be a colony of Great Britain. If, before the outbreak of the French Revolution, the king had introduced a measure of reform of the most flagrant abuses, the monarchy might well have survived. Had the Czar of Russia liberalized his government of Russia in 1905 or 1917, he could with impunity have preserved a large measure of his privileges and powers. The tyrant refuses to bend and must be broken—a law of history that is the secret of liberty. It also explains why men must suffer, in order that they may be driven to achieve freedom.

This insight the Bible reveals through the classic epic of liberation—the Exodus from Egypt. In connection with the long-drawnout duel between Moses and Pharaoh, a striking phrase occurs frequently: "The Lord hardened the heart of Pharaoh." To be sure, Biblical thought, which traces all phenomena directly to God, uses this idiom synonymously with another oft-repeated phrase: "Pharaoh hardened his heart." But the wording of the first phrase enshrines a great truth—the hardening of Pharaoh's heart was as essential an element in the process of Israel's liberation as Moses' stout courage. Had Pharaoh mitigated the rigors of bondage and granted his Israelite slaves a few days' respite in the wilderness, some "extremists" might not have been satisfied, but the masses would have been "reasonable" and returned to their task-masters. The proof of this contention lies in the fact that this was precisely the reaction of the Israelites a little later when the memory of slavery had dimmed ever so slightly. The Divine plan of liberation demanded that Pharaoh be cruel and unrelenting, so that ultimately slavery might fall.

In sum, suffering performs several indispensable functions in human life—as a force for moral discipline, a spur to creative achievement, and an instrument for progress toward justice and freedom.

We have discussed suffering theologically in terms of sin, and pragmatically as a means for the attainment of higher ends. Evil also may be approached genetically, as the vestigial remains of the lower stages of human evolution. Like the appendix in man's body that is apparently of no value today, although it performed significant functions earlier in his evolutionary career, many antisocial traits that are the source of so much suffering today are remnants of the past, from which man has not yet emancipated himself. Hatred, suspicion, and combativeness are part of man's jungle inheritance necessary for his survival in the past. They are now a hindrance to be overcome, or at least controlled and sublimated.

Underlying our entire discussion is a vivid, indeed painful, awareness of the reality of evil. There have been metaphysical and religious thinkers who have defined evil simply as the absence of good. This approach has been particularly congenial to the mystic. Thus the mystic classic, the *Zohar*, conceives of evil as the disharmony which arose in the universe during the process of creation, when the Divine Judgment was separated from the Divine Mercy. The Kabbalist Rabbi Isaac Luria describes evil as the result of "the breaking of the vessels" which led to the encrustation of the sparks of goodness within hard shells of darkness in the material world. He sees the duty of man as the liberation of these "sparks" and their return to their Divine source. Hasidism perhaps went furthest in denying the reality of evil, when it described evil as simply the lowest rung on the ladder of good, and therefore capable of redemption through man's efforts. It is noteworthy, however, that evil was never dismissed as an illusion. What the mystics taught was that evil was temporary and superficial, and that it needed to be redeemed rather than destroyed. It is one of Martin Buber's most fruitful insights that evil is real, yet capable of redemption, since it is never permanently or completely divorced from the good. The profane, in his words, is the not-yet-hallowed.

This double character of evil has been sensed on the level of ordinary human experience. Men often speak of a trying experience as being "a blessing in disguise." They have found that the perspective of time often reveals the positive value of suffering that has been undergone unwillingly. It is this recognition that often converts suffering into a stepping-stone to nobler living.

We must confess that we find ourselves unable to accept the mystic's approach as the full answer to the problem of evil. The suffering of the innocent in painful disease, the death of a child, the cutting off of genius or talent before its fulfillment—all these categories of evil are too agonizing to yield to any of the views already expressed. Here suffering is manifestly not the consequence of the sufferer's sin, being much too cruel to be a fair penalty for error, and much too intense to be justified either as a discipline or as a spur to achievement. Some forms of human suffering we can understand, however imperfectly. But tragedies such as these are beyond all the resources of the human intellect. We walk in the cavern of darkness with only the flickering lantern of reason in our hand. Without it, we should be plunged into uttermost gloom, but with it we can see only a little ahead, and often in the shape of distorted shadows flickering upon the walls. The justifications of human suffering offered by Job's Friends and by Elihu are not without merit, but they do not fully dissolve this mystery, to which only God holds the key. Hence the Lord himself needs to appear in the whirlwind and speak to Job. The burden of the great God-speeches, as we have seen, is not to overwhelm Job with the power of God, but rather to evoke his awe at the spectacle of the beauty and order of nature, which serves as a clue to the moral order of the universe. As the natural order is mystery as well as miracle, so the moral order is miracle as well as mystery. Both are revelations of the will of God, which man can comprehend only in part, yet both are capable of evoking man's reverence and joy in life.

Though many of the manifestations of evil in a world created by a good God of righteousness are within the power of our reason to grasp, an irreducible core of mystery remains. Here the creative vision of the artist, the poet, and the musician offers us the only anodyne from suffering, by bringing us a recognition of the beauty and harmony of the world. The universe is a work of art, the pattern of which cannot be discerned if the spectator stands too close to the painting. Only as one moves back a distance, do the scales and blotches dissolve and the design of the artist emerges in all its fullness. In the world which is our home, we are too close to the pattern of existence, too deeply involved in it, to be able to achieve the perspective which is God's alone. Though we must always be conscious of the pain of all living creatures and not only of our own suffering, we can feel that the structure we see is real, and the lineaments of suffering have their place in the total picture.

To be sure, no neatly articulated system of man can fully comprehend either the grandeur or the misery of existence. Particularly when tragedy strikes, it is not easy to share Phillips Brooks's cheerful conviction that the checkerboard of life is made up of black squares on a white background, not of white squares on a black board. Yet it is then that this faith justifies itself, commended not merely by the promptings of faith, but also by the voice of reason.

Perhaps the truest word was spoken by a third-century sage, Yannai: "It is not in our power fully to explain either the well-being of the wicked or the suffering of the righteous" (*Abot* 4:15). Nonetheless, we are not called upon to abdicate reason and reflection in pondering on the nature of evil and comprehending as much of it as we can. What still remains a mystery may then be borne with resignation in a world where so much may be experienced with joy. Man's efforts must never cease to transform the evil in the world and reduce its dimensions. Yet what cannot be transformed can be transcended, through the vision of a world which is the handiwork of God.

SIMON GREENBERG invokes human psychology and biblical teachings in order to propose that the God-faith is the only viable explanation and inspiration for human altruism. Since the only reasonable acts of man are those of self-preservation and the avoidance of pain, it is difficult, psychologically speaking, to defend one's sacrifice for ideals. Some say that an act is reasonable simply if it contributes toward the survival of one's group, but this still does not rationally explain why members of different groups should concern themselves with mankind as a whole. The Torah teaches that man's destiny is to be God-like and thus to help his fellow man. Greenberg's reverence for the self-sacrificing saints of history brought him to God. Though he admits that he cannot know that the Torah is absolutely true, he affirms: "I do know with an absolute certainty that if it were not for the Torah and its teachings, human life generally and Jewish life in particular would for me be bereft not only of all its nobility but of all conceivable meaning." Man, the Torah proclaims, is created in God's image. The interaction of many free beings can never be perfect; hence human suffering. But man must "strive ceaselessly to approximate God by exercising his capacities to their maximum perfection."

VI.

God and Man

SIMON GREENBERG

EACH MAN FINDS God in his own way. The Midrash (Genesis Rabbah 39:1) relates that Abraham's search for God started with the question "Is it possible that a well-ordered, smoothly running castle has no lord?" Some become aware of God by experiencing the sense of "radical amazement" when confronting the mysteries and the majesty of life and the universe. In what follows, I shall indicate the path that led me to God.

It is not enough for a human being to say "I do this because I *feel* like doing it." Human behavior is peculiarly human when it is consciously related to articulated ideas or principles. There is that in man which irresistibly goads him on to "prove" at least to his own satisfaction that what he does "makes sense," that it is "reasonable." We consider an act to be reasonable when we believe it to be reasonably related to a principle whose validity we accept for what we consider to be adequate reasons. The more self-evident the principle and the more universally accepted, the more adequate is it as a standard for judging the reasonableness of an act.

A primary task, therefore, of human thought has been the search for self-evident, universally accepted principles. A principle is self-evident when every term used in its formulation and when it, as a whole, has precise, universally accepted meaning. A principle is said to be "universally accepted" if all who subject it to meticulous scrutiny find it to be valid beyond reaonsable doubt.

Unfortunately, however, the American Declaration of Independence notwithstanding, no "self-evident truths" involving value judgments have thus far been formulated. The wide acceptance and "self-evidence" of some moral principles are illusory, for the concepts employed in their formulation are not subject to precise definition and each one accepts the principle on the basis of his own definition of the concepts involved.

The following two principles fulfill the requirements of being self-evident and universally accepted in greater measure than any other known to me. They "justify" more acts to the satisfaction of the doer and the observer than any other principle or principles known to me.

(1) An act is considered reasonable if it contributes towards the preservation of the actor's physical existence upon this earth.

(2) An act is considered reasonable if it helps the actor to avoid physical pain.

The meaning of every word in each of these two principles is clear and is beyond reasonable doubt, as is the meaning of the statement as a whole. Nor are there any goals more universally accepted as reasonable validations of human acts than the preservation of one's physical existence and the avoidance of physical pain.

However, they obviously are not considered as adequate guides under all conditions and circumstances. Not only do all men not act in accordance with them at all times, but few believe that they should. Human beings repeatedly, knowingly and wilfully, perform acts that either terminate or hasten the termination of their physical existence, or cause them physical pain. Men in the thousands have not only willingly suffered physical pain but even risked life and accepted death, believing that in so doing they were acting reasonably. Socrates drank the hemlock as a matter of conscious choice. Rabbi Akiba knowingly risked and accepted martyrdom. Countless numbers of great and humble men and women daily accept physical pain or discomfort and even risk life itself so that someone else may be spared pain or granted life. If asked why they behave as they do, they would not all give the same answer. But they would all try to refer their acts to a principle, in accordance with which the act would appear to be adequately rationalized.

The inevitable question that presses itself upon us then is this: Is there any principle which is at least as nearly self-evident and as nearly universally accepted as the two mentioned, in the light of which actions which are inimical to the preservation of the physical existence of the individual, or which subject him to physical pain, might be rationalized? For this is the crux of the ethical problem that each of us must face. I do not know of any such principle.

I am compelled therefore to choose one of two possible alternatives. I must either declare all acts which an individual willingly performs though he knows them to be both bearers of physical pain and inimical to physical preservation, as irrational, or I must—for what appears to me to be adequate reason—accept as a guiding principle for my action one which is neither self-evident nor universally accepted.

There are those who maintain that all man's acts if they are to be declared reasonable must conform to the requirements of the two above-mentioned, universally accepted, self-evident principles. They implicitly or explicitly declare the act of the martyr, the saint or the hero, to be the act either of a naive, or a misguided, or a foolish individual.

Some reformulate the principles as follows: An act is considered reasonable if it contributes towards the physical preservation of the group (family, people, nation) of which the actor is a member, or of mankind as a whole, or if it helps his group or mankind to avoid physical pain, even though it may not do the same for the actor.

In being thus modified, universal acceptability is obviously sacrificed. For the principle that one should be ready to sacrifice his physical existence and comfort for that of the group, even though he can avoid doing it, is certainly not validated by its mere statement. It has to be proved. I know of no self-evident, universally accepted principle, in accordance with which it is reasonable to assume that when there is a real choice possible between one's own physical existence and comfort and that of any group, be it nation or mankind, one should *prefer the group*.

Moreover, mankind being divided into various distinct and often mutually hostile groups, many individuals in each group have the choice of abandoning their own group and finding greater physical security and comfort through joining another group. If one has the opportunity to do that, is there any self-evident, universally accepted principle in accordance with which such an act could be declared unreasonable?

In addition, in deciding upon acts that would contribute most towards the preservation of the physical existence of the group (whether the group be less than or the whole of mankind), differences of opinion inevitably arise. For the ultimate outcome of any act cannot possibly be foreseen. Hence, in advocating one act over against another, an element of the unknown is inescapably present. Under such circumstances, in accordance with what principle does it become reasonable for one to accept mistreatment, as Jeremiah did, and even death, as Socrates did, at the hands of the very group he seeks to serve, in order to press upon it his own particular version of what will make for its physical preservation and well-being?

Finally, in a world divided among differing groups, what principle should guide the group as a whole in its relations to other groups, or to mankind as a whole? Few who today rationalize the death of the individual in behalf of his group, by the "life" which he thus bequeaths to his group, are ready to rationalize the possible death of the group by the "life" it may thus bequeath unto the rest of mankind. The analogy we so frequently draw between the relationship of the individual to the group and the group to other groups in human society stops short at its most crucial point. And the individual may well inquire why the group which demands of him to sacrifice himself for it, does not at the same time declare its readiness as a group to sacrifice itself for the good of mankind as a whole, whenever mankind may call upon it to do so.

Let us note that this line of thought, which modifies the original two principles by substituting the group or mankind for the individual, continues to justify acts only in terms of physical security and freedom from physical pain. It merely transfers the point of reference of the pain and the security from the individual to a group. But the transfer is purely arbitrary, in no way rationalized by any self-evident, universally accepted principle. Moreover, there is no way of proving that the act of the martyr or saint makes for the physical welfare of his group. Socrates' death did not save Athens nor did Akiba's martyrdom bring physical security to his generation. Indeed, the group is most often of the opinion that the actions of its saints, its prophets and its martyrs are inimical to its own physical welfare, as witness the treatment usually meted out to their contemporaries.

The rationality of one's reverence for qualities which often endanger and even terminate physical security and comfort cannot then be validated either empirically or by any self-evident, universally accepted principle known to me. But everyone who experiences such reverence profoundly and inescapably, must, out of an irrepressible need to preserve his sanity, formulate for himself a principle in the light of which that reverence makes sense.

For what does reverence for the saints, the martyrs and the willing, humble sufferer imply? When that reverence is sincere and is confirmed by reflection, it implies the belief that though the qualities which make for saintliness and enable one to contemplate and serenely accept physical suffering and even martyrdom, may, and most often do, contribute to the physical welfare of the individual, or of his group, it is not that which makes them desirable or gives them significance. On the contrary, the physical welfare of the individual or of the group, be it even the whole of mankind, are of significance only as they serve those qualities, for only they endow life with significance above that of the beast.

What are these qualities and why are they supremely desirable? I found the answer to these questions in the Torah. While all of my childhood experiences and early training predisposed me to my final decision, they did not in themselves determine it. As I matured, I was exposed to other very powerful influences as were all the young Jews who, like me, grew to manhood in democratic America and received their general education from the first grade through the University in secular institutions. The final decision could not therefore have been made without considerable intellectual wrestling and without a large element of conscious choice.

It was the Torah that set before me the doctrine that man's highest destiny is to strive to be Godlike, for only as he approximates God, who is Ultimate Being, does he, as man, have Being. It was the Torah that taught me that not every act that involves physical suffering or death helps man approximate God. Nor do only those acts which involve physical suffering or death help man become Godlike. The Torah taught me that man approximates Ultimate Being only as he "does justly, loves mercy, walks humbly," as he "speaks truth in his heart," as he "loves his fellow man as himself," and as he strives to understand and fulfill the precept: "Be ye holy for I the Lord Thy God am holy" (Micah 6:8; Psalms 15:2; Leviticus 19:18, 19:2). What justice, love, mercy, and holiness require of me, I shall not now discuss. But of one thing I am certain. The significance of the acts they enjoin, and therefore their own significance, may be suggested or foreshadowed in terms of humanly measurable results, but cannot be validated or exhausted by them. Their significance derives ultimately from their association with a realm which transcends man's mundane experiences. Their significance derives ultimately from God.

Thus it was my irrepressible reverence for the saints and martyrs of human history; for the lovers of mankind who ever strive to serve "the stranger, the orphan and the widow"; for the humble who remain loyal to a sick parent, child, spouse, or friend at a painful price of personal physical discomfort; for lovers of freedom who risk and give their lives that freedom may prevail; for the self-sacrificing pioneers of science in search of truth; for the honest artisans and tradesmen who forego opportunities to take advantage of the ignorance or need of others; and my inability to rationalize their acts in terms of the two most self-evident and most universally accepted principles—regardless of how they themselves might have rationalized their acts—it was that which opened for me the only door leading to God which was never again closed even temporarily. Other doors had also been opened that beckoned me on to God. The heavens and their hosts did speak to me of Him. But the doors they opened did not remain as stubbornly resistant to the repeated, irrepressible efforts of reason and self-interest to close them as did the door which the saints, the martyrs and the humble good, had opened.

Though I can never know with an absolute, communicable certainty that what the Torah thus teaches me about God and about the path leading to Godliness is true, I do know with an absolute certainty that if it were not for the Torah and its teachings, human life generally and Jewish life in particular would for me be bereft not only of all its nobility but of all conceivable meaning.

Man can at best only approximate Ultimate Being, or God. An insuperable chasm separates man from God. Man is a creature and God is his Creator, and man can never be God. For God's omnipotence has but one necessary limitation: He cannot create another God. He cannot bestow upon His creatures the qualities of His own non-creaturehood. But because I believe that He created and sustains His creation in Love, I believe He did bestow upon it the capacity to approximate Him. To the best of our present knowledge, man has been most amply thus endowed. That is what our Bible means to convey to us by telling us that man was created "in God's image" (Genesis 1:27).

I see in the capacity to approximate God the highest expression of God's love for His creatures. To the extent that we exercise this God-given capacity to approximate Him, to that extent do we experience God's love for us. Man may some day achieve that perfection of Knowledge, Power and Will and that perfection of interaction among them which would regularly result in acts conforming to the requirements of justice, love, truth, and holiness. The distance between man and his Creator would thus be reduced to its theoretically minimal proportions. There is, however, no absolute assurance that he will attain such perfection.

Did God then bestow favor upon His creation by bringing it into being even though He cannot endow it with His own perfection? I do not know an answer to that question which is fully communicable and logically beyond all possible doubt. But I do know that for me there is only one answer possible. It is to believe with a perfect faith that in granting me life as a human being, God bestowed His greatest blessing upon me; for what greater gift could He have granted me than the maximum possibility of approximating Him![1]

Inherent in this possibility is the attribute of Freedom for Freedom is of God's essence and where there is no Freedom there is no possibility to approximate God in any measure. In stating that God created Man "in His image," Scripture, I believe, is telling us that Man has been so much more abundantly endowed with the attribute of Freedom than any other of God's creatures as to enable him to approximate God in greater measure than any other creature. But Scripture does not deny some element of Freedom to the rest of creation. In comparison to man all the rest of creation, both animate and inanimate, appear to be completely devoid of Freedom and our modern science with its immutable—more recently, not so absolutely immutable—natural laws has reinforced that commonplace observation. For reasons that I cannot here discuss, I believe that every electron—or however else we shall finally designate the ultimate primary component of all observable phenomena—exercises a measure of freedom, however small it may be.[2]

The existence, therefore, of all of the natural phenomena which we observe is in part dependent upon the free cooperation of the infinite number of electrons which compose them. Every cell of the human body exercises its measure of freedom. To that extent, the normal functioning of the human body depends upon the free cooperation of the countless cells which compose it. Thus also every human being exercises his freedom, and the free cooperation of large numbers of human beings constitutes a human society. This cooperation among electrons or cells or human beings is never perfect. Hence the many tragedies and near tragedies in the universe. I see in the travail of God's creation, His travail, in that He cannot bestow upon His creatures the perfection which is His and His only as the non-created Creator of all. Man, who has been endowed with a greater measure of freedom, as well as with a more ample capacity to know, to will and to do, than any other creature as far as it is known to us, must thus strive ceaselessly to approximate God by exercising his capacities to their maximum perfection. Therein lies his duty and his opportunity. He can find courage in the performance of his duty and in the exercise of his opportunity, in the faith that his Creator is Himself striving to aid him, that He finds divine delight as man succeeds in approximating Him and that He suffers as man fails. *"Bekhol tsaratam lo tsar,"* "In all their affliction He is afflicted" (Isaiah 63:9). The depth of tragedy and degradation into which man can fall is in proportion to the heights of joy and exaltation to which he can climb. God could not offer His creatures the blessings of the heights without exposing them to the dangers of the depths. If He could, He would, for He created them in love.[3]

In man's ceaseless effort to approximate God, the needs of the physical aspect of his being cannot be accepted as the ultimate arbiters of the reasonable. Neither are they to be viewed as its inveterate antagonists. The assumption that man as Being is not identical with his body should not be interpreted to mean that the body is in reality antithetical to man's Being, leading to the conclusion that man achieves his ultimate Being as he denies or destroys the body.

I find meaning in the human experience only as I accept the Rabbinic concept of the essential unity of body and soul. Both are inseparably interwoven in one another's very essence. Both together can strive to approximate God, but can never—either together or singly—become identical with Him. I reject any and all types of monistic philosophy because it identifies the whole of the universe, and man as part of the universe, with God. Nor can I accept any philosophy which posits a fundamentally dualistic conception of man, declaring one aspect of man—his soul—to be in essence divine, and the other aspect—the body—to be non-divine. In all monistic philosophies, man really never loses his essential godliness. Body and soul are merely aspects of the two divine attributes of extension and thought. In all dualistic concepts of man, the soul is, as it were, a divine "spark" imprisoned in a dark cell, destined to return to the original "flame" from which it was but temporarily separated. Hence the soul is really never less than divine while the body can never be anything more than the very antithesis of the divine. No part of me is either God or completely devoid of Godliness.

In praying for life on the High Holidays, we say "The soul is Thine and the body is Thy handiwork. Have mercy upon Thy creature." Both body and soul are God's creations and we ask His mercy upon both of them equally. It is this complete interdependence of body and soul which makes concern for the body's welfare spiritually acceptable and rationally defensible, without making it ultimately determinative. For the martyr, in choosing death rather than physical life, is thus not deciding between body and soul, but between an action which would help him in his totality to approximate God, and one which would seriously impair or completely destroy his capacity to approximate God.

Just as I cannot accept the body's security and comfort as the ultimate guides for my actions, because I would thus identify my essential Being with my physical body, even so do I find it impossible to view what we call death as the utter and irretrievable annihilation of the Being which has its visible presence in the body. For that too would imply an identification of my Being with my tangible, visible body which disintegrates in death. Moreover, if that were so, I see no possible rational refutation of Louis XV's position *"Après moi le déluge"* ("After me, the deluge"). It can be rationally rejected only if we assume that there really is no *après moi.*

What happens to the *moi* after death, we have no way of knowing. Regarding the realm beyond the grave, Rabbinic tradition teaches that even the Prophets were granted no insight into its nature (Shabbat 63a). But I believe that the essential Being of every individual persists in some manner more real than merely as an item in the memory of a descendant or the "race." Moreover, I believe that the *moi* after death is in some significant manner related to the *moi* of before death. To the extent that the body is an integral part of the *moi*, it too must have Being after death. The nature of our Being in the realm "from whose bourn no traveller returns" we cannot know.

Will those who once walked this planet again walk upon it in the form of physical Being that was once theirs? I find no intellectual or spiritual need to deny it or affirm it. I do not find it theoretically impossible because I can think of no necessary limits upon the creative powers of God other than the one I previously mentioned. But I do not affirm it because I do not find it indispensable to a rationalization of my basic belief that my life upon this earth "makes sense" only as I strive to approximate God.

NOTES

1. See Eruvin 13b for the discussion of the question of whether it were better that man had not been created at all.

2. See Hans Jonas, *The Phenomenon of Life* (New York: Harper and Row, 1966), pp. 83-86 and the Index there under "Freedom."

3. The subject of evil and suffering is discussed more fully in Simon Greenberg's *The Ideals of the Jewish Prayer Book* (New York: The National Academy for Adult Jewish Studies, 1942), pp. 80-117.

MONFORD HARRIS observes that while the Bible and Talmud are not concerned with proving God's existence (the concern of modern philosophy), the ancients were not necessarily naive. He points to the weaknesses of various proofs of God's existence, and adds that different arguments appeal to different men. Building on Heschel's philosophy, Harris concludes that if God is embraced as "Holy Personality," proof of His existence is unnecessary. We do not even think of "proving" the existence of a person with whom we have a relationship, lest we reduce him to an object. God cannot be so reduced by humans. Thus, as the ancients perceived, the problem is not whether or not we prove His existence, but whether or not we seek Him.

VII.

On Proving God's Existence

MONFORD HARRIS

I

THAT BIBLE AND TALMUD are supremely indifferent to the problem of proving the existence of God, while philosophers have been deeply concerned with the problem of proof, is itself remarkable. Since for the Jewish Scriptures rejecting God is a sin, one would have expected them to be particularly attentive to this question.

Their silence has been attributed by many to their inherent naiveté, that the issue of proof was beyond their intellectual ability, or, what amounts to the same thing, that they did not reflect on their basic premise. This is untenable. Bible and Talmud are not primitive, precritical works. Should the modern documentary theory of the Pentateuch's composition be established, the view that the Torah is a postcritical work would be strengthened. For that theory, that the Pentateuch is a relatively late and final redaction of various earlier documents and strands, presupposes a redactor, or redactors, with critical acumen and standards as to what should be rejected and what should be accepted. This implies a point of view beyond naiveté. Should a post-modern theory emerge, still lacking a name but explored by such critics as E. Robertson Smith in England and Israeli thinkers like Kaufman, Cassutto, S. D. Goitein, Adar and others, then the Pentateuch, with all its subtle themes and controlled nuances of idea and style, is certainly not the product of a naive outlook.

The Talmud, too, still awaiting sustained modern scholarly analysis, is clearly not a naive book. Its carefully controlled depth-analysis of the Bible, its high attention to detail, its acute probing of words, the necessity for decision as to what part of the Oral Tradition was to be written down and what was to be excluded—all this clearly indicates that it is the product, not of naive minds, but of highly critical thinkers. The fact, then, that the Bible and Talmud do not deal with the problem of God's existence, perhaps the central concern of Jewish and Western philosophy, merits reflection all the more.

II

Proving anything, even the simplest things, is, as every student of philosophy knows, a very difficult process. Bertrand Russell has stated somewhere that on logical grounds it is impossible to prove that when we are dreaming we are only dreaming. A medieval Chinese poet formulated the problem in a peculiarly tantalizing way when he said, "Last night I dreamt I was a golden butterfly. Am I today a man who last night dreamt he was a golden butterfly, or am I a golden butterfly who is now dreaming he is a man?" How much more, difficult, then, is it to prove God's existence.

Many attempts have, nonetheless, been made. At the beginning of the modern era the deists formulated a proof of God's existence which is still used. Breaking with Christianity, they believed that God's existence could be proved by Man's reason; for them the idea of revelation was nothing more than superstition. Their argument for God's existence was that, as every artifact must have a maker, so, too, the universe, the most remarkable artifact, must have a maker. This maker is God. David Hume, in his *Dialogue Concerning Natural Religion*, destroyed the deist argument. He argued that a watch, the deist's favorite example, told us nothing about the nature of its maker. It might have been made by an evil craftsman. On the basis of the deist argument, the world, too, may have been made by a devil, not by God. Secondly, from an artifact one cannot logically conclude that there was only one maker. A group of craftsmen may have made it, particularly when dealing with so delicate an instrument as a watch. Thus, too, many craftsmen may have made the world. Deism, therefore, could not logically exclude polytheism. Thirdly, and most incisively, Hume argued that when it came to raising the question as to who created God the deists stopped by saying God always was; He was uncreated. But if they were willing to stop at a given point, it was equally logical to stop with the universe and say that it always was; it was uncreated. Hume's arguments are ultimately unanswerable on logical grounds.

The deist argument, despite its untenability, has filtered down to the masses of our day. It is repeated by those who know nothing of its origin. We can dismiss it not only because Hume destroyed it but because we know that its appeal was due to the fact that the deists, for all their denial of their Christian predecessors, depended on prior affirmations of Western civilization. Their logical arguments were ultimately no more than psychological bolsterings for a view they were committed to on non-rational grounds.

An argument for God's existence more interesting by its very daring and finesse is Anselm's ontological argument (1033-1109). Anselm argued: I have an idea of a perfect Being; one of the attributes of perfection is existence; therefore, this perfect Being must exist. This perfect Being is God. God exists. The argument was attacked, when first presented, by the monk Gaunilon on the basis of its sheer subjectivity. Yet it had merit. Students of philosophy have pointed to the fact that it lived on in so important a founder of the modern world as Descartes. One might even detect echoes of Anselm in modern religious existentialism.

For our purposes Anselm's argument presupposes that one has an idea of a perfect Being. Presumably we do not. Or to state it somewhat differently: it cannot convince the atheist; and it does not need to convince the believer.

III

It is chastening to reflect on the arguments for God's existence, for it brings one to the realization that there is no final argument that will convince all men. There are, at best, different arguments that will appeal to different men. Perhaps there can be no final absolute proof for all men. It is, nevertheless, the task of the faithful thinker to deal not only with the questions posed by the skeptic but to deal with his own skepticism, too. How is it then that Bible and Talmud do not deal with the problem of proof?

It has been rightly said that in the ancient world there is no problem of atheism. For the Bible, not atheism but polytheism is the problem. Hence the problem is not to demonstrate the existence of divinity; the problem is one of rejecting an *embarras de richnesses* of gods. All types of arguments are used to convince the loyal Hebrew that he should reject the false gods. Yet, while this is true, human being must have had their more fundamental doubts as well; the most faithful believers have often doubted.

In fact, the biblical-rabbinic tradition makes no effort to prove God's existence because it is clearly and critically committed to the proposition that God's existence is inherently unprovable.

The central categories of this tradition are God as Holy Personality. Professor Heschel has analyzed this conception of God as Personality in his analysis of the divine pathos.* That He is characterized by pathos means, as Heschel puts it, that He stands in "personal and intimate relation to the world." God, as Personality, however, is counterbalanced by the conception of the Holy God. *Kadosh*, as is well known, means "separate," "apart," "distinct from." For along with His quality of pathos, He is also separate, apart, distinct from all else. If God were only a God of pathos, He would be nothing more than a most sensitive, loving, though vaster and all-powerful, human being. As a Holy God He is radically different from everything. But if he were only the Holy God He would not be the God of relationships, the God who is ultimately and passionately involved with His creatures.

By virtue of these two categories, the biblical-rabbinic tradition, because of its very affirmation, precludes proof of God's existence.

God as Personality cannot be proved because of two basic presuppositions. When personalities become objects of proof they are just that: objects. A person with whom I have a relationship need not be proved; as soon as I attempt to do so I am not treating him as a person. He is being treated as an It, an object of proof, a datum. He is transformed from person into a thing.

Not only is the other person transformed into an It, but also something must be done by the I that is attempting the proof. To proceed to prove the existence of the personality with whom I have a relationship necessitates stepping outside of that relationship. For in a relationship knowledge of the other is immediate and cannot be proved. Proof demands objective detachment. It means at least a temporary breaking of relationship. In the case of a person proving God's existence it means a breaking of the relationship (however temporary) with God. To break the relationship with God, if only for a moment, has the momentous meaning for the classical Jewish tradition of sin. The existence of God as Personality cannot and must not be proved.

As the God of relationship must not and cannot be proved, so, too, God as the Holy God must not and cannot be proved. An obviously absurd example will serve to clarify this. Imagine a contemporary scientist claiming that he had captured a fragment of the divine in his retort. A classically oriented response to this claim would be that the scientist undoubtedly has something in his retort, but in the nature of the case it cannot be God; for God cannot be "captured" by man. To capture (or to contain partially in a test tube) would mean that one controls. It cannot, therefore, be a fragment of God (though it may be something non-earthly), for God as a Holy God cannot be controlled by

*"The Divine Pathos," JUDAISM, Winter 1963, pp. 61-67.

human beings. Proving God by some formula is a kind of grasping of God, semantically controlling God. It is the essence of the classical view of God as Holy God that He is apart, distinct from, separate from everything else, that He cannot be grasped by retorts or formulae, which are, in effect verbal test tubes. God as Holy God cannot, in the nature of the case, be proved.

IV

The term holy personality is not a formula that grasps God. Firstly, it is not proof that this God exists; it simply tells us about God. But the nature of this telling is in itself significant. That He is Personality tells us not about God objectively but that He is the God of relationship-with-us. That He is Holy tells us that all formulations, even pathos, are inadequate or partial. Holiness is, therefore, a counterbalance to everything, even to Personality.

Secondly, Holy Personality is not a formula of humans that grasps God. Men may have reached out for the gods, as the history of human culture would indicate. But the traditional Jewish understanding has been that the Holy God above and beyond our grasp has reached out to grasp us.

V

The skeptical Jew who seeks for proof of God's existence misunderstands the issue. No proof can prove the existence of the Holy Personality God. At best it proves the philosopher's God, who is neither the God of relationships, for he is a metaphysical objective datum, nor is he the Holy God, since he is grasped by formula. The skeptical Jew—dear to us, for we are all he to a lesser or greater extent—must give up the quest for proof of God's existence. He must quest God. For, the tradition assures us that "when ye quest Me ye shall surely find Me." This assumes, of course, that the quest is sincere. Since there is evidence that no man knows himself as he truly is, one can assume that only God judges one's sincerity. The skeptic who strives, therefore, to be sincere in striving for God does not quest to grasp God in a proof formula but prays that God grasp him in genuine relationship.

The classical problem, therefore, is not the problem of proof but the problem of prayer, that is, the dialogue between the skeptic and the Holy Personality God. Or, to state it somewhat differently, for the modern skeptic the beginning of wisdom is to become skeptical of his skepticism.

Modern man, WILL HERBERG laments, generally understands the "God-idea" in the light of Greek metaphysics and medieval scholasticism. God thus becomes an all-embracing cosmic force on the one hand, or the "divine in us" on the other. Yet the God of Hebraic tradition is the God of the Bible, a "Living God," a dynamic personal power. Defending the anthropomorphism of the Bible against its rational detractors, Herberg makes use of Heschel's notion that the divine reveals itself as "emotional-personal."

"The God of the Hebraic tradition," Herberg observes, "is either a living, active and 'feeling' God or he is nothing." Herberg attempts to trace the reasons for the modernist inability to think of God as "personal." Apart from the influence of the Greek tradition, modern man, according to Herberg, is influenced by the "antipersonalistic bias of our culture." Herberg warns: "To deny personality to God, as the modern mind is prone to do, is . . . at bottom, to deny the reality and worth of personality in man."

Herberg explores the implications of the biblical account of creation, observing that "the pronouncements of science in this regard are not only dubious but irrelevant." The biblical doctrine of creation is understood by Herberg as an "indispensable ground for any conception of nature that does justice to its reality and value without losing sight of its contingent and conditional character."

The affirmation of divine sovereignty, Herberg concludes, "makes available a perspective that transcends the immediate and partial interests of life and is thus a most potent force for sanity in individual and social existence."

VIII.

The "God-Idea" and the Living God

WILL HERBERG

ONE OF THE GREATEST obstacles in the way of modern man's appropriating or even understanding the religious tradition to which he is heir is the fact that the only "God-idea" made available to him by contemporary culture is one that can possess very little significance for his life or for the larger destiny of the world he lives in. We are all of us more or less involved in this strange situation. Even when we have succeeded in breaking through current secularist prejudice to the point of being ready to think seriously about God, we only too easily fall into a conception of the divine that has virtually no power or meaning in human existence. That is the only conception, apparently, of which we, in our modern-mindedness, are capable, and yet it is a conception that leads nowhere. The biblical teaching about God, even when we read and ponder the Scriptures, seems somehow to elude our comprehension, but it is the only teaching that can make our affirmation of God a potent transforming force in our lives.

The "God-idea" that comes, so to speak, naturally to modern man is an idea out of Greek metaphysics and medieval scholasticism, recast here and there by the rationalism of the past two centuries. It sees "God" as, on the one hand, a sort of all-embracing cosmic force or "soul of the universe" and, on the other, as the "divine in us," the exalted ideals toward which we strive. Religion then becomes indeed what Matthew Arnold called it, "morality touched with emotion"—a kind of sentimentalized ethic afloat in a vague, heart-warming sea of cosmic piety. But if that is God and that is religion, of what possible significance can either be? No wonder so many today who are earnestly searching for something beyond the prevalent secularism can make nothing of religion. The religion that reaches us is somehow too tenuous to be relevant to the burning interests of our time, too etherealized to give us an understanding of the permanent crisis in which we find ourselves or the resources with which to cope with it. Something very different is required.

And something very different is available. The "God-idea" of contemporary spirituality is not the God of Hebraic religion. The God of Hebraic religion is not a philosophical principle, an ethical ideal or a cosmic process. The God of Hebraic religion, the God of the Bible, is a *Living God*. In this tremendous phrase—the Living God—which has become so strange to our ears but which occurs repeatedly in the Bible and continues right through rabbinic tradition,[1] is concentrated the full potency of the Hebraic "God-idea." Only, it is no longer a mere "God-idea"; it is the Living God himself.

When Judaism speaks of the Living God, it means to affirm that the transcendent Absolute which is the ultimate reality is not an abstract idea or an intellectual principal but a *dynamic Power* in life and history— and a dynamic power that is *personal*. The God of Judaism is thus best understood as a transcendent Person whose very "essence" is activity, activity not in some superworld of disembodied souls but in the actual world of men and things.

Attribution of personality to God is a scandal to modern minds. The religiously inclined man of today can understand and "appreciate" a God who—or rather, *which*—is some impersonal process or metaphysical concept. But a God who is personal, a person: that seems to be the grossest "anthropomorphism" and therefore the grossest superstition. Who can believe in any such thing?

The embarrassment of modern man when confronted with a personal God casts a revealing light on his entire outlook. In a certain sense, of course, every statement we make about God is bound to be both misleading and paradoxical. For the language we employ is of necessity the language of nature, while that to which we apply it is beyond nature; such usage must therefore necessarily be in some sense figurative and burdened with a heavy load of ambiguity. The transcendent Absolute obviously cannot be comprehended in any formula devised by the mind of man. Attempting to express or communicate what one wants to say about God is very much like trying to represent three-dimensional reality on a flat surface, by perspective drawing or projection. The representation is both true and false, significant and misleading: true and significant if taken in terms of the symbolism employed, false and misleading if taken literally. In speaking of God and religion, the words or phrases we use are symbols in a very special sense: they serve to point to a super-dimensional reality that cannot be grasped in idea or perception. They do more; if they are adequate to the purpose, they serve also to reveal some of its reality and meaning for us. We thus express what is beyond nature in terms of the natural, what is unconditioned in terms of the conditioned, what is eternal in terms of the temporal, what is absolute in terms of the relative.[2] No wonder that every such expression of ours ends up in paradox; paradox can penetrate where the self-consistent speculations of reason can never reach.

In whatever way we speak of God, whether we speak of him as a cosmic force or as a transcendent Person, we are making use of religious symbols. Everything depends upon the kind of symbols we use, for the symbols we use indicate not only the kind of God we affirm but also—what is very much the same thing in the end—our entire outlook on the universe. What do we mean when we speak of God as a Person? We mean that we meet God in life and history, not as an object, not as a thing, not as an *It*—to use Buber's pregnant distinction[3]—but as a Thou, with whom we can enter into genuine person-to-person relations. Indeed, it is this I-Thou encounter with God that constitutes the primary life-giving experience of faith: God, as Buber points out, can never be expressed; he can only be addressed.[4] This personal encounter with God—"the Being that is directly, most nearly and lastingly over against us"[5]—is not "merely" subjective, as naturalistic oversimplification would have it; it is an immediate self-validating encounter which transcends the ordinary distinction between subject and object, just as does any genuine encounter between man and man. For there are two ways of "knowing": knowing a *person* by *encounter* and communication, and knowing a *thing* by *using* it. When one man meets another as person to person, is it not absurd to speak of this encounter as either subjective or objective? Is it not absurd to speak of it as if the encounter itself, as well as the person we meet, were no more than a state of mind of ours or, on the other hand, as if the other person were an object about whose existence we have to assure ourselves through the objective procedures of scientific method? Is not this a total falsification of the real meaning of the I-Thou encounter, which is primary and self-revealing and prior to all distinctions of the understanding? What is true between man and man is true equally, or rather pre-eminently, between man and God.[6]

The ascription of personality to God is thus an affirmation of the fact that in the encounter of faith God meets us as person to person. It means, too, that the divine Person we meet in this encounter confronts us as a source of free dynamic activity and purpose. It is this freedom and purpose that, within limits—for the human spirit is conditioned by all the circumstances of life—exhibits itself in our own existence as an essential part of the meaning of personality. In God, these limitations are, of course, stripped away, and the free activity of personality manifests itself in consummate form. The Scriptural writers—whether legalist, priestly or prophetic—simply take the full personality of God as axiomatic. God speaks and is spoken to; he is jealous, angry, compassionate and forgiving; he acts and is acted upon; he has aims and purposes which he executes in history: he is, in short, a "decision-making person who has communication with and care for decision-making persons on this earth."[7] Later philosophers and to some extent even rabbinic writers were embarrassed by biblical expressions reflecting this "conception" of God and tried to explain them away as merely figurative or poetical;[8] modern apologists have generally followed the same line. But this will not do. Remove the "anthropomorphic"—or rather anthropo*pathic*—features from the biblical account of God and nothing whatever is left, not even a philosophical concept. "The divine reveals itself," writes A. J. Heschel, discussing the prophetic experience, "in a characteristically conditioned manner. . . . It reveals itself in its 'pathetic,' that is, emotional-personal bearing. God does not merely command and require obedience, he is also moved and affected; he does not simply go on ruling the world impassively, he also experiences it."[9] The God of Hebraic religion is either a living, active, "feeling" God or he is nothing.

Why is it that we, modern-minded men, are so scandalized when we are seriously asked to think of God as personal? To some extent, it is probably due to the fact that we have inherited the Greek metaphysical conception of God as Pure Being, incapable of change, modification, affection or outgoing action; after all, as Brunner points out, are not the Greeks the "tutors of our age" so that "even the thinking of the common man . . . is thoroughly pervaded by their thought"?[10] But fundamentally, it seems to me, this embarrassment of ours is to be traced to the pervasive antipersonalistic bias of our culture. The whole tendency of mechanistic science and technology in the past two centuries has been to "dehumanize" our thinking and to imbue us with the conviction that personality is "merely subjective" and therefore unreal, since *real* reality, the reality presented to us by science, is impersonal. It is not seen how ambiguous, how dangerous, this term "impersonal" is, implying, as it does, both what is above and what is below personality. It may be proper to hesitate to attribute personality unconditionally to the divine because God's superpersonal being takes in and transcends all aspects of personality, but it is sheer stultification to relegate the divine to a *sub*personal level.[11] How far must the depersonalization, the dehumanization, of our culture have gone that we have come to regard it as a mark of enlightenment and sophistication to picture the highest reality in terms of such subhuman concepts as a tendency of development or a field of force!

To deny personality to God, as the modern mind is prone to do, is thus, at bottom, to deny the reality and worth of personality in man. On the other hand, the affirmation of God as personal is not only dictated by the reality of the divine-human encounter but is also a vindication of the pre-eminence of personal being as we find it in human existence over the nonpersonal categories of science and philosophy. This conclusion is significant of a general relation we shall find repeated in various contexts: the denial of God leads inexorably to the devaluation and destruction of man.

God is thus not some "spiritual" abstraction or principle for man to reach through intellectual illumination; God, in Hebraic religion, is an active, living "decision-making" Being who plunges into human history and personally encounters men in their activity. But this God, let us not forget, is a transcendent God never to be simply identified with, or found inside of, the world of nature and man. This paradox of a God who is beyond everything in nature and history, and yet is ever actively involved in both, goes to the heart of Hebraic religion, especially as revealed in the prophetic writings. It is the dialectical paradox of the Wholly Other/Wholly Present that we meet on all levels of life and experience.[12]

This paradox is most profoundly expressed in the biblical teaching on creation, which is in more than one sense the beginning of all that follows. According to the Scriptural account, God creates the world, and, in later interpretation, creates it *out of nothing*. All existence that is not God is thus affirmed to be conditioned by and dependent upon God, the Unconditioned: God as Creator is Lord over all. This is the foundation of biblical theology.

Modern man finds it difficult to understand this or any other concept of creation because science seems to him to teach the infinity of time and space, the beginninglessness and endlessness and therefore the essential changelessness of things.[13] But the pronouncements of science in this regard are not only dubious but irrelevant, for what the biblical doctrine of creation is intended to express is not so much an event in time as the presupposition of all temporal existence. Creation is thus in the first place an affirmation that "nature" or the world is not self-subsistent and autonomous but owes its being to its transcendent source. The Creator God, however, is not the absentee divinity of deism, who, having once completed his work, retires from the universe. God re-creates the universe at every moment, rabbinic tradition tells us,[14] and this is meant to express not only the pregnant insight that creation continues but also the fundamental fact that, even after it has come into being, the created universe can make no claim to self-subsistence. Creation continues because the universe remains open and novelty ever emerges, because no system of closed mechanical determinism can ever be final. For the same reason, the universe can never lay claim to autonomy unless "Nature," as with Spinoza and other pantheists, is taken to be divine. It is precisely this type of idolatry—the worship of the world, its powers and "laws"—that the biblical doctrine of creation protects us against.

Between the Creator God and the world that is his creation there is a vast gulf that can be bridged only from the side of the divine: all significance, all value, all power is an endowment from God. This, in the last analysis, is the meaning of the holiness of God which the Scriptural and rabbinical writers are never tired of exalting.[15]

The absolute transcendence of God [H. Frankfort declares] is the foundation of Hebrew religious thought. God is absolute, unqualified, ineffable, transcending every phenomenon, the one and only cause of all existence. God, moreover, is holy, which means that all values are ultimately his. . . . To Hebrew thought, nature appears void of divinity . . . God is not in sun and stars, rain and wind; they are his creatures and serve him. Every alleviation of the stern belief in God's transcendence is corruption. In Hebrew religion, and in Hebrew religion alone, the ancient [pagan] bond between man and nature is destroyed. . . . Man remains outside nature. . . .[16]

As Waxman puts it, in Judaism "man is freed from subjection to nature."[17] And indeed faith in the transcendent God who is Lord of nature saves man from standing in superstitious terror before the powers of nature or from being swallowed up in sentimental-mystical ecstasy by its mysterious rhythms. Nature is neither divine nor corrupt; sustained in this belief, man can confront it without fear and master it.[18]

The traditional doctrine of creation *out of nothing* expresses the conviction that there is no ultimate principle in the universe aside from God. It is thus an utter rejection of the dualism or polytheism that underlies all religions but those stemming from Hebraic sources. Because God created the universe, existence as such must be good;[19] indeed, the Scriptural account presents God as making this pronouncement at every stage of the creative process. Hebraic teaching has no place for the Greco-Oriental notion, so influential in our thinking, that matter is the eternal source of evil. There is nothing eternal but God; moreover, the created universe, the natural, the "material" universe in all its aspects, is not evil. Evil, of course, there is, but this evil cannot be inherent in existence. It cannot be part of the eternal order of creation but must rather represent a disruption of it.

Taking it in its larger meaning, the biblical doctrine of creation can thus be seen to be the indispensable ground for any conception of nature that does justice to its reality and value without losing sight of its contingent and conditioned character.

The affirmation of God as Creator is associated with the affirmation of the divine sovereignty. No appellation for God is more common in biblical-rabbinical literature or in Jewish liturgy than the term King; no concept is more characteristic of the Hebraic outlook than the Kingdom—that is, the kingship—of God. David's prayer, as recorded in Chronicles, communicates something of the intensity and exaltation of spirit behind these phrases: "Thine, O Lord, is the greatness and the power and the glory and the victory and the majesty; for all that is in the heaven and in the earth is Thine; Thine is the kingdom, O Lord, and Thou art exalted as head above all" (I Chron. 29:11). The formula introducing virtually every prayer in the liturgy is: "Blessed art Thou, O Lord our God, King of the Universe. . . ."[20]

What does the kingship of God mean in the context of Hebraic religion? Its implications are inexhaustible, but above everything else it means that the God who created the universe is the absolute Lord over nature, life and history. No aspect of existence escapes his sovereign rule: "*All* men must bring *all* their lives under the whole will of God."[21] Life cannot be departmentalized into secular and sacred, material and spiritual, with the latter alone falling under divine jurisdiction. No such distinction is recognized in Hebraic religion; the attempt to withdraw anything, no matter how seemingly insignificant, from divine rule is branded as an attempt to set up a rival, an idolatrous, claim against the sovereignty of God: "I am the Lord thy God . . .; thou shalt have no other gods before me" (Exod. 20:2-3). All life, all existence, is governed by one ultimate principle and that principle is the will of the Living God.

The affirmation of the divine sovereignty taken seriously means, of course, that *only* God is absolute. This simple statement has the widest ramifications. It implies immediately that everything which is *not* God is "relativized." Nothing but God possesses any value in its own right. Whatever is not God—and that means everything in the world, every society, institution, belief or movement—is infected with relativity and can at best claim only a passing and partial validity. This God-centered relativism does justice to whatever is valid in the relativistic emphasis of modern thought without falling into the self-destructive nihilism to which the latter invariably leads. It makes available a perspective that transcends the immediacies and partial interests of life and is thus a most potent force for sanity in individual and social existence.

Moreover, if God is the sovereign Lord of existence, it follows that the whole duty of man is comprised in single-minded obedience and service to him. God is master; man, his servant—with all that this implies. This exaltation of the absolute sovereignty of God and the unrelieved emphasis on man's utter subjection and dependence, so characteristic of Hebraic spirituality, comes rather as a shock to the modern mind, which finds such notions "archaic," not to say offensive to democratic decency. Indeed, one very popular writer on religion finds it un-American. "A religion that will emphasize man's nothingness and God's omnipotence, that calls upon us to deny our own powers and glorify his," he proclaims, "may have fitted the needs of many Europeans but it will not satisfy the growing self-confident character of America. . . . We Americans have had little of the feeling of helplessness and dependence that characterizes so much of Oriental and European religion."[22] There is no occasion here to examine what the religious tradition of America really is; it is obviously something very different from the brash and superficial chauvinism this writer makes it out to be. What is much more important is to bring to light the utter confusion as to the nature of religion and the nature of man involved in this type of criticism. For the democratic idea makes sense only in a society of equals and not even the most zealous liberal would venture to assert such a relation between man and God. As a matter of fact, as we shall see later, the very concept of human equality has no meaning and democracy no validity except in terms of the common subjection of all men to the sovereignty of God. It is through loyal and devoted acknowledgment of this sovereignty that man finds his true freedom and personal dignity. Pretensions to self-sufficiency and attempts to measure himself against his Maker can only lead, as they have always led in the past, to utter chaos within the soul of man and the community he attempts to create. Denial of the divine sovereignty leads directly and inexorably to the disruption of human life. No one should know this better than the man of today who is heir to all the devastation that the fatal Prometheanism of the modern age has brought upon the world.

NOTES

1. See, e.g., Deut. 5:23; Jer. 10:10, 23, 36; Hos. 2:1; Pss., 42: 2-3; 84:3.—The term is particularly frequent in the liturgy.

2. "Religious symbols always use a finite reality in order to express our relation to the infinite. But the finite reality they use is not an arbitrary means for an end, something strange to it. It participates in the power of the ultimate for which it stands. A religious symbol is double-edged. It expresses not only that

which is symbolized but also that through which it is symbolized." Paul Tillich, "Religion and Secular Culture," *The Journal of Religion*, Vol. XXVI (April, 1946), No. 2.

3. Martin Buber, *I and Thou* (T. & T. Clark: Edinburgh, 1937), *passim*.

4. Buber, *op. cit.*, p. 81.

5. Buber, *op. cit.*, p. 80.

6. That is what makes attempts to "prove" the existence of God such an impertinence. "So rather let us mock God out and out," says Kierkegaard; "this is always preferable to the disparaging air of importance with which one would prove God's existence. For to prove the existence of one who is present is the most shameless affront, since it is an attempt to make him ridiculous. . . . How could it occur to anybody to prove that he exists unless one had permitted oneself to ignore him and now makes the thing all the worse by proving his existence before his very nose? The existence of a king or his presence is commonly acknowledged by an appropriate expression of subjection and submission; what if, in his presence, one were to prove that he existed? . . . One proves God's existence by worship." *Concluding Unscientific Postscript* (Princeton University: Princeton, N.J., 1944), p. 485.

7. J. P. Hyatt, *Prophetic Religion* (Abingdon-Cokesbury: Nashville, Tenn., 1947), p. 154.

8. The efforts of Philo, Maimonides and other philosophers to get rid of or explain away the anthropomorphisms of Scripture are well known. Even Judah Halevi is so far carried away by the philosophic conception of the impassive, immutable deity that he actually denies God the attribute of *mercy*: "They attribute to him mercy and compassion, although this is, in our conception, surely nothing but a weakness of the soul and a quick movement of nature. This cannot be applied to God, ordaining the poverty of one individual and the wealth of another. His nature remains quite unaffected by it. He has no sympathy with one nor anger against another." *Kitab Al-Khazari*, tr. by Hartwig Hirschfeld (Bernard G. Richards: New York, 1927), ii. 2.

9. A. J. Heschel, *Die Prophetie* (Polish Academy of Sciences: Cracow, 1936), p. 131.

10. Emil Brunner, "Die Bedeutung des Alten Testaments," *Zwischen den Zeiten*, Vol. VIII (1930).

11. "The depth of being cannot be symbolized by objects taken from a realm which is lower than the personal, from the realm of things and subpersonal living beings. The supra-personal is not an 'It,' or more correctly it is a 'He' as much as it is an 'It' and it is above both of them. But if the 'He' element is left out, the 'It' element transforms the alleged suprapersonal into a sub-personal, as it usually happens in monism and pantheism." Tillich, "The Idea of the Personal God," *Union Review* (November, 1940).

12. Buber, *I and Thou*, p. 79.

13. It is significant, as E. Frank points out, that "although modern man does doubt creative power in God, he certainly does not doubt the possibility of such a creative power in himself. And how could he doubt the possibility of a free will and of the power of self-determination in himself if without it his own thinking would be without truth and meaning?" "Time and Eternity," *Review of Metaphysics*, Vol. 1 (September 1948), No. 5.

14. "God is not only the sole creator of the world, he alone upholds it and maintains in existence by his immediate will and power everything that is. This universal teaching of the Bible is equally the doctrine of Judaism: 'God created and he provides; he made and he sustains.' The maintenance of the world is a

kind of continuous creation: God in his goodness makes new every day continually the work of creation." G. F. Moore, *Judaism* (Harvard University: Cambridge, Mass, 1927), I, 384; Moore provides the documentation.

"[The Prophets] proclaimed God's work in nature in the creation as sustaining of the cosmos . . . Second Isaiah did not believe that Yahweh's work in creation was an absolutely finished thing; Yahweh was ever creating in history that which could be proclaimed as *new.*" J. P. Hyatt, *Prophetic Religion,* p. 158.

15. E.g., Lev. 19:2: "I, the Lord your God, am holy"; Isa. 6:3: "Holy, holy, holy is the Lord of Hosts." *The Holy One Blessed is He* is one of the most familiar appellations of God in rabbinic literature.—See Moore, *Judaism,* II, 101 ff., 109 ff.

"According to this attribute [the "Holy One of Israel," as used by Isaiah], YHVH is not only holy but *the* Holy, that is to say, everything in the world which is to be named holy is so because it is hallowed by him." Buber, *The Prophetic Faith* (Macmillan: New York, 1949), pp. 206-07.

16. Henri Frankfort, *Kingship and the Gods* (University of Chicago: Chicago, 1948, pp. 342-44. Some tenses have been changed in the quotation.

17. Meyer Waxman, *A Handbook of Judaism* (Bloch: New York, 1947), p. 136.

18. E. A. Burtt shows how conceptions of God and his creative work derived from Hebraic tradition served to provide the metaphysical foundations of early modern science. *The Metaphysical Foundations of Early Modern Science* (Harcourt, Brace: New York, 1932), esp. pp. 148, 256, 293.

19. Waxman, *A Handbook of Judaism,* p. 140.

20. Particularly significant are the *Malkuyot* (Kingdom verses) in the liturgy for Rosh Hashanah.—Rosh Hashanah, echoing the ancient festival of the enthronement of Yahweh, is in fact the celebration of the Kingship of God.

21. J. P. Hyatt, *Prophetic Religion,* p. 51.

22. Joshua Loth Liebman, *Peace of Mind* (Simon & Schuster: New York, 1946), p. 173.

According to ABRAHAM J. HESCHEL, the prophet is one who regarded history as revealing the work of God, and who knew God as a person, as a subject, rather than as an object. The God of the prophets had a personal and "intimate" relationship with the world, and reacted to human events. The theme of the divine mission was divine pathos, understood as "an act formed with intention, depending on free will, the result of decision and determination." Divine pathos, to the prophets, was not selfish (as in the case of the gods of mythology), but "directed outward" to the people. God's pathos was an "expression of his will," a "form of expression of God's absolute values." The prophets, according to Heschel, "knew two different kinds of divine *pathos:* from the point of view of man, the *pathos* of redemption and that of affliction; from the point of view of God, the *pathos* of sympathy and that of rejection."

Heschel contrasts the unique prophetic concept of divine pathos and the moral order with the theologies of other ancient civilizations. He then points to historical forces that have led Bible critics to underplay the prophetic concept of divine pathos. Modern man, Heschel suggests, can benefit from the prophetic suggestion that "God can be experienced by us only if and when we are aware of His attention to us, of His being concerned with us."

IX

The Divine Pathos

ABRAHAM J. HESCHEL
(ed. William Wolf)

HOW CAN we define the prophetic consciousness in relation to God? The prophetic consciousness was, of course, a consciousness about the world, but the prophets did not see the world as a superficial succession of causes and effects in the world; they saw it rather as a meaningful relation among events. History revealed the work of God and therefore needed interpretation. To the prophet God is never an object; He is always a person, a subject. The prophet does not think of God as of something absolute in the sense of unrelated; he thinks of Him primarily as of One who takes a direct part in the events of the world.

The prophets never ask: "*What* is God?" They are interested only in His activity and influence in human affairs. Even their views of what we would call basic principles took the form of concrete aims and tasks. It is from this point of view that we must try to answer the questions: What is typically prophetic theology like? What attitude to God defines the meaning of prophecy? Which aspect of the monotheism they affirmed had the most decisive influence upon their thought and feeling?

To the prophet, as we have noted, God does not reveal himself in an abstract absoluteness, but in a specific and unique way—in a personal and *intimate* relation to the world. God does not simply command and expect obedience; he is also moved and affected by what happens in the world and he *reacts* accordingly. Events and human actions arouse in Him joy or sorrow, pleasure or wrath. He is not conceived as judging facts so to speak "objectively," in detached impassivity. He reacts in an intimate and subjective manner, and thus determines the value of events. Quite obviously in the biblical view man's deeds can move Him, affect Him, grieve Him, or, on the other hand, gladden and please Him.

114

This notion that God can be intimately affected, that he possesses not merely intelligence and will, but also feeling and *pathos*, basically defines the prophetic consciousness of God.

Pathos is not, however, to be understood as mere feeling. Pathos is an act formed with intention, depending on free will, the result of decision and determination. The divine *pathos* is the theme of the prophetic mission. The aim of the prophet is to reorient the people by communicating to them the divine *pathos* which, by impelling the people to "return," is itself transformed. Even "in the moment of anger" (Jer. 18:7), what God intends is not that His anger should be executed but that it should be appeased and annulled by the people's repentance.

The divine *pathos* is not merely intentional; it is also transitive. The gods of mythology are self-centered, egoistic. Their passions—erotic love, jealousy, envy—are determined by considerations of self. *Pathos*, on the other hand, is not a self-centered and self-contained state; it is always, in prophetic thinking, directed outward; it always expresses a relation to man. It is therefore not one of God's attributes as such. It has not a reflective, but rather a transitive character. Hence, whereas in the mythological genealogy of the gods man plays no part, the "history" of God cannot be separated from the history of the People Israel: the history of the divine *pathos* is embedded in human affairs.

In primitive religion, God's anger is something arbitrary, and unrelated to any conditions. The prophetic thought that human actions bring about divine *pathos*, emphasizes the unique position that man occupies in his relation to God. The divine *pathos* rooted though it is in God's free will, emerges in the context of conditions which are quite clearly human conditions.

The prophets know two different kinds of divine *pathos:* from the point of view of man, the *pathos* of redemption and that of affliction; from the point of view of God, the *pathos* of sympathy and that of rejection. But the fact that rejection seems to occur more frequently in the biblical account should not be taken to prove that wrath is inherently one of God's chief attributes. On the contrary, prophecy aims at the annulment of the *pathos* of affliction and rejection. The prophets experience God's wrath as suffering which He receives at the hand of man. It is the incredible disloyalty of His people which arouses in Him the *pathos* which afflicts. God's word comes as an appeal and a warning to His people not to arouse His anger.

The basic features emerging from the above analysis indicate that the divine *pathos* is not conceived as an essential attribute of God. The *pathos* is not felt as something objective, as a finality with which man is confronted, but as an expression of God's will; it is a functional rather than a substantial reality. The prophets never identify God's *pathos* with

His essence, because it is for them not something absolute, but a form of relation. Indeed, prophecy would be impossible were the divine *pathos* in its particular structure a necessary attribute of God. If the structure of the *pathos* were immutable and remained unchanged even after the people had "turned," prophecy would lose its function, which is precisely so to influence men as to bring about a change in the divine pathos of rejection and affliction.

God's *pathos* is obviously not to be understood as a powerful wave of emotion which overwhelms and sweeps everything away since for the prophets justice is a basic feature of God's ways. *Pathos* and *ethos* do not simply exist side by side, opposing one another; they pass into each other. Because God is the absolute source of value, His *pathos* is always ethical. The divine *pathos* is a form of expression of God's absolute value.

Pathos is not something created arbitrarily. Its inner law is the moral law, for *ethos* is immanent in *pathos*. God is concerned about the world and shares in its fate. How could His *ethos* express itself more deeply and more immediately than by this intimate and emotional participation? But to identify God with the moral idea would be contrary to the very meaning of prophetic theology. God is not the appointed guardian of the moral order. He is not an intermediary between a transcendental idea of the good and man. The prophet does not think of Him as a being whose function it is to supervise the moral order and to bring about the realization of an autonomous morality. Morality is the norm, not the structure of the relation between God and man. As love cannot be identified with the values found in it, so the relation between God and man cannot be associated simply with the value of the moral idea. The *pathos*-structure of divine *ethos* implied and follows from the unlimited sovereignty of God. If the moral law were something absolute and final, it would represent a destiny to which God Himself would be subject. Far from being sovereign, God would then fall into dependence on rigid, objective norms.

The subjection of the moral idea to the divine *pathos* is the indispensable assumption of prophetic religion. Mercy, repentance, forgiveness, would be impossible if moral principle were held to be superior to God. God's call to man, which figures so frequently in the writings of the prophets, presupposes subjective ethics. God's repenting a decision which was based on moral grounds clearly shows the supremacy of *pathos*. Let us take the idea of retaliation as an example. Whereas in Hindu religion retaliation is automatic, punishment following crime; in prophetic religion, it is seen not as a blind movement of mechanical power, but as directed by the *pathos* of conscience and will. This is why it was only in Biblical religion that the powerful and paradoxical idea could be developed.

A comparison with other theological systems can help to reveal the uniqueness of the prophetic idea of God. The Stoics considered *pathos* to be unreasonable and unnatural emotion, whereas apathy—the subduing and the overcoming of the emotions—was taken to be the supreme moral task. Spinoza held feeling to be "confused ideas." Laotse's *Tao* (the "divine way") is the eternal silence, the everlasting calm and the unchangeable law of the cosmic order. In accordance with *Tao*, man is to rid himself of desire and sympathy, greed and passion, and humbly and quietly become like *Tao*. Zeal and unrest are to be avoided. To live according to *Tao* means to live passively. The God of the prophets, however, is not the Law, but the Lawgiver. The order emanating from Him is not a rigid, unchangeable structure, but a historic-dynamical reality. Aristotle's god ever rests in itself. Things long for it and thus are set into motion; it is in this sense the "prime mover," but is itself immovable. Aristotle's God knows no feeling or suffering; it is simply pure thought thinking itself. The prophet's God is concerned with the world, and His thoughts are about it. He is the God of the fathers, the God of the covenant, The divine *pathos* expresses itself in the relation between God and His people. God is the "Holy One of Israel."

Many civilizations too, know an inescapable, unyielding power standing above the gods. Fate is supreme; it cannot be evaded. The divine *pathos*, on the other hand, strives at overcoming destiny. Its dynamic character, which makes every decision provisional, conquers fate. In Greek theology, the highest power does not need man. Events are a monologue. But Jewish religion starts with the covenant: God *and* man. An apathetical, immobile conception of God could not possibly fit into prophetic religion.

The divine *pathos*, though it is rooted in His freedom, is not simply will. God as pure will is found in Islam. In the Koran, Allah is represented as a will removed from all considerations, working without any relation to actuality. Since everything is rigorously determined, the dialogue is again reduced to a monologue. Central is not the relation between Allah and man, but simply Allah himself. The prophets explicitly fought against the idea, widespread even in Palestine, that God was the Creator of the world but did not interfere with the course of nature and history. This essentially deistic notion has no place for any genuine connection between God and the world.

The decisive importance of the idea of divine *pathos* emerges clearly when we consider the possible forms in which God's relation to the world may present itself. A purely ethical monotheism in which God, the guardian of the moral order, keeps the world subject to the law, would restrict the scope of God's knowledge and concern to what is of ethical significance. God's relation to man would, in general, run along the lines of a universal principle. The divine *pathos* alone is able to break through this rigidity and create new dimensions for the unique, the specific, and the particular.

The idea of divine *pathos* throws light on many types of relation between God and man unknown in apathetic religion. The covenant between God and Israel is an example. The category of divine *pathos* leads to the basic affirmation that God is interested in human history, that every deed and event in the world concerns Him and arouses His reaction. What is characteristic of the prophets is not foreknowledge of the future but insight into the present *pathos* of God.

The idea of divine *pathos* has also its anthropological significance. Man has his relation to God. A religion without man is as impossible as a religion without God. That God takes man seriously is shown by his concern for human existence. It finds its deepest expression in the fact that God can actually suffer. At the heart of the prophetic affirmation is the certainty that God is concerned about the world to the point of suffering.

In sum, the divine *pathos* is the unity of the eternal and the temporal, of the rational and the irrational, of the metaphysical and the historical. It is the real basis of the relation between God and man, of the correlation of Creator and creation, of the dialogue between the Holy One of Israel and His people.

The meaning of the divine *pathos* was often misunderstood by Jewish as well as by Christian and Islamic religious philosophy, which tended to overlook its specific form and content and to interpret it as simply an aspect of anthropomorphism, or to be more precise, of anthropopathism.

Marcion, the gnostic leader, bitterly assailed anthropopathism. In the polemics of Jews and Christians against heathenism, the emotions of the pagan gods formed a favorite target of attack. In more modern times, too, exception was frequently taken to God's wrath, which was held to be incompatible with His justice and love. But, of course, God's wrath is not something in itself but is part of the entire structure of the divine *pathos*. God's anger is conditioned by God's will and aroused by man's sins; it can be dissipated by the "return" of the people. Divine wrath is not opposed to love, but rather its counterpart. It is the very evidence of God's love. Only because God loves His people is He capable of being kindled with anger against them. God's love, justice, and wrath are part of the same structure of divine *pathos*.

Embarrassment over the "emotional" and irrational features of the biblical account of God induced the so-called historical school of Bible criticism to assume an evolutionary development. In ancient times, it was alleged, Israel knew only the awe-inspiring God; in later times, however, they came to think of God as a kind and loving God. This view is neither true to fact nor in line with the fundamental biblical outlook. It likewise ignores the crucial polarity—love and anger, justice and mercy—which characterizes the divine *pathos.*

Whether philosophical or historical, the objections to anthropopathism have generally prevailed. Why? What has been the strength of this opposition to the idea of divine *pathos?* It seems to us to be due to a combination of various tendencies which have their origin in Greek classical philosophy. The Eleatics taught that whatever exists is unchangeable. This ontological view was very soon put to use to determine the nature of God. Xenophanes, Anaxagoras, Plato, and Aristotle followed in much the same line. The principle that mutability cannot be attributed to God is thus an ontological dogma, and as such it has become the common property of religious philosophers.

It is easy to see how on the basis of the ontological view of the Eleatics there emerged a static conception of God. According to Greek thinking, impassivity and immobility are characteristic of the divine. Now since in Greek psychology, affects or feelings are described as emotions (movements) of the soul, it is obvious that they cannot be brought into harmony with the idea of God. The ontological basis of this system of thought may, of course, be challenged by another ontological system which sees in changeability the very sign of real being. Such a system will lead to a dynamic rather than static idea of God.

Since Plato, we have become familiar with the distinction between a rational immortal component of the human soul and one that is irrational and mortal. The rational component is believed to be indivisible, whereas the irrational one is usually subdivided into a noble and a less noble part, the former comprising the passions, the latter the evil desires. In medieval philosophy, the three elements are reduced to two, but in either case the life of the emotions is separated from the realm of the rational. The dualism of values thus engendered has deeply penetrated Western thinking. To the degree that theology has subscribed to this dualism of values, it has attributed to God the power of thinking, but excluded the emotions. But this dualism is utterly foreign to Biblical thinking. The emotions are part of the entire spiritual structure, and Scripture never demeans them.

The wisdom of the Greek exalted reason above the passions. Zeno even demanded the complete extinction of the feelings on moral grounds. All the other schools of Greek ethics acknowledged the inferior character of the irrational emotions as against the rational part of the soul. This opinion was projected into theology. The ideal of the sage was made to find its realization in God. Plato constantly stressed the notion that the gods are without emotions, desires, or needs.

The Greek word *pathos* implies suffering. In the Greek view, *pathos* is necessarily passive; in the state of *pathos,* one is affected and directed by another from the outside. From very early times, it was felt that God could not be affected in such a way. God, the Supreme Cause, could not possibly suffer from or be affected by something which is effected by Himself. Passivity was held to be incompatible with the dignity of the Divine. It was on these grounds that anthropopathism was rejected. But this whole line of thinking makes little sense in biblical terms. In the Bible, God desires to be loved.

Authentic Jewish thought evaluates the emotions in a manner diametrically opposed to the Greek view. The emotions have often been regarded as inspirations from God, as the reflection of a higher power. Neither in the legal nor in the moral parts of the Bible is there a suggestion that the desires and the passions are to be negated. Asceticism was not the ideal of biblical man. Since the feelings were considered valuable, there was no reason to eliminate them from the conception of God. An apathetic and ascetic God would have struck biblical man with a sense not of dignity and grandeur but rather of poverty and emptiness. Only through arbitrary allegorizing was later religious philosophy able to find an apathetic God in the Bible.

Recognizing the motives lying behind the Greek rejection of anthropopathism helps us get an insight into the meaning of the teaching itself. We can see how very questionable are the presuppositions in terms of which anthropopathism was for centuries repudiated by religious philosophy. Present-day philosophy has abandoned many of these axioms taken over from ancient Greek philosophy and it will also have to revise its attitude towards anthropopathism.

The mystic strives to experience God as something final, immediate, In mythical thinking, too, God Himself is the object of the imagination. For the aborigines, indeed, God dwells in the visible symbol. Once religious thinking proclaimed God to be invisible and different from man, there would seem to be no escaping agnosticism. The prophets overcame this dilemma by separating essence and expression. They were not out to experience God Himself, but rather His expressions in the image of vision, in the word of inspiration, in the acts of history. Prophetic revelation, indeed, does not reveal anything about God's essence. What the prophet knows about God is God's *pathos,* but this is not experienced as a part of the divine essence. Not God Himself is the object of understanding, but only His relation to Israel and to the world. Hence revelation means not that God makes Himself known, but that He makes His will known. In the separation of essence and relation the prophetic knowledge of God becomes possible.

The prophets are familiar with various forms of the divine *pathos:* love and anger, mercy and indignation, kindness and wrath. But what is, so to speak, the intrinsic property of the divine *pathos?*

In every one of its forms, the divine *pathos* points to a connection between God and man—a connection which originates with God. God "looks at" the world and its events. He experiences and judges them; this means that He is concerned with man and is somehow related to His people. The basic feature of the divine *pathos* is God's transcendental attention to man.

Yet even here we must not think that we reach God's essence. God's transcendental attention merely defines the limits of the prophet's understanding of God. The prophet never speculates about God's real being. In the divine *pathos,* which is a manifestation of God's transcendental attention, he finds the answer to the events of life. For in it is implied God's interest in the world and His concern for it.

The world is looked upon by God. God knows us. God can be experienced by us only if and when we are aware of His attention to us, of His being concerned with us. The prophet is impressed by God's concern with the world. This is the ultimate reality for prophetic spirituality.

God's transcendental attention engenders in man the sense of being the object of the divine subject. In all that the prophets knew about God, they never found in Him a desire which did not bear upon man. God is not the object of religious discovery, but the sovereign subject of revelation. He is the supreme subject.

LOUIS JACOBS points out that in the biblical period, the Hebrew word for "faith," *emunah,* was a synonym for "trust" in God. In the Middle Ages, however, *emunah* became the term for belief that there *is* a God, whereas *bittahon* came to refer exclusively to trust *in* God. Jacobs proceeds to observe that whereas medieval Jewish thought emphasizes faith as trust, moderns are more concerned with the problem of faith as belief-in. He traces the medieval Jewish quietism that arose from preoccupation with the question of how much trust man is to put in God, and how much in his own abilities. Jacobs observes that, to moderns, "trust in God cannot be equated with a facile optimism that because God is in His heaven all will be well in the physical or material sense." Trust in God, as the best in Jewish tradition understands it, and as modern man will regard it, is an attitude of "relationship with God" which enables one to "live as God's ally, as it were, in the struggle against evil."

X

Faith and Trust

LOUIS JACOBS

THE HEBREW WORD for "faith," *emunah,* was, in the Biblical period, a synonym for "trust" in God. When, during the Middle Ages, *"emunah"* became reserved for the cognitive aspect of faith, for belief that there is a God, the Biblical term *bittahon* continued to serve, as it did in the earlier period, for the idea of trust in and reliance on God. *Emunah* has now come to mean that man affirms God's existence, *bittahon* that man places his trust in God. The famous mediaeval work on this theme, *"Sepher Ha-Emunah We-Ha-Bittahon"* ("The Book on Faith and Trust," written by Jacob Ibn Shesheth though incorrectly attributed to Nahmanides) states: Faith *(emunah)* is the tree, trust *(bittahon)* the fruit.[1] There can be no fruit without a tree, there can be no trust without faith. Man cannot trust in God unless he believes that there is a God to be trusted. But there can be a tree without fruit. It is possible for man to believe that there is a God and yet fail to trust in Him.

This may be for a variety of reasons. It may be that his belief in God is too weak and vague to produce the more passionate, committed affirmative relationship suggested by trust. Or, as Ibn Shesheth writes,[2] it may be because, while believing without reservation in God's power to help, man cannot bring himself to believe that he, in his sinfulness, is worthy of being helped. This latter reason is the heart of the problem of trust in God. How far should the believer rely on God and how much reliance should he place on his own efforts? If it is irreligious to fail to place one's trust in God is it not either arrogance or naïvety to believe that God will help in all circumstances? This is the central religious problem regarding the life of trust. When is trust a virtue and when does it cease to be a virtue? When is trust to be embraced and when rejected? No sane believer would face an oncoming express train trusting God to save him

124

from injury. He would regard this as an act of impiety, of testing God, of failing in the God-ordained duty that he take care of himself. Where, then, is the line to be drawn between courageous reliance and foolhardiness? Religious teachers have given to this question various answers ranging from the most extreme attitude of complete quietism, in which man does nothing for himself, to so great a confidence in the power of human effort as to nullify trust in God.[3]

A PROPER BALANCE

"Trust in God and keep your powder dry." This implies that it is both proper and desirable to strike the correct balance between the view that only human effort avails and that which sees all human effort as futile. But, as in all matters regarding the attainment of a delicate balance, the problem is extremely complicated. Where is the emphasis to be placed? On the whole it is correct to say that during the Middle Ages the stress was on the "trust in God" while in modern times even the most religious of men have been rather more concerned with keeping the powder dry.[4]

The historical background to the marked shift in emphasis is not at all difficult to trace. From the Renaissance, man's newly discovered powers of self-expression led him increasingly from a God-centered to a man-centered universe, with man acquiring progressively greater self-confidence. The view that this life was a school where man had to train himself to enjoy God forever yielded increasingly to the view that this life was good in itself. There was a new flowering of the human spirit, expressing itself in the beginnings of accurate scientific investigation and in new forms in art, literature and music. With the advent of modern science and technology and their world-transforming achievements, from the building of great roads, railways, bridges and ships to the splitting of the atom, it is not surprising that the mediaeval view of human effort as a mere concession to human frailty, as a necessary evil,[5] receded more and more into the background. There is obviously a vast difference in outlook between the mediaeval Islamic view that a man should regard himself as a corpse in the hand of God, with no will of his own at all, to the *religious* motivation behind the rise of modern capitalism.[6] For the modern believer the whole idea of trust in God has been called into question in a way inconceivable in the Middle Ages. And yet, unless they are spiritually insensitive, modern men must surely see that such a tremendous idea cannot be abandoned by the believer without the greatest impoverishment. They must sense the incongruity between their protestations in the house of worship that all depends on God and their daily conduct of life as if they had no need of that hypothesis.

In making this distinction between the modern and the mediaeval attitude we are not suggesting that the distinction is always neatly chronological. An attitude of quietism is not entirely unknown among modern Jews and famous mediaeval thinkers like Saadiah Gaon rejected it. In Saadiah's chapter on "Worship"[7] there is a very modern-sounding analysis of the whole question. Many assert, observes Saadiah, that the highest endeavour of the servant of God ought to be to devote himself exclusively to God's service, singing His praises and worshipping Him in prayer and study, while abandoning all mundane concerns in his confidence that God will provide. Saadiah does not deny that the ideal is a lofty one but he takes strong exception to its exclusiveness. If, for instance, man takes no concern for his food he will die. If all the members of a particular generation failed to concern themselves with the begetting of offspring divine worship would eventually cease altogether for there would be no one left to engage in it. Furthermore, the hermit saint is unable to fulfill what Saadiah calls the "rational" commands of the *Torah* such as the laws governing business relations and the conduct of man in society, the laws of just measures and the duties of charity. Nor will Saadiah allow an exception to be made for the individual saint on the grounds that his special kind of devotion will equip him the better to serve as a teacher of others and thus repay his debt to society. For this would mean that it is not he but those others who serve God in the particular way the *Torah* enjoins, that is the way in which God wishes to be served. Nor is attention to one's material needs in any way irreligious since this is the way God has laid it down for man to follow. If one is to be consistent in an attitude of quietism it would have to be applied to man's spiritual as well as his material concerns. Unless one accepts that there is a God-ordained way for man why pray or study? Why not remain entirely inactive, trusting God to reward man with eternal bliss without his being obliged to engage in any effort whatsoever? But if one accepts the idea of a God-ordained way then it can only be the way of the *Torah* and this is clearly not that of quietism.

Saadiah, then, is a mediaeval opponent of quietism. One of the most influential of modern religious thinkers, Kierkegaard, holds the opposite view to that of Saadiah. In comparing these two thinkers we are not suggesting that there is a clear-cut distinction in this matter between Judaism and Christianity. The problem is far too complicated for any such neat distinction and it is obvious that individual temperament enters into the picture. The point of the comparison is to demonstrate that while, generally speaking, our distinction between the mediaeval and the modern world on this question of trust in God is sound, it must not be pressed too far. Saadiah, the mediaevalist, is very modern while

Kierkegaard, the modern, is completely mediaeval. Moreover, it is significant that, rightly or wrongly, Kierkegaard states that his own position is the only authentic Christian doctrine and that the opposite view is pure Judaism.

"Judaism," writes Kierkegaard,[8] "is really of all religions outspoken optimism. Certainly Greek paganism was also an enjoyment of life, but it was uncertain and filled with melancholy, and above all it had not divine authority. But Judaism is divinely sanctioned optimism, sheer promise for this life." On the question of marriage he observes: "That Christ was born of a Virgin would not have scandalised the pagans, but for Judaism it was bound to be a scandal. For Judaism culminates in regarding marriage as so divine that it is God himself who has instituted it. Judaism has ideas of the propagation of the species as a kind of religion. And then to be born of a Virgin! Basically this is a denial of the whole of the Old Testament, a removal of its essential powers." Kierkegaard's determined opposition to marriage is expressed with the vehemence so typical of this existentialist thinker: "The error in Catholicism is not that the priest is celibate; no, the error is that a qualitative difference between the layman and the priest has been introduced, which goes clean against the New Testament, and is a concession of weakness in relation to numbers. Certainly the error is not that the priest is celibate—a Christian should be celibate. 'But if you hold to this you will have no Christians at all!' If that is so, it is all one to me. 'And on the other hand, if you make Christianity consist of marriage, then you will get millions of Christians!' It is all one to me."

Protestant Orthodoxy, with its demand that man marry and propagate the species, Kierkegaard considers to be "heart twaddle, mediocrity with a dash of sugar." In another passage he remarks: "But in Christianity married people are consecrated, and the ceremony sanctifies this relation. How charming! So bandits in the south sanctify murder by kneeling down beforehand at the altar." Saadiah, as any representative Jewish teacher, would have been horrified that marriage could be compared, even by illustration, with murder. In the Talmud (*Yeb.* 63b) it is said that R. Eliezer stated that he who does *not* engage in the propagation of the race is as though he sheds blood.

It is worth noting, however, that the ideal of the hermit saint is not entirely unknown in Rabbinic Judaism, as evidenced by the example of Ben Azzai (second cent.) who preached eloquently on the virtues of marriage while himself remaining unmarried. Excusing his lack of consistency this teacher is said to have protested that his soul was in love with the *Torah* and the world would have to be established by others.[9] It is strange that Saadiah makes no mention of this at all and he may have been influenced by the need to combat contemporary ideas of quietism. But his silence is further evidence that on a complex issue such as this it is precarious to talk of *the* Jewish point of view.

Prior to the time of Saadiah there is a debate, recorded in the Talmudic literature,[10] in which the second-century teacher, Rabbi Simeon ben Yohai, taught that the man who "does God's will" can afford to neglect his material responsibilities, relying on God to provide. Rabbi Ishmael, his contemporary, retorted by quoting: *"That thou gather in thy corn"* (Deut. 11:14) to demonstrate that human effort is indispensable. A later teacher remarked[11] that many have tried to follow Rabbi Simeon without success but many have followed Rabbi Ishmael with success. The background to the debate should not be overlooked. Both teachers lived at a time when the wars with Rome and the sporadic attempts at Jewish revolt had brought great devastation to the land. At this period there was so considerable an economic decline in Palestine that there are sparse references in the sources of the period to commercial undertakings there. In such periods it is usual to find teachers like Rabbi Simeon advocating a completely negative attitude towards human effort, rejecting it as fruitless in favour of a life of prayer and contemplation. What does emerge clearly from the earlier sources is that both quietism and its opposite had their advocates among Jewish teachers and that the differing attitudes were not uninfluenced by cultural and economic considerations.

MUSAR AND QUIETISM

Even into the twentieth century the more extreme attitude on trust found its exponent in the saintly Rabbi Yoizel Hurwitz of Novogrudok (called Navaradok) in the Government of Minsk. Rabbi Yoizel (*c.* 1848-1919) was a distinguished representative of the *Musar* movement, the Lithuanian moralistic movement founded in the last century by Rabbi Israel Lipkin of Salant.

Rabbi Yoizel, a successful business man in his youth, came under the influence of the *Musar* movement and eventually relinquished his commercial interests to devote himself entirely to moral improvement and divine worship. For a time he lived as a hermit in a little hut with two holes in the wall, through which sympathisers would place meat or dairy dishes (the two apertures were for the purpose of keeping the two separate in compliance with the dietary laws which forbid the mixing of meat and milk). He became the particular target of *Maskillim*, the advocates of Westernisation among the Russian Jews. Eventually Rabbi Yoizel emerged from seclusion to found a Talmudical Academy in Navaradok in which his particular approach to Judaism was extensively cultivated. Chaim Grade's short Yiddish story: "My Quarrel with Hirsh Rasseyner" is a vivid account of the views of the Navaradok students.[12] Rabbi Yoizel's ideas on trust in God are to be found chiefly in his *"Madregath Ha-Adam"* ("Man's Spiritual Stage") published for the first time just before his death and reprinted some years ago.[13]

Rabbi Yoizel was particularly concerned that men with the necessary qualifications should devote themselves unreservedly to *Torah* study, taking no thought of the morrow, ready to sacrifice every worldly ambition and thought of career. It is said that in Rabbi Yoizel's extremism he prayed for the economic downfall of those of his pupils who engaged in trade so that they would be obliged to devote themselves to *Torah* study. A pupil of Rabbi Yoizel named Joel Barantschick once opened a small shop in Riga. When the master heard of it he prayed that Rabbi Barantschick would become bankrupt.[14] Two typical sayings of Rabbi Yoizel are: "Man must be capable of giving up all his tomorrows for today; so that he should not have to spend all his todays for one tomorrow." "He who worries about this world may be likened to one who sits in a train and pushes his finger against the carriage wall to make the train go faster."[15]

It is notorious that the Navaradok students engaged in bizarre practices inviting ridicule so as to cultivate an attitude of complete indifference to worldly opinion. Some would dress as tramps, neglecting cleanliness. Some would go to a chemist's shop and ask for nails. Others again would make ridiculous proclamations in public. It was believed that by thus inviting scorn a man learned to view with equanimity the disdain and praise of others and so equip himself for a life of sincere devotion to the truth regardless of public opinion.[16] Navaradok, however, did not preach quietism in spiritual matters. Here, it was taught, all depends on human effort. The Navaradok students came to a Jewish hamlet and lodged in one of the Study Houses; when the resident Jews came to Synagogue they found chalked on its doors: "Jews, Repent!" A Navaradok student would stand in the market place publicly confessing his sins, particularly that in his endeavors on behalf of others the ego had reared its head and he therefore was the lowest of the low.[17] In this way trust in God served the interests of a strong revivalist movement.

To the question, widely discussed by the mediaeval thinkers, of why human effort is required if God provides, Rabbi Yoizel replies that it all depends on man's own attitude. Rabbi Yoizel advocated the most extreme attitude of trust. He believed that if a man really has this strong sense of God's power to help and relies upon it without qualification then God provides without any human effort being required. Human effort only becomes obligatory when trust in God is weak.[18] Rabbi Yoizel knows, of course, that the Talmudic authorities quoted earlier state that many have followed Rabbi Simeon ben Yohai without success but he replies that, indeed, his way is not for the *many*. The few chosen individuals, however, prepared to follow this way can proceed in complete safety. When a man wishes to swim, observes Rabbi Yoizel,[19] he must plunge into the water and surrender to the experience. If his hand or foot is always groping for the security of a hold he will never learn to swim. The pious man who trusts in God with reservations, always leaving scope for human effort, will never know what it really means to trust in God. Rabbi Yoizel, a great master of the parable, had a favourite illustration in reply to the objection that human experience teaches that success is only possible through human effort.[20] A blacksmith said that it was a good thing he had never taken up the trade of goldsmith for he would have starved, since during his whole career no one had ever brought him gold to fashion. The man who lives without complete trust in God does, indeed, require human effort but a higher life is possible for those courageous enough to cast their burdens on the Lord.

TRUST IN GOD

To come to the contemporary attitude, it is clear that trust in God cannot be equated with a facile optimism that because God is in His heaven all will be well in the physical or material sense. Such an attitude, psychologically and theologically unsound, despite Rabbi Yoizel, is totally unsupported by experience. Trust in God cannot mean this. It is obvious that however we understand the difficult question of divine providence, there is no guarantee that justice and righteousness will immediately win out. Moreover, even if a man believed his cause to be just he would have no right to expect God to come to his immediate vindication. There may be a large number of complex factors, which the believer is bound to take into account (the needs of others, the divine economy in which nature is not suspended by the prayers of the just, etc.) preventing an immediate remedy in an unjust situation. Further, the man so sure that his cause is right as to demand immediate vindication is lacking in the humility that should be the hallmark of the religious man, if the accounts of Theistic faith are to be trusted. Confidence that one's needs will be satisfied partakes more of trust in oneself than trust in God. To trust in God without the slightest attempt at keeping the powder dry is to trust in Him without using powder at all. It is to step in the path of the oncoming train. It is to rely on a miracle, which, as the Rabbis remind us, is an act of impiety.[21]

Trust in God is best seen not as a course of action to be pursued but as an attitude of mind to be cultivated. The man who trusts in his friend is aware that sometimes there may be reasons for the friend being of little help, but this does not affect the trustful relationship between them. Each is fortified by the knowledge that there he has an ally. Indeed, the very notion of trust implies a degree of uncertainty. It is an affirmation in spite of circumstances. By analogy it is possible to see one's attitude towards trust in God in this way. It is an attitude based on the Theistic premise that God loves man and is not at war with His creation. It does not ignore the Rabbinic idea that man is co-partner with God,[22] that human effort is itself God-ordained. The man of faith believes that in any ultimate sense his pursuit of the good and rejection of evil will conquer, will bring him nearer to God, will make its contribution to the fulfillment of God's purposes. The chief concern of the man of faith is to have that relationship with God which makes him live as God's ally, as it were, in the struggle against evil.

Tillich[23] has defined "faith" as "ultimate concern" and rightly sees this as the Biblical meaning of trust in God. He remarks[24] that idolatrous faiths (the worship of the nation or of success) fail precisely because they try to make ultimate that which is finite and they therefore *ultimately* disillusion the believer. Of Biblical faith Tillich says:[25] "An example—and more than an example—is the faith manifest in the religion of the Old Testament. It also has the character of ultimate concern in demand, threat and promise. The content of the concern is not the nation—although Jewish nationalism has sometimes tried to distort it into that—but the content is the God of justice, who, because he represents justice for everybody, and every nation, is called the universal God, the God of the universe. He is the ultimate concern of every pious Jew, and therefore in his name the great commandment is given: 'You shall love the Lord your God with all your heart, and with all your soul, and with all your might' (Deut. 6:5). This is what ultimate concern means and from these words the term 'ultimate concern' is derived. They state unambiguously the character of genuine faith, the demand of total surrender to the object of ultimate concern."

The tension between reliance on God and the need for human effort is never entirely abolished. If it were the dynamics of faith would be at an end. And the true man of faith would not wish it to be otherwise. For trust in God, as any other vital relationship, is a matter of constant challenge and response, approach and withdrawal, relinquishing and possessing. Something of this is without doubt implied in the most famous statement in the Bible on trust in God:

> Blessed is the man that trusteth in the Lord,
> And whose trust the Lord is.
> For he shall be as a tree planted by the waters,

And that spreadeth out its roots by the river,
And shall not be anxious in the year of drought,
Neither shall cease from yielding fruit.

(*Jer.* 17:7-8).

Or, in the words of another prophet:

For though the fig-tree shall not blossom,
Neither shall fruit be in the vines;
The labour of the olive shall fail,
And the fields shall yield no food;
The flock shall be cut off from the fold,
And there shall be no herd in the stalls;
Yet I will rejoice in the Lord,
I will exult in the God of my salvation

(*Hab.* 3:17-18).

NOTES

1. *"Sepher Ha-Emunah We-Ha-Bittahon,"* ed. B. Chavel, in *Kithbhe Ha-Ramban,* Vol. II, pp. 341–448. The illustration of the tree and its fruit is given in Chapter 1, ed. Chavel, p. 353. The author illustrates this by Hillel's saying (*Abhoth,* I, 5) that the unlearned man cannot be a saint. The saint must be learned but it does not follow that the learned man is a saint.

2. *Op cit.,* Chapter 1, ed. Chavel, p. 353.

3. For a splendid summary of the whole question see R. J. Zvi Werblowski: "Faith, Hope and Trust: A Study in the Concept of Bittahon" in *Papers of the Institute of Jewish Studies,* ed. J. G. Weiss, London: Magnes Press, Hebrew University, Jer., 1964, pp. 95-139.

4. See the very interesting Responsum of Rabbi Moshe Feinstein (Vol. *Hoshen Mishpat* etc., New York, 1963, section *O.H.,* No. 111, pp. 299–300) dated Heshvan 27th, 5724 (1963) on whether it is indicative of lack of trust in God to take out a life insurance policy. The question is posed as follows: "Is there any advantage in, or is there a prohibition against, taking out an insurance policy because, God forfend, it may appear to be a lack of trust in God in whose power it lies to make a man rich enough to leave a substantial sum to his heirs?" The reply is that it is obviously permitted and is no different from any other business enterprise. Rabbi Feinstein quotes *Ber.* 60 that it is a "vain prayer" to pray for a miracle. Bittahon, he argues, means that all is from God but *on condition* that human effort is first expended. The whole idea of insurance is God's "advice" to this generation on how to prosper. *Bittahon* comes into it, too, that one will be able to pay the premiums. The same applies to other forms of insurance e.g., car insurance and against fire and theft. All God-fearing people, concludes Rabbi Feinstein, who take out insurance policies understand this.

5. See the sources quoted by Werblowski, *op. cit.,* pp. 124–125.

6. See R. H. Tawney: *Religion and the Rise of Capitalism.* For the Islamic doctrine of *tawakkul* ("trust," "contentment," "resignation") see Werblowski *op. cit.,* p.

121 who quotes the famous saying of Sahl of Tustari; "The first stage of *tawakkul* is that one should be in God's hand like a corpse in the hand of the washer, which he turns to and fro as he wills without any movement or violition on his part." Werblowski rightly points out that this attitude is incompatible with that of the Bible and the Rabbis.

7. *Emunoth We-Deoth (The Book of Beliefs and Opinions)*, X, 15, trans. S. Rosenblatt, pp. 395–397.

8. This and the following quotations are from *The Last Years—Journals 1853–55* by Søren Kierkegaard, edited and trans., by Ronald Gregor Smith, (p. 67; p. 79; p. 264; pp. 119–120).

9. *Yeb.* 63b. See Maimonides, *Yad, Hil. Ishuth*, XV, 3 and *Shulhan Arukh*, Ebhen Ha-Ezer, I, 5, that this attitude did not entirely die out even at a much later date.

10. *Siphre, Ekebh*, sec. 42, *Ber.* 35b. See my *Jewish Values* pp. 86–98, for a fuller discussion.

11. *Ber., ibid.*

12. Published in an English translation in: *A Treasury of Yiddish Stories* edited by Irving Howe and Eliezer Greenberg, pp. 579–606. On Rabbi Yoizel see: "Rabbi Israel Salanter: Religious-Ethical Thinker" by Menahem G. Glenn, pp. 82-90 and Dobh Katz, *Tenuath Ha-Musar*, Vol. IV, Tel-Aviv, 1957, Chapters 10–24, pp. 179–351.

13. *Madregath Ha-Adam*, New York: Kedem Press Co., 1947.

14. Katz, *op. cit.*, p. 238 note 10.

15. Glenn, *op. cit.*, p. 87.

16. For further details see Katz, *op. cit.*, pp. 257f.

17. Glenn, *op. cit.*, pp. 89-90.

18. See Katz, *op. cit.*, Chapter 15, pp. 241–251.

19. *Madregath Ha-Adam*, p. 196.

20. Katz, *op. cit.*, p. 243.

21. See *Pes.* 64b.

22. *Sabb*, 119b. See *supra*, p. 142.

23. Paul Tillich: *Dynamics of Faith.*

24. *Op. cit.*, pp. 11-12.

25. *Op. cit.*, pp. 2-3.

In Biblical and Rabbinic literature, the "supernatural datum" was regarded as the main source of human awareness of God. In the Middle Ages, religious thinkers sought "rational proof" of God's existence. Today, most people retain some form of belief in God out of upbringing and habit, since modern thought questions the historicity of biblical miracles and theophanies, and modern philosophy points to weaknesses in the classical "proofs" of God's existence. Indeed, behaviorist psychology questions the existence of the human self, just as people once questioned belief in God.

Against this historical background, MORDECAI M. KAPLAN asserts that man derives his belief in self or God from a will-to-live pointing to a quest for "salvation," a term that Kaplan chooses to designate "what man actually strives after, or should deliberately strive after, if he wants to be true to his essential nature as man." Social, rational, and spiritual interests propel man toward such salvation. Common to human spiritual interests is the "sense of holiness," which is called forth when we feel that achieving or experiencing certain values provides us with inner growth and social growth.

Belief in God, according to Kaplan, "derives from the intuition that the cosmos may be depended upon to help us achieve salvation." The prophets and philosophers have attempted to inform such belief with reason. Kaplan also notes that culture, civilization, or religion attempts to transmit its experience of "godhood or cosmic dependability" through special sancta, which ensure survival or continuity of faith when they are reinterpreted once traditional explanations become outgrown. World events reveal that any conception of "this-worldly salvation" worth preserving must stress the dignity of the human person, the unity of mankind, and "the transcendence of God as reflected in man's eternal striving to transcend himself." Religious life must not be based on the authority of tradition, but on personal conviction, and application of personal reflection to the traditions, hopes, and experiences of the Jewish people.

XI.

How Man Comes to Know God

MORDECAI M. KAPLAN

I

JEWISH TRADITION CONTAINS accounts of visions in which men are said to have actually beheld God. The Torah records that what the Israelites saw and heard at Sinai was a direct self-manifestation of God. Even though they saw no form they heard "the sound of words." Those words are said to have been uttered by no one but God. That same God had appeared to Moses in a burning bush, and many centuries later spoke to Elijah in a thin small voice. These theophanies are assumed to have been direct self-manifestations of God.

According to that same tradition, God revealed himself also indirectly. The miraculous events which took place for Israel's sake were regarded as proof of God's power. The prophets who felt impelled, often against their own will to deliver oracles to the people, were certain that God had put those oracles into their mouths. Thus empirical evidence of a sensate character is assumed in traditional religion to be the main source of men's knowledge of God's existence. Only few remote references to reason or reflection as the source of that knowledge are found in the Bible. We may therefore say that, according to traditional Judaism, the main source of man's awareness of God is some supernatural datum, in the form of sensate experience of God's actual reality, or in the form of some unmistakable sensate evidence of His power.

In Judaism, Philo may be said to have been the first to recognize an additional source of men's awareness of God. That traditional source is reasoned reflection, as developed by thinkers like Plato and Aristotle. These thinkers, in the course of their effort to comprehend all of reality under a single concept that would give it unity and meaning, were led to assume the existence of God. In this they differed from other Greek thinkers who regarded reality as inherently blind and meaningless mechanism or inexorable fate. According to Plato, only the assumption of the idea of the Good as the highest world principle, and according to Aristotle, only the assumption of some eternal, immovable and wholly independent first mover, can render reality intelligible. God was thus to them the principle of intelligibility. They did not infer his existence from sense data, but from the compelling demand of reason.

During the Middle Ages, the three historical religions, Judaism, Christianity, and Islam, struggled to achieve a synthesis of what came to be regarded as the two main sources of man's awareness of God: empirical evidence and reasoned reflection. That synthesis assumed the historicity of the supernatural phenomena which pointed to the existence of God as a sense datum of supernatural character. At the same time, it tried to reckon with the demand of reason. In compliance with that demand the medieval theologians formulated three types of rational proof for the existence of God: the cosmological, the teleological and the ontological.

The cosmological proof derives from the principle that every effect must have a cause; from that it follows that the universe as a whole must have a first cause. The teleological proof is based on the many evidences of adaptation of means to ends. Such adaptation implies purpose and purpose implies one who purposes. The ontological proof starts with the assumption that the very idea of God implies perfection. What would so impair this perfection as non-existence? Hence God necessarily exists.

Most people, who come under the influence of modern thought, question the historicity of the theophanies and the miracles on which traditional religion bases its belief in God. They also know too much about the fallacies which modern philosophy has pointed out in each of the three so-called rational proofs for the existence of God to be wholly convinced. Nevertheless, they somehow manage to retain their belief in God. Were anyone to suggest to them that they do so because of their upbringing or force of habit, they would be the first to spurn such an explanation. Of course, that would not prove anything, since we are not, as a rule, qualified to account for our own beliefs and actions. Nevertheless, they owe it to themselves to justify their beliefs on grounds that would clear them of the suspicion of acting irrationally. It is therefore important for any modern person, who feels strongly the need for believing in God, to produce the credentials which validate that belief. It is the purpose of the following argument to indicate the nature of such credentials.

II.

The fact is that neither traditional religion nor pre-modern philosophy itself was really aware of how man came to believe in God. The study of the various religions of mankind points to an altogether different source of that awareness from the ones which they assume. The source of man's belief in God happens to be the same as that which yields the belief in the existence of human selfhood or personality.

We ordinarily maintain that we are sure of the existence of the self, because we experience it. But how do we experience it? The self is the object neither of empirical evidence nor of rational inference. It is neither tangible nor visible. What we speak of as "I" is not something which any of the evident manifestations of our bodies by themselves could prove to be real. Cleverly constructed automata might be made to behave in a manner similar to human bodies, yet we would not ascribe personality to them. Least of all do we depend on philosophical or metaphysical arguments to verify the existence of self-hood. Yet there is nothing of which we can be as certain as of the reality of the self.

It is interesting to note that the very existence of the self, or human personality, has of late been seriously questioned, not of course to the same extent, but virtually for the same reasons that people have come to question the belief in God. The type of psychology known as "behaviorist" assumes that the belief in the existence of the self derives either from a mistaken interpretation of the phenomena of the body, or from philosophical inference which is based on false reasoning. Behaviorists have accordingly come to the conclusion that there is no such thing as a self. They claim that the self is no more than the sensation of a catch in the throat. They maintain that there is no need whatever, when dealing scientifically with the human being, to reckon with the element of consciousness. Hence the saying that "psychology first lost its soul, then its mind, and finally its consciousness." If man were merely a complex system of conditioned reflexes as the behaviorists claim, he would think as accurately as a counting machine figures. The truth is that the very act of denying the self proves its existence. One is reminded of the fable of the water and the jug. Said the water to the jug, "You don't exist, because you're not like me." To which the jug replied, "If I didn't hold you, you wouldn't have the strength or the courage to utter a single word." By now, behaviorism has turned out to be so bankrupt that few psychologists are willing to act as its receivers. This should be a lesson for those who want to divest human life as a whole of the belief in God.

If we want to know whence men derive their belief either in the self or in God, we must look to a source hitherto neglected. That source is the will-to-live which the human being possesses in common with other living beings. In one extremely important respect, however, man's will-to-live differs from the will-to-live of the sub-human creature. Thanks to his extraordinary mental powers, man has been able to transform his will-to-live into the will-to-maximum-life or the will to make the optimum use of life. Man can remember past situations, imagine possible future situations, draw inferences and form judgments. Beside carrying on these mental processes in his own mind, he can communicate their products to his fellows through the medium of symbols, and transmit them as social heritage from generation to generation. The very experience of living so sharpen's man's will-to-maximum-life that it gives rise to a number of beliefs concerning realities which are invisible. Among the most important of these realities are the self and God. Without the belief in those realities, man would not be able to act humanly or sanely. In order, therefore, to comprehend what is meant by believing in God, we shall have to examine how man's will-to-maximum life, or his relentless urge to make the optimum use of life, actually functions.

The object of man's will to achieve the optimum as well as maximum use of life is known by various names. The ethicists call it "happiness," "summum bonum," or "growth." The traditionalists call it "a share in the world-to-come," "life abundant," or "salvation." These terms designate what man actually strives after, or should deliberately strive after, if he wants to be true to his essential nature as man. In this discussion, the term "salvation" will be used, because it is the widest in scope and depth.

The quest for salvation, whether as fact or as norm, is more distinctively human than any other differentia. Whatever else has been named as the human differentia turns out upon close scrutiny to be possessed, even if in a very minute degree, also by the sub-human. But the very nature of salvation precludes it from being an object of striving, even in the minutest degree, of any creature but man. In fact, even man began to engage in that quest only in the comparatively recent stages of his career on earth. The reason the quest for salvation is so uniquely human is that it necessarily involves making conscious choices among entire patterns of living, with a view to determining which pattern will yield most life. This is not possible for any but a highly developed human mind. To conceive an entire pattern of living implies being self-conscious, that is, capable of holding in one's mental grasp a cluster of remembered situations as well as a quickly changing complex of imagined situations. The mind must be able to abstract from both the remembered and the possible situations enough elements to weave into a pattern which shall include what is most likely to satisfy our various hungers and needs to a maximum degree.

The function of the historical religions and of the various philosophies of life has been to present to later generations the kind of life-pattern which seemed to satisfy the earlier generations in their quest for salvation. A time comes when those religions and philosophies are challenged. That means that new conditions have arisen which offer alternatives to the ideas and habits that have come down from the past. These alternative ideas and habits may either be assimilated by the traditional religions and philosophies, or form the content of new religions and philosophies. Both possibilities are being realized in our day.

III.

The basic interest in salvation, as such, is at present without a scientific discipline. To inaugurate such a discipline would be entirely in order; it might go by the name of "Soterics." One of its functions would be to make a systematic study of all forms of striving after salvation, as that striving has manifested itself in the life of mankind. We might then discover the traits which all those strivings have in common and wherein they differ. In the meantime, I venture to submit what I have discovered to be the case with all life-patterns which are organized with a view to salvation. All such life patterns are three-dimensional in character, in that they reckon with three types of human interest. Though organically interrelated with one another, and incapable of operating independently, these interests cannot be resolved into or equated with one another. The term "human interest" here refers to an entire psychic configuration which includes 1) a drive or impulse, 2) a want, hunger or feeling of lack, and 3) a value, or goal toward which the drive is directed.

Whenever a human being consciously refuses to yield to some dominant desire or ambition, in order to be or do his best or to live up to some standard of what is expected of him, he is engaged in making the most of his life. It is then that not only his will to live but his will to make the most of life, or the will to salvation, is active. Now the striking fact about the human being is that, whenever the will to salvation is active in him, he is more or less aware of interests which are such distinct types that they may be said to lie in entirely different dimensions of living. The *awareness* may be affirmative, as when an interest is accepted as legitimate, or negative, as when the interest in question is regarded as too obstreperous or altogether illegitimate. The *interests* may be classified into three distinct categories, each category constituting, as it were, a different dimension of human life. In so far as man strives to achieve not only the "good life," but "the full life," or "life abundant," his life possesses breadth, depth, and elevation.

The dimension of breadth is the dimension of functional or welfare interests; the dimension of depth is the dimension of rational interests, and the dimension of height is the dimension of spiritual interests. The purpose in designating them as belonging to three dimensions is to imply that the interests of one dimension are so incommensurate with those in either of the other two as to be in no way capable of being derived from, equated with or reduced to them. Insofar as it is at all possible to isolate from the stream of human living any one experience or event to which we give a name, we shall find that, to deal adequately with it, we have to reckon with it as having the three foregoing dimensions. By ignoring any one of them, we shall fail to grasp the experience or event as alive and know it only as a dead specimen of life.

First, the welfare interests included all those which aim to achieve security, health, mating, social recognition and the utilization of excess function in play and the creative arts. This is the realm wherein fear, the sense of danger, and libido, the craving for prestige and self-expression, constitute springs of action. Efficiency in satisfying these interests depends upon knowledge of the relationships, cause-and-effect and of means-and-ends.

Secondly, the rational interests are those which seek to satisfy two demands of human nature in its will to salvation. They are the demand 1) for truth as contrasted with illusion or error, and 2) for righteousness or justice, as contrasted with all that is unethical. Efficiency in the pursuit of these interests implies a hunger for rational objectivity and for righteousness, and the ability to satisfy them.

Take, for example, the case of two wounded soldiers on the battle field who find themselves alongside each other with a few precious drops of water in the canteen of only one of them. The natural prompting of the one who has the water to drink all of it himself belongs to the physical interests which we identify under the heading of "welfare." But at that very moment he may be prompted to share it with the wounded soldier next to him. It is then that the need to act ethically and spiritually asserts itself. He would regard himself as contemptible, if he were to ignore his comrade's need. When he shares the water, even if it means that he reduces his own chances of surviving, he has lived as a human being more fully than if he manages to survive by not yielding to what we speak of as his higher promptings.

Note the inevitable use of the term "higher promptings" to describe the foregoing situation. The term "higher," applied to the act of kindness in comparison with the tendency to quench one's own thirst, is our way of expressing the fact that the act of kindness belongs to a different order or category of values.

Thirdly, the dimension of the spiritual interests. It is among the interests in this dimension that we shall find the objective which forms the basis of man's belief in the existence of God.

The spiritual interests revolve about three objectives of which men become aware in the striving after salvation. These objectives are: 1) The experience of being a center of initiative. That is the experience of "selfhood." If successfully fostered it gives rise to a sense of personality. The process of fostering it involves focusing on the aspect of responsibility, which is a corollary of being a center of initiative, or of freedom to choose among different courses of action. 2) The experience of being integrally related to a social context. This is the experience of "otherhood." If successfully fostered it gives rise to a sense of family, of country, of church and possibly of humanity as a whole. The process of fostering it involves focusing on the aspect of loyalty. 3) The experience of finding the world dependable, from the standpoint of the will to salvation. This means that by conforming to what we assume, or discover, to be the direction in which the world is moving, we fulfill ourselves, or realize to the maximum our creative potentialities. If successfully fostered, that experience makes us aware of godhood in the world. The process of fostering it involves focusing on the aspect of piety.

Common to all these three groups of spiritual interests is the sense of holiness. We might also attribute the quality of holiness to the dimension of reason, for the pursuit of truth and justice for their own sake is likewise often experienced as uniquely indispensable to salvation. We might well ask: what in all these values which are consciously related to salvation calls forth the sense of holiness? The answer is: it is the feeling that in achieving or experiencing these values we are experiencing inner growth, and that the same time, we are reaching out for a type of reality which transcends human life. The urge to salvation and its progressive attainment in the process of growth thus yields intimations of the transcendent. But the transcendent is not necessarily synonymous with the supernatural. The supernatural is that which contravenes the known laws and processes of nature. The transcendent is merely that which lies beyond their domain.

GOD AS THE POWER THAT MAKES FOR SALVATION

IV.

The belief in God derives from the intuition that the cosmos may be depended upon to help us achieve salvation. This intuition is as real an experience as our experience of the visible objects around us. The object of this intuition comes in the form of a feeling; it lacks the definiteness which the experience of visible objects possesses. This fact explains why the intuition that the cosmos may be depended upon to help us achieve salvation is interpreted in a thousand different ways, depending upon our intellectual, moral and spiritual development. The one thing in common, however, to all these interpretations is the conception of godhood as manifest in the belief in one or in many gods. The conception of godhood answers the universal urge in men to make the most of their lives. But when they try to describe the experience of godhood and the circumstances attending that experience, they do so in all kinds of possible ways. Each group or people interprets its experience of the dependability of the cosmos in accordance with what happens to be of greater importance to it. The history of religion is the history of those interpretations.

At the present time, most of the traditional interpretations given to men's intuition or experience of the dependability of the cosmos have come to be unacceptable; they conflict with the now familiar facts about the world and human nature. To deal intelligently with the problem of religion, we must know what gave rise to the erroneous notions which form part of the traditional interpretations of religious experience. We shall then be able to salvage the element of abiding truth that they possess.

The first important fact we observe when we study the early stages of man's existence on earth is that, during the greater part of it, the welfare interests seemed to monopolize his life. Nevertheless, even in the most savage types of society we can discern the beginnings of rational and spiritual interests, if we look closely enough. But until very recently, man was unable to differentiate among those interests. As a result he entertained the most bizarre notions concerning the dependability of the cosmos, or of the fact of godhood in the world, and of how to avail himself of that dependability in order to make the most of his life.

To understand how early man came to worship as gods all kinds of objects both real and imaginary, we must bear in mind that he was for a long time unable to distinguish his social environment from the cosmos as a whole. His social environment included all objects, animate and inanimate that he saw about him, as well as the human beings living or dead that figured in his consciousness. It was nothing unusual for him to regard sun, moon, stars, trees, springs and animals as members of his own clan or tribe. Insofar as those objects or human beings enabled him to satisfy his yearning for salvation, they were to him the means of experiencing godhood. Even in the more developed stages of civilization, gods are essentially the superhuman members of one's own people or church. By now, even though man has achieved an awareness of cosmic dependability as distinct from the help which he receives from his own group, it is still mainly through his own group that he expects to achieve salvation or to experience the dependability of the cosmos.

The truth is that a full grown awareness of cosmic dependability as transcending national or churchly limitations is the achievement thus far only of a limited number of prophets and philosophers, and of those who accept their teachings. The ancient prophets and philosophers were the harbingers of what we hope will ultimately become a universal awareness of an inner demand to reckon with the dimension of reason. The philosophers concentrated on the interest in the attainment of truth, in their effort to understand reality as such, apart from the way it is refracted by the physical and spiritual interests of man. The prophets concentrated on the interest in the attainment of justice, in their effort to free men's dealings with one another from the dominant influence of selfishness and pride.

The effect of the explicit regard for both truth and justice upon the spiritual interests has been to purify them of falsehood and group selfishness. When men acquire an interest in truth and justice, they are more likely to cultivate personality for the sake of human dignity and freedom, to maintain social life in a spirit of international unity and responsibility, and to foster religion as a guide to human salvation irrespective of race, people or church.

V.

A further noteworthy fact with regard to the experience of cosmic dependability is that it never takes place in a vacuum, as it were, but is always mediated through specific persons, objects, places, events, texts, etc. These media come to be regarded as holy. They become foci of entire patterns of behavior involving a wide range of duties and prohibitions. These are the sancta which figure in the life of a group, be it tribe, nation or church, as indispensable to the salvation of the group as a whole, and of every one of its members in particular. These same sancta constitute the elements which give to any culture or civilization its individual character and differentiate it from other civilizations. The sancta are the vehicles through which a culture, a civilization or a religion is transmitted from one generation to another. So long as they are relevant to actual needs and convey an acceptable meaning, they continue to be a source of inspiration for all the forms of creative activity within the group in whose life they figure as the media of salvation.

There comes a time, however, in the life of a culture or civilization, when the explanations why the particular persons, objects, events, texts should serve as media for experiencing godhood or cosmic dependability are no longer acceptable. If the particular group which has evolved that system of sancta has sufficient incentive to preserve its solidarity and individuality, it will refuse to give up those sancta, even when the traditional explanations for their being regarded as such are no longer valid. It is then that the process of reinterpretation sets in. The sancta are then interpreted figuratively or symbolically, so that they might continue to serve as media for the experience of godhood. Consequently, the growth in rationality or enlightenment is by no means a sufficient cause for the breaking up of historical constellations of sancta, or more simply stated, for the liquidation of a historical religion. The fate of a historical religion is entirely in the hands of its adherents. If they possess sufficient intellectual plasticity and moral sympathy to be capable of reinterpreting the sancta of the group to which they belong, they can manage to give those sancta an indefinite lease on life.

Accordingly, the essential distinction between one religious tradition and another is to be found neither in the conception of God, nor in the interpretation of the experience of cosmic dependability, from the standpoint of salvation. Each religious tradition has its own constellation of sancta which has historically served for its adherents as the medium for experiencing godhood. From this it follows that there should be as little occasion for referring to a Jewish, or a Christian, or a Mohammedan conception of God as there is now for referring to a Jewish, a Christian, or a Mohammedan conception of the earth or of the heavens. The intuition which is the basis for the belief in God is an experience common to all human beings, when they attain a certain stage of mental and social development. The interpretation of that intuition likewise depends not so much upon the group into which the individual is born, as upon his own general outlook on life. The real distinction between one religion and another is either one of difference in the conception of salvation or one of otherness, that is, one of belonging to another society.

For practical purposes it should be sufficient to trust the spiritual experience of cosmic dependability, or of the immediate awareness of a Power not ourselves, that makes for salvation. The most important problem from that point on is not how to interpret that experience or intuition with a view to rendering it compatible with some particular philosophical outlook on life; this is a problem only for philosophers and theologians. For the generality of mankind, including the philosophers and theologians themselves, the burning problem at the present time is: what constitutes salvation? To be able to answer that question is to know what demands the cosmos makes upon us.

Until modern times there was one uniform conception of salvation. Jews, Christians and Mohammedans were agreed that salvation was unattainable in this world. They were equally agreed that only in the hereafter was the true bliss, which constitutes the life abundant, attainable. The most violent revolution in human history has taken place neither in the political sphere nor in the economic, but in the idea of salvation. The number of those who repudiate the traditional idea of salvation has been increasing in geometric ratio during the last hundred years. The present cataclysm is in a large measure the effect of the conflict of rival theories of this-worldly salvation. The traditional theory of other-worldly salvation is no longer acceptable. Fascism, Nazism, Communism have come forward with conceptions of this-worldly salvation which have captivated entire nations. If democracy is to make any headway, it will have to become equally articulate and convinced of the particular conception of this-worldly salvation which is compatible with it. Events have proved that the only conception of this-worldly salvation in which it will be possible to organize human life is one in which the spiritual interests that center about the self, society and the cosmos will give rise respectively to the values of 1) the dignity of the human person, 2) the unity of mankind and 3) the transcendence of God as reflected in man's eternal striving to transcend himself.

VI.

Formerly the conscientious rabbi might say with the poet,

> Ah, the men of my own race
> Bitter bad they may be,
> But at least they hear
> The things I hear,
> And they see the things I see.

Those halcyon days when rabbis and congregation heard and saw the same things in Jewish life are long past. Now they hear and see the same things only in the movies, which furnish some of their main sermon topics. That the rabbi and the congregation nowadays live in different universes of discourse is nobody's fault but the rabbi's. As a spiritual leader, he should have made it his business to guide and instruct his people in what they ought to know, and not merely to voice their wishful thinking.

The entire structure of religious belief has been undermined by the contemporary man's assumptions concerning what is historical and what is legendary. We have to rebuild the entire framework of our religious life. *Our religious life will henceforth have to be based not on the authority of tradition but on personal conviction.* All education in religion, whether elementary or advanced, will have to reckon with traditional religion only as part of the material on which to base personal conviction.

Personal conviction in Jewish religion will have to result from a twofold educational process. First, the process of reflection which is common to all men who think; second, the process of applying the results of such reflection to the traditions, experiences and hopes of the Jewish people.

The process of reflection which is to yield a tenable and workable conception of God will have to be kept free from the intricacies of metaphysics and theories of knowledge. Metaphysically, Whitehead and Alexander have formulated ideas of God which probably come nearest to objective reality. But how can such ideas ever serve as the basis of religion for the millions?

I venture, accordingly, to propose a different approach to the problem of basing religion on personal conviction.

In the first place, we should be cognizant of an important fact that emerges from the entire history and anthropology of religion. That fact is that human beings identify as "divine" whatever renders life worth living. Thanks to his powers of memory, imagination and abstract thought, man is more sensitive than other creatures to the evils of life. Thanks, however, to his exceptionally strong will to live, he learns either to transform or to transcend those evils. In the very process of doing so, he affirms the worthwhileness of life. The manner of his affirmation, the ideas, emotions, and actions which enter into it are determined by his cultural attainments. The term "God" helps to give, within each people, continuity to the process of affirming the worthwhileness of life. It also serves as a means of communicating that process from one people to another and from one civilization to another.

To believe in God is, accordingly, the exact equivalent of affirming the worthwhileness of life to such an extent that we regard life as deserving to elicit from us the best we can be and do, and to have us endure bravely the worst that can befall us. All praises and hymns to God are essentially affirmations of the inherent goodness and worthwhileness of life.

But the crucial question is: what renders life worthwhile? The ancients looked to their traditions for the answer. They took for granted that their traditions had come from God—the source of life's worthwhileness—and they asked no further questions. The changes, however, that have taken place in human life have rendered whole populations dissatisfied with the answers given by their traditions. They want to arrive at the answer for themselves. And so we have different philosophies of life at war with one another, each claiming to be divine, or absolute, or capable of rendering life worthwhile. To choose from among them one which we can believe in with all our hearts, and at the same time find congenial to our status as Jews, is the second stage in the reflective process in which we must engage.

Only after having achieved the outlines of a philosophy that indicates what it is that renders life worthwhile—and therefore godlike—are we ready to revitalize Jewish religion. Revitalizing Jewish religion means reinterpreting the Jewish tradition in the light of that philosophy. It means creating a literature and art in which that modern philosophy is given sanction and depth by the abiding values in Jewish teaching. It means, above all, extending the scope of Jewish worship and prayer to include the ever-widening range of human needs.

According to JACOB KOHN, "God is not one in addition to the infinite multiplicity that makes up the world, neither is God One as the mere sum of these multiplicities." Rather, God's Unity is "that unity by virtue of which every element actual or possible, ideal and physical, finds its relation to every other, through which every novelty in nature or history emerges out of the settled background of what already is, and points to some beyond yet to be." God's Being is "supreme and *all inclusive being*" (Kohn's italics).

Every individual attains its individuality from some whole—whether biological, geological, etc.—and relates itself to other beings in many ways. The whole, while never really apart from the many, is never exhausted by their multiplicity, either. To Kohn, the Whole is a given, evinced from a rational approach to the universe. The question for theology is not whether the Whole exists, but whether it can be identified with God "as He functions in the religious life."

The mystery of God's Unity is, according to Kohn, that "He is *in* nature but not *within* its confines." Kohn cites various examples from classical Jewish literature to support his claim. He also examines briefly the works of Spinoza, Samuel Alexander, Whitehead, and Paul Weiss, in order to show how leading thinkers seem to be gravitating toward the approach to God that he suggests.

XII.

God as the Whole

PRELIMINARY DEFINITIONS OF GOD AS THE WHOLE

WE ARE SEEKING a view of God and His unity which will avoid the necessity of trying to prove how *in the course of time* from the simple and the unitary the many came into being. The following statement despite its sketchy character expresses such a view. The whole of reality in its distributive multifariousness—this, that and the other indefinitely—is the universe or the world of our experience, the same reality in its primal or transcendental wholeness or singularity is God. This, that and the other, things, their relatedness, their processes of becoming, are all of them, phases or modes of His being.

God is not one in addition to the infinite multiplicity that makes up the world, neither is God one as the mere sum of these multiplicities. His unity again is not the additive unity of the parts combined to make a whole. Rather is it that unity by virtue of which every element actual or possible, ideal and physical, finds its relation to every other; through which every novelty in nature or history emerges out of the settled background of what already is, and points to some beyond yet to be. It is, therefore, the unity through which all the characteristics and phases, concrete and universal, can be recognized in their separateness and yet forever connect with one another the further our explorations reach. His is supreme and *all inclusive Being.* God's presence in them all gives them being; their presence in God gives them unity.

The logical as in fact the psychological priority of the Whole and, therefore, its transcendence over any part or combination of parts, is apparent wherever we turn. Nothing has individual significance or can be imagined to have such significance save within a larger unity which endows it with particular meaning. It is an error to think of the mind as originally aware of a multiplicity of things in varied relations one to another. The area of awareness in the infant is at first an undifferentiated and unbounded extension within which it finally carves out many objects held together in various relationships and distinguished by many qualities. The experience of depth or of the space continuum is brought about only as the child wriggles its body and stretches forth its hands and strains to focus its eyes. At last it discovers *itself* as one more thing in a continuous space which has no breach but only a beyond. Finally, the subject claims its object. The ego is born and the child uses not only the third person or the mere verb "baby wants" but "I want," "I feel," "I hurt." The many concrete things, their qualities and their relation and transformation come to our attention only as *abstractions from a whole region of awareness.*

The mass and the molecule, the atom and the quantum are only a series of successive diminishing fields of energy within larger fields of space-time existence. The larger, as we have noted, is not compounded of once unrelated parts. On the contrary, the latter must be viewed as abstracted from the more inclusive. Science and philosophy get to know the microscopic by and through analysis of the macroscopic. Qualities— redness, loudness, beauty—become known by abstraction from the concrete entities which they qualify. They are not ever seen independently and then, as it were, pasted on to the object that displays them. So abstract a concept as peace becomes a social ideal only because we sometimes do discover it either within ourselves or in a society at peace and carry it with us as an ideal through centuries filled with war and the desolations of war.

Environment and the life it environs are not found originally apart from one another. They too are abstractions. Can we imagine an amoeba without environment and then suddenly introduced to an environment as a guest to a drawing room? *Environment enters into the very definition of life and life into the definition of environment.* They are again abstractions from a history in which they are both involved. We hold them apart only for purposes of definition so that we may again unite them for purposes of explanation.

No cells ever generated a living organism except insofar as they were first involved in a living organism from which they emerged or from which they parted company, to enter into relations with a common environment to which the previous organism was also related. This does not imply that protoplasm may not have originated through some synthesis of inorganic substance. The fact remains however that the inorganic matter so synthesized as well as the organism now making its appearance, were elements of a substance which was neither organism or environment, before the transformation took place, but had the potential of both. Such synthesis cannot be called generation. The young of no animal was ever born into a vacuum but always within some biological family or ethnic group—some Whole that had previously existed and now claims it and determines its status.

In other words, every individual thing of whatever kind—a mountain, a coral reef, a grain of sand—attains its concrete individuality, emerging from some Whole previously existent and relating itself to other beings within a wide skein of relations (qualitative, quantitative, causal and rational), which themselves make possible new emergents and new transformations that may today still lie beyond all ken.

The whole of being is never something apart from the many of which it is the whole and yet *it is never exhausted by their multiplicity*, actual or possible.

The main question of theology remains: is there anything about this whole of being which would justify us in identifying it with God as He functions in the religious life?

In Jewish theology, I have often pointed out, the dominant theme is always the mystery of the Unity. So far from considering the unity of God, a simple creed easier to understand than the gorgeous multiplicity of a heathen pantheon or even the paradox of the Christian trinity, Jewish thinkers were keenly aware of the difficulties in the affirmation of the unity. In some stanzas of The Royal Crown by the philosopher-poet Ibn Gabirol, that philosophical perplexity is beautifully expressed:

> Thou art One, the beginning of all computa-
> tion, the base of all construction.
> Thou art One, and in the mystery of Thy
> Oneness the wise of heart are astonished,
> for they know not what it is.
> Thou art One, and Thy Oneness neither
> diminishes nor increases, neither lacks
> nor exceeds.
> Thou art One, but not as the One that is
> counted or owned, for number and change
> cannot reach Thee, nor attribute, nor
> form.
> Thou art One, but my mind is too feeble
> to set Thee a law or a limit.[1]

Gabirol, as we have seen, was both a philosopher and a poet of the synagogue. As philosopher, he was claimed by Moslems and Christians alike before the original Hebrew of his manuscript Fountain of Life, was finally identified. He is usually classed among the neo-Platonists of the scholastic period, yet the same philosophic wonder characterizes the Aristotelians, especially those who refused to grant primal matter co-eternity with God. The mystery as we have already seen, consists largely in how this primal transcendent unity could be the essence or source or creator of the multifarious and imperfect world. They proposed several solutions upon which we cannot dilate at this point.

For us, I think, the mystery must be stated differently. We ask, how can the rich multiplicity of the universe with all its striking contrasts and contradictions yet give some hint as to the nature of the One and even lead to the idea of unity as a *rational explanation for their togetherness in multiplicity.*

Frankly, this idea of God's unity must result in a kind of pantheism provided the emphasis is placed on *theism and not on pan.* All of nature, all phases of the physical universe are within God and God is in them all.

Yet we dare not say that He is contained within their boundaries. God, from our point of view, is the realm of the possible, the creative and the actual insofar as they have relevance to one another. The infinite multiplicity of His creatures and the processes determining their becoming do not limit the scope of His being. He is *in* nature but not *within* its confines.

Some hint of this kind of pantheism runs throughout the Judeo-Christian tradition—both prophetic, mystical and philosophic. The logicians are as prone to it as are the romanticists. Some allusions to such systems of thought I had sketchily introduced into *The Moral Life of Man.*[2] I repeat them here somewhat expanded and with many recent additions because they are germane to the idea of God we are here developing in relation to the cosmic process known as the evolution of life.

The 90th Psalm begins

> Lord thou has been our dwelling place in all
> generations,
> Before the mountains were brought forth
> Or ever thou has formed the earth and the world
> Even from everlasting to everlasting thou art God.

INSTANCES IN MEDIEVAL AND MODERN THOUGHT

We have, furthermore, the luminous interpretation in rabbinic literature of God's omnipresence. He is frequently called "The Place" and this is interpreted to mean neither His heavenly abode, as in the third chapter of Ezekiel, nor merely His being everywhere, but more precisely "the

Holy One, Blessed be He, is the *Place* of His *universe* and not the universe the place of Him." Spinoza ascribes this view both to the ancient Jews and to Saint Paul when he affirms, "I assert that all things live and move in God."[3]

The following lines from the *Song of the Unity*[4] are eloquent with this description of the unity of God. Life and nature find their being in Him.

> All that was at first
> And all that at last shall be
> All the creatures and all their deeds
> And all their spoken words and thought
> From beginning to end
> Thou knowest them all.
> And thou forgettest not
> For thou art co-present with them.
> There is nothing so secret that it is hidden
>   from Thee
> Events of the future and of the past
> With Thee are they one . . .
> For thou art from eternity to eternity
> *They are all in Thee and Thou art in them all.*

The last lines we have quoted remind one of Meister Eckhart who is very nearly contemporary with the Jewish circles from which our mystic poem derives. Rabbi Judah Ben Samuel, to whom the above verses are usually attributed, died in Regensberg in 1217. Eckhart was born in 1260 and is usually acclaimed as the earliest speculative mystic of Western Christianity. He is said to have remarked, "God is all things, all things are God. . . . The eye with which I see God is the same eye with which God sees me. My eye and God's are one eye." Brinton speaks of this attitude as "aggressive mystical pantheism."[5]

The subconscious logic of medieval Jewish mysticism, especially that of the Kabbalah, as well as strains of certain Oriental thought, show a similar attitude. Thus the impression one receives from this literature, especially from the Zohar,[6] is that the Absolute, the *Undifferentiated Infinite (the En Sof)* cannot possibly account for the world and cannot become an object of worship and adoration. Where everything is equally possible, nothing can actually happen. In this sense, the infinite is sometimes equated with nothingness by some of the mystics (as in certain forms of modern existentialism). God, however, to the author of the Zohar, is not merely the infinite. He is the infinite as defined by His self-revelation in the Sefirot. These are attributes of His which eternally emanate from the infinite, not as divine persons but as creative poten-

cies. They are ten in number. (The word Sefirah in early Jewish speculation means number or dimension as in the Sefer Yezirah.)[7] To wit:
Wisdom, Understanding and Knowledge, Love, Power and Splendor,
Victory, Majesty and Sovereignty and, last of all, the Foundation—then
we arrive at the mundane world of man. Together, they constitute the
realm of Divine Being.

In this scheme, man plays his part not only as the end product of the
divine travail but as a participant helping by his deeds to activate the
higher realms upon which his being depends. All reality, we might say,
becomes a *spiritual field of force* with the Unknown Infinite at one pole
and man at the other.

In a new climate of thought, disclaiming all mystic feeling and
repudiating both revelation and scholastic rationalism, Spinoza becomes
the champion of a thoroughgoing pantheism. The substance of the
world is one, infinite and absolutely free and that substance is God. Its
attributes are infinite in number though the human mind distinguishes
but two—thought and extension. All particular things, all actual entities
are *modes* of substance in one or more of its infinite attributes. There is
not only an infinity of attributes but each attribute is infinite. Each mode
is what it is by virtue of its necessary place in the being of God. Such a
God, if properly loved through intellectual apprehension and joy in His
eternal perfection (where nothing can possibly be other than it is), can
also be said to love man since, in loving Himself (which to Spinoza
means enjoying, in thought, His own perfection) He must love all the
creatures who are modes of His own thought. The will, it seems, is only
seemingly free but thought can and does accept truth and in the course
of such acceptance, man attains Blessedness.

This is not the occasion to attempt a critical appraisal of Spinoza or to
point out how we may be inclined to deviate from some of the conclusions he reaches. The *Ethics* remains, however, a magnum opus of
deductive logic.

It will always be a moot question among interpreters of Spinoza
whether Spinoza, who aims at complete repudiation of the supernatural, only uses the term God as a sort of courteous gesture to placate the
prevailing religious tradition, whereas he means only to describe substance; or whether as in the closing paragraphs of the *Ethics* where *love*
and *blessedness* become key concepts, he uses the term Substance for
philosophical clarification but means God all along. My impression is
that Wolfson in his great work on Spinoza, holds the former view. On
the other hand, a very interesting little book by Ruth Lydia Saw of the
University of London, on *The Vindication of Metaphysics—a Study in the
Philosophy of Spinoza*, takes quite the opposite point of view. I find
myself, on the whole, in agreement with her conclusion though I would

not make so good a Christian of him as she attempts to do. "Infinite substance" she explains, "turns out to be a person, a fit object for love, veneration and worship and when Spinoza comes to the end of the *Ethics,* he allows his language to become suitable for the description of such a person. I think this is a legitimate process. Having in mind a person known to his forefathers by revelation, even though he rejects their ways of speaking of this person, Spinoza deduces from the idea of being such a description that can fit only this person."[8]

Both Samuel Alexander in *Space-Time and Deity,* and Whitehead who sometimes calls himself a pluralist, confess their indebtedness to Spinoza in more ways than one. Says Alexander, "Space-Time can only be described not as one and still less as *a* one but as *the* one; and only then because the quasi-universal adjective serves once more to designate not its number but its infinite singularity; or, as is more clearly still expressed by calling it *Substance,* that it is not so much an individual or a singular as the one and only matrix of generation to which no rival is possible because rivalry itself is fashioned within the same matrix."[9] "Space and time are, *in the words of Spinoza,* though not with the significance which he attaches to the phrase, attributes of the universe of Space-Time."[10] God is the whole world as possessing the *quality* of deity; of such a being God is the body and deity the mind. But this possessing of deity is not actual but ideal. As an actual existent, God is the infinite world with a nisus towards deity (the quality of deity is always some higher value still to be achieved—J.K.) I understand this to mean not that God is *non*existent but that He is not merely existent. He is real in another sense. Nor can existence ever actually contain all those infinite gradations of ascending qualities which are the hallmark of Deity.

Another statement of Alexander's where his pantheism takes on a humanistic tinge is the following, "Our minds, therefore, and everything else are the organic sensa of God. All we, are the hunger and the thirst, the heartbeat and sweat of God. This is what Rabbi Ben Ezra says in Browning's poem when he protests that he has never mistaken his end, to slake God's thirst." It is interesting to observe how easily modern thinkers who deal with mathematics and logic grope for illustrative material in poetry and mysticism.

Whitehead, though he differs greatly from the absolute monism of Spinoza, nevertheless concedes large areas of agreement. "The Philosophy of organism (the name he gives his own) is closely allied to Spinoza's scheme of thought." "The attraction of Spinoza's philosophy lies in its modification of Descartes' position into greater coherence. He starts with one substance, causa sui, and considers its essential attributes and its individualized modes." "In all philosophical theory, there is an ultimate which is actual by virtue of its accidents. In the philosophy of organism, this ultimate is termed creativity and God is its primordial non-temporal accident. In monistic philosophy, *Spinoza's* or absolute idealism, this ultimate is God." "One side makes processes ultimate, the other side makes fact ultimate."[11]

It is evident that from our point of view, the ultimate is not process but God as Being. On the other hand, we refuse to assign to the ultimate mere actuality. It transcends the actual since it also embraces the possible, known or unknown, and that decision between possibilities which evokes the actual and thus the cosmic process.

We cannot but wonder whether Whitehead's "creativity" is very different from Spinoza's emphasis on *natura naturans*. It must not be overlooked that Whitehead is also responsible for the statement, "The safest general characterization of European philosophical tradition is that it consists of a series of footnotes to Plato." In reference to his *eternal objects*,[12] he ventures upon such a footnote, "The things which are temporal arise by their participation in the things that are eternal. The two sets are mediated by a thing which combines the actuality of what is temporal with a timelessness of what is potential. This final entity is the Divine element in the world."[13]

A theistic thinker today is likely to reflect either the epistemological systems of Kant, Hegel or the absolute idealists such as Royce, or he may build upon the pragmatists from Peirce to Dewey who have all made important contributions to which we shall occasionally allude. Then again, he may accept some form of existentialism which would rule out altogether philosophic and conceptual thought as a suitable approach to God. Otherwise, only some form of Spinozism is left him, modified perhaps, by the deeper insights of Platonism. The word Substance has too static a connotation today and will, doubtless, be replaced by some word which connotes process as well as form.

Quite recently, a new book has appeared by Paul Weiss who had previously published a volume on *Reality* and on *The Nature of Man* as well as a number of other philosophical dissertations. The title, *Modes of Being*, and its unabashed metaphysical tone again suggests a union of Spinoza and ontological Platonism. It begins with a challenge: "This is a book in philosophy. As a philosophical work should, it attempts to articulate a vision of the whole of things."[14] Such daring in an age characterized by the mock modesty of over specialization is indeed welcome.

His main thesis is: "One had, I became convinced, to distinguish and assume, in turn, the perspectives of four distinct realities—Actuality, Ideality, Existence, and God. All four, one had to affirm, are final and irreducible modes of being with their own integrity and career."

As I understand this rather complex and somewhat ambiguous nomenclature, it means, not that any of these things is real apart from the other, but that every fact has its place in the being of God, in the world of the actual, in the field of existence, and, of course, in the realm of ideas or possibility. "God is that being who among other things makes unity of what otherwise would be a detached set of occurrences. He sees to it that the ideal is realized and that actualities are perfected." I can see no objection to this description of the functioning of God. From the point of view we have been developing, such functioning would be too grandiose a task for a god who is merely a *mode of being*.

I still can think of no better phrase than the "Infinite Unity of all Being" which Feibleman uses in his *Ontology*.[15] Feibleman is a realist in the Platonic sense—essences are as real as things. God then becomes what He has popularly been called all along—*Supreme Being*.

NOTES

1. Solomon Ibn Gabirol, *The Kingly Crown*, translated by Bernard Lewis (London: Valentine-Mitchell, 1961).

2. Jacob Kohn, *The Moral Life of Man* (New York: Philosophical Library, 1956).

3. Cf. Harry Austryn Wolfson, *The Philosophy of Spinoza*, Vol. I (Massachusetts: Harvard University Press, 1934), p. 196.

4. Read in the Synagogue on the eve of the Day of Atonement.

5. Cf. Crane Brinton, *A History of Western Morals* (New York: Harcourt, Brace and Co., 1959), p. 191, note 18.

6. The Book of Splendour is the central text of Kabbalism.

7. *Sefer Yezirah—Book of Creation*—One of the earlier mystical classics in Jewish literature.

8. Ruth Lydia Saw, *The Vindication of Metaphysics—A Study in the Philosophy of Spinoza* (London: Macmillan & Co., 1951). Cf. p. 68 for further views of Spinoza on the inner nature of individual reality.

9. Samuel Alexander, *Space, Time and Deity* (London: Macmillan & Co., 1927) p. 339.

10. *Ibid.*, p. 342.

11. Alfred North Whitehead, *Process and Reality* (New York: Macmillan and Co., 1930).

12. Ibid., p. 32.

13. Ibid., p. 63.

14. Paul Weiss, *Modes of Being* (Carbondale: Southern Illinois University Press, 1958).

15. James K. Feibleman, *Ontology* (Baltimore: Johns Hopkins Press, 1951), pp. 190, 195.

Citing the Bible, Rabbinic authorities, and other sources from Jewish history, ISRAEL H. LEVINTHAL argues that the Jewish tradition has always put great stock in human inquisitiveness, and that, throughout the ages, the tradition has reflected man's attempts to sharpen his perceptions about God and His will. Levinthal's sophisticated sermon affirms that "Judaism believes in the evolution of the human mind. Judaism teaches that with the gradual evolution and perfection of the human mind and with the enrichment of the human spirit, more and more will there be progress in the glimpses that we shall catch of the Divine; and more and more will our conceptions of Him be developed and refined." Levinthal cites many remarkable sources from the classic Jewish tradition in order to support his affirmations.

XIII.

The Development of the God-Idea

ISRAEL H. LEVINTHAL

THE JEWS CAME to their recognition of God not so much through philosophic reasoning or metaphysical speculation, but rather by instinct, by what psychologists might call intuition, and what religionists might term Divine manifestation or revelation.

Among the unique features of this God Idea of the Jew, above all, its ethical distinctiveness. God to the Jew was what Matthew Arnold called "the Power, not ourselves, that maketh for righteousness."[1] He was the essence of all holiness and all morality, that driving force in us and in the world making for justice and righteousness. To quote Professor Moore again: "Jewish monotheism was reached through the belief that the will of God for righteousness is supreme in the history of the world; one will rules it all to one end—the world as it ought to be! . . . Its origin was thus, to put it in a word, moral rather than physical or metaphysical."[2]

The Jew, being of a practical nature, did not delve into the mystery of what God is, which he knew was beyond human ken, but instead was vitally concerned to know the Will of God, which to him was revealed in the Torah, in the teachings of his inspired spiritual giants—that Will of God which would aid him to become Godlike, holy even as God is holy.

Now it is true that Judaism accepted without protest the decree, as recorded in the Biblical tale we interpreted in our last discussion, "For man shall not see Me and live!"[3] It is also true that the Jewish spirit, being pragmatic in its aim, was content with a God who functioned in the daily lives of men without attempting theological descriptions of that God. Nevertheless, we must understand that human nature is inquisi-

160

tive, that man, even though he knows his search is futile, is determined to get some glimpse of the Divine Being who plays such an important role in his life. That is how we can understand the Bible story that makes Moses plead before God: "Show me, I pray Thee, Thy glory!"[4]

Now in that same story, you recall, God says to Moses: "And I will take away My hand, and thou shalt see My back, but My face shall not be seen."[5] In this mystic sentence, filled with such anthropomorphic allusions, I believe, is contained a great philosophic truth, which we must fully appreciate if we are to understand the development of the God conception in Judaism. While we cannot grasp God's being in all His glory—for "My face shall not be seen"—we do catch glimpses of that Godliness, even though these glimpses do not reveal His real essence but are the creations of our own minds and hearts. We *must* create an image of Him because we *want* to image Him, because we want to know and behold Him. The poet, whose Hymn of Glory we still chant in the Synagogue, expressed it truly when he says: "I will declare Thy glory tho I have not seen Thee; under images will I describe Thee, tho I have not know Thee. . . . In images they told of Thee, but not according to Thine essence; they but likened Thee in accordance with Thy works."[6]

That is how we can explain the various descriptions of God that are found in the Bible and in all our sacred literature. They are only glimpses of God revealed by the limited powers of the human mind. While it is true that the Jewish teachers protested and warned against anthropomorphic conceptions of God—we need only recall the words of Maimonides that "Whosoever conceives God to be a corporeal being is an apostate"[7]—men had to create images of Him in their thoughts to satisfy the yearning of their minds powerless to visualize Him. It was because of the recognition of this failing of the human mind that Rabbi Abraham ben David of Posquières severely criticized Maimonides for the above opinion.[8] We find in the Bible descriptions and designations of God as a warrior, a shepherd, a king, a judge, a father—all human concepts. How can we explain such portrayals, knowing that God is beyond the realm of portrayal? The peoples of those days simply put their own images into their concept of God in a desire to come closer unto Him. The Rabbis are all emphatic in their assertions that the Torah, when using such descriptions, merely intends to assist the simple-minded, that all such expressions concerning God must never be taken literally; they are simply due to the inadequacy of human language;[9] or, as one Rabbi puts it, "to make the ear listen to what it can hear!"[10] Even when we say today that God is all-knowing or all-good, we must realize that we are using a terminology which in philosophic strictness is inapplicable to God. We use such terminology because, with the inadequacy of human speech, we have none better.

We must understand this, if we want to study the various conceptions of God that have been evolved. When people lived a pastoral life, they naturally conceived of God as a shepherd. When they lived a monarchical life, and the king was to them the embodiment of all that was great and powerful, it was but natural that they should image their God as king. When they idealized the love and devotion of a father, God to them was the father; and when they appreciated the role of judge in dispensing justice, God was conceived as the supreme judge. As F. Max Müller observes: "Man devised means as varied as nature herself to express the idea of God within him."[11]

I emphasize this point in our discussion for various reasons. Some people childishly assume that we have but one defined conception of God, and that unless you accept that conception, you must surrender any claim to a belief in God. There is no fixed concept of God in Judaism; conceptions of Him have grown and developed and changed from the dawn of Jewish life to our own day! It is the same with mankind as it is with an individual. When you talk to a child about God, you talk to him in childish language, in the language of fairy tales, if you will, in language that his tender mind can grasp. When he grows older, you speak to him of the same theme in an altogether different language. So, too, with mankind—and so, too, with the Jewish people. In the childhood stage of their national development, their conceptions of God may have been childish. But these conceptions grew with the growth of their national genius and experience. He is the same God, but our concepts of Him changed and grew with every richer experience. With the same poet of the Synagogue we can say: "Tho men imagined Thee in many visions, Thou art one in all likenesses."[12]

The Rabbis, indeed, state this truth in their own inimitable way. Commenting upon the words of the Psalmist, "The voice of the Lord is *Ba'Ko-ah,* powerful," they say that God reveals Himself not with His own overwhelming might, but *L'fi Koho Shel Kal Ehad W'ehad—according to each man's individual power and capacity"*[13]—and, we might add, according to the stage of true civilization the age has attained.

If you study the Bible intelligently, you will be able to trace the various stages of this growth. You will see there the God Idea, *L'fi Koho Shel Kal Ehad W'ehad,* as all, the lowliest and the loftiest, have visioned Him. You will see Him conceived as but one of many gods; then you will see Him as the greatest of all gods; then, the God of Israel only, and finally, you will see Him as conceived by the Prophets and spiritual giants—the God of all humanity and all the universe—the one, eternal, everlasting God, ruler of the destinies of all mankind. The Bible records all these views, because the Bible mirrors the life of our people, their ideas and ideals in the course of more than a thousand years. Primitive views appear side by side with the most advanced prophetic conceptions. In searching for the true Jewish conceptions, we must know how to differentiate between the pure gold and the dross. We must look for the noblest conceptions which the Jews reached in the loftiest moments of their existence; we must look to the concepts taught by their God-conscious geniuses rather than to the descriptions offered by the ordinary man in their midst.

And I emphasize this fact because I want to bring home to you the progressive spirit that marks the Jewish teaching of the God Idea. Judaism believes in the evolution of the human mind. Judaism teaches that with the gradual evolution and perfection of the human mind and with the enrichment of the human spirit, more and more will there be progress in the glimpses that we shall catch of the Divine; and more and more will our conceptions of Him be developed and refined.

Some of you may recall the fact that a few years ago, a professor in one of our colleges[14] startled a convention of scientists and savants with the declaration that science today demands a new conception of God, and that this newer view must be formulated in the light of contemporary astrophysics, which seems to be in conflict with so many of the traditional theological and cosmological ideas. I remember quite vividly what a furor this statement made in the newspaper stories, how a high and distinguished prelate of the Church denounced in most emphatic language the very idea of such a demand. What would be the answer of traditional, historic Judaism to such a challenge? Judaism would say: "If you can give the world a new, a clearer glimpse of the Divine, if you have a new conception that you can offer to the human heart athirst for God, by all means let us have it, and the world shall be your debtor for all time!" That is the beauty of Judaism. Judaism has never been, and is not now, and never will be opposed to any new conception of God which the human mind may formulate, as long as that conception is still that of God and not of something that is to serve as a substitute for God. It believes that man's conception of God must grow with the growth of the human mind and with the enrichment of the human heart.

There is a striking passage in the Bible that I believe reveals in remarkable fashion the true teaching of Judaism on this subject. When Moses was sent on the historic mission to bring the message of liberty to his enslaved brethren, he said to God: "When I come unto the children of Israel and shall say unto them, The God of your fathers hath sent me unto you, and they shall say to me *Mah Sh'mo*, What is His Name? *Mah Amar Alehem*, What shall I say unto them?"[15] What can such words mean? Did not the Jews in Egypt know God? Does not the Bible itself say that their lives were so embittered that they cried unto God?[16] How is it possible to conceive that when Moses will come and speak to them in the name of the God of their fathers, the God to whom they cried in their anguish, they will ask: "What is His name?"—as if He were a total stranger unto them! And the answer which God gives to Moses is even more remarkable. *"Ehe-ye Asher Ehe-ye,* I am that I am! Thus shalt thou say to the children of Israel, *Ehe-ye* hath sent me unto you!"[17] But you have in this dialogue, in language that hides a deeper thought, the very essence of the Jewish attitude toward the conception of God. The Israelites in Egypt knew their God, the God of their fathers. But they were seeking a new conception of that God. *Mah Sh'mo,* What is His name now? Under what concept do you image Him today, when the experiences of our life call for an enlargement of that concept, for an enrichment of our vision? And God gives the true answer. The English translation of God's answer—*"I Am That I Am"*—is not the literal translation; it is in fact, a translation that is questionable and whose meaning is doubtful. *Ehe-ye Asher Ehe-ye* literally means *"I shall be what I shall be!"* There is no fixed concept. I shall be what the future will unfold of Me. "Thus shalt thou say unto the children of Israel, *Ehe-ye* hath sent me unto you!" The important thing is that *Ehe-ye—I shall be*—I shall always be God! As to My name, the future alone will tell—I shall be whatever the human mind and heart will be able to fathom of My mystery.

The Jewish God conception is not static or fixed. As the Rabbis interpret these words: *Zeh Sh'mi L'fi Sha'ah, Ehe-ye Asher Ehe-ye*—As for My name, as for the human conception of Me—*L'fi Sha'ah,* it is according to the time,[18] to the stage of civilization that men shall have attained; *Ehe-ye Asher Ehe-ye* "I shall be whatever I shall be"—it depends not upon Me but upon the spiritual heights to which you will ascend!

Now please do not look upon this interpretation of the Biblical dialogue as a bit of pulpit hair-splitting. I have given you what I believe to be the true meaning of these Biblical words. You will find the same thought emphasized again a little further along in the Biblical story. God again appears unto Moses and says to him: "I am Jehovah, and I appeared unto Abraham, unto Isaac and unto Jacob *B'El Shaddai,* as the God Shaddai. *Ushmi Jehovah Lo Nodati Lahem,* but by My name Jehovah I made Me not known to them."[19] Again, what does all this mean? According to the Rabbis,[20] the various names of God represent different conceptions. *Elohim* emphasizes the God who dispenses justice; *Jehovah,* the God who displays mercy and compassion; *Shaddai,* the God of power and might. The Israelites in Egypt knew God as *El Shaddai,* the God who rules the universe, the philosophic or cosmic God. But now they had reached the stage in their spiritual experience where they caught a new glimpse of God, where they were able to think of Him in a new concept—the concept of Jehovah or the God who is the essence of mercy and kindliness. The Jews could not understand why they continued to be enslaved, and why the God of their fathers should permit such a condition to continue. A God who is *El Shaddai*—the Power who rules the heavens and the earth, but who has no sway in the life of men—is not enough. That very conception of God as the Supreme Power could almost justify the Egyptian rulers in their philosophy that might is right, that because they had the power they were justified in enslaving the weak. They knew now that God must be more than *Shaddai*—and for the first time in their national experience He became known unto them as *Jehovah*, the God of mercy, who took the side of the weak against the strong, the few against the many, the enslaved against the rulers who forced upon them their chains.

Such revelations of the deeper concepts of God are not just thrust upon man. Rashi, the great commentator, wisely points out to us[21] that our text says *Lo Nodati* (in the passive sense—"I have not been known"), not *Hodati* (in the active sense—"I have not made myself known"), to teach us this very truth—that these new concepts are not just given to man automatically. We cannot achieve new conceptions of God by just saying we want a new conception. We must be spiritually prepared for the new revelation. *Nodati, "I am made known"*—I am revealed through the human soul, the human heart and the human mind!

Our Rabbinic literature offers us a number of such examples to illustrate the historic development and growth of the God concept. To quote but one: "From the day that God created the world until the days of Abraham no one called God as *Adon*, Master or Lord, until Abraham came and so termed him."[22] It was a new conception of the Divine, according to the sages, that was first revealed through Abraham—God as the *Adon*, the Master Will of the Universe. And the founder of Hassidism, the Baal Shem Tob, in a beautiful interpretation asks why we say in the introductory part of the *Eighteen Benedictions*, "The God of our fathers, the God of Abraham, the God of Isaac and the God of Jacob!" Why this repetition of the word God? Would it not suffice to say "the God of Abraham, Isaac and Jacob?" But the word is repeated, he tells us, to impress upon us the thought that though He is our fathers' God—the same God through all the ages—Abraham put his impress upon our understanding of God, so that He is in truth the God of Abraham. Isaac received that conception, but added his own vision to it, so that He is also the God of Isaac; and Jacob, receiving the conceptions of his fathers, put his spiritual stamp upon them, so that He is also the God of Jacob.[23] In other words, every generation, if it be but spiritually attuned, can give its added vision, its new glimpse, of the glory of the Divine.

Herein lies the unique greatness of Judaism. It has faith in the evolution of the human mind and heart. Judaism believes in the sublime enlargement and unfoldment of our spiritual vision in the future. Nay, more, Judaism asks us to be honest in our God conception. There is a passage in the Talmud that we dare not overlook in our present discussion. "Moses called God 'the great and mighty and terrible.' Then came Jeremiah and he said: 'Foreign idolaters are dancing in His Temple; where is His terror?' And he dropped the appellation 'terrible' from the description of Moses. Then came Daniel, and he said: 'Idolatrous invaders have reduced His children to servitude; where is His mightiness?' And he did not call God 'mighty'." The Talmud adds that the Men of the Great Synagogue restored these attributes or conceptions of God, by pointing out the defects in the reasoning of Jeremiah and Daniel. The Rabbis significantly ask, nevertheless, "How dared these Prophets to contradict that which Moses spoke?" And Rabbi Isaac answers: "Because they knew that God *Amiti Hu* is the essence of truth, they therefore could not lie to Him!"[24] What a glorious message comes to us from this Talmudic tale! Judaism demands sincerity and truth in all our teachings concerning God.

Yes, if any professor, through his researches in new fields, can give to us a new conception of God that shall bring added spiritual satisfaction to the yearning hearts of men, the world will indeed make him its debtor! Such revelations, however, we fear will not come from the scientist or from the philosopher, but from the God-intoxicated man—the man of Divine vision. Tolstoy saw this clearly when he told us that "Neither philosophy nor science can establish man's relation to the universe. . . . Man's relation to the world is defined not by intellect alone, but also by feeling, and by the whole combination of his spiritual forces. . . . The qualities which make some men more suited to receive the rising truth are not any special, active qualities of heart, rarely coinciding with a great and inquisitive intellect: renunciation of the cares of the world, consciousness of one's own material insignificance, and great sincerity, as we see exemplified by all the founders of religion."[25]

Judaism has faith in the future. You recall those beautiful words of the Prophet, with which the Jew concludes his every prayer service: "And the Lord shall be king over all the earth; in that day shall the Lord be One and His name One."[26] Ask the Rabbis: "And now is not God One? What mean the words 'In that day God shall be One and His name shall be One'?" And they answer beautifully: "Now God is One, but His names are many. Everyone conceives Him according to his own vision. But in the world that is to be—in that glorious future that is yet to come—not only will God be One; His Name, too, will then be One."[27] All mankind will have advanced to the loftiest heights of spiritual truth, all will catch the vision that hitherto was reserved for the chosen few, a vision that will turn the world into a realm of blessedness.

In the meantime, whatever new concept of God may be revealed, we know, we are confident, that it will be but a new glimpse of that God who is the God of our fathers, and who, we hope, will remain the God of our children!

NOTES

1. Matthew Arnold, *Literature and Dogma.*
2. Moore, *Judaism*, I, 361.
3. Exod. 33:20.
4. *Ibid.* 18.
5. *Ibid.* 23.
6. Ane'im Zemirot, *Singer's Prayer Book,* p. 78, London, 1912.
7. Maimonides, *Mishne Torah,* Teshubah, III, 7.
8. RaBaD *ad loc.*
9. Abot d'R. Nathan, version 1, ch. 2; version 2, ch. 3, p. 7a, ed. Schechter.
10. *Ibid.;* 32 Middot of R. Eliezer, No. 14, ed. Wilna.
11. Quoted by S. S. Cohon, *What We Jews Believe,* p. 138; *cf.* F. Max Müller, *Chips from a German Workshop,* I, 350, and *Life and Religion,* p. 55.
12. Ane'im Zemirot, *Singer's Prayer Book,* p. 79.
13. Midr. Tanh., Yitro, sec. 17, ed. Buber—commenting on Ps. 29:4.
14. Harry Elmer Barnes.
15. Exod. 3:13.
16. *Ibid.* 2:23.
17. *Ibid.* 3:14.
18. Midr. Lev. R., ch. 11, sec. 5, Warsaw 1867.
19. Exod. 6, vs. 2-3.
20. Midr. Gen. R., ch. 33, sec. 4, Warsaw 1867; Abot d'R. Nathan, version 2, ch. 38, pp. 50b-51a, ed. Schechter.
21. Rashi, Exod. *ibid.*
22. Berakot 7b, top.
23. The commentary "Ez Yosef" to the *Prayer Book 'Ozar ha-Tefilot,* p. 155a, Wilna 1923. *Cf.* "Panim Me'irot" (Responsa), I, 39; *cf.* also similar interpretation in M. Amiel's *Derashot 'el 'Ami* I., p. 107.
24. Yoma 69b. *Cf.* Talm. Yer., Megillah, end of ch. 3, col. 74c, ed. Krotoshin; Deutr. 10:17; Jeremiah 32:18; Daniel 9:4.
25. Tolstoy, *Essay on Religion and Morality.*
26. Zech. 14:9.
27. Pesahim 50a.

YOCHANAN MUFFS attempts to evolve a "Jewish approach to the conflict between the spirit and the world." In so doing, he defines "spirit" as "that creative potential in man—and according to some, in nature as well—that makes for self-transcendence." Spirit manifests itself in art, religion, and philosophy.

Muffs affirms that "it is God's sovereign power and will which invests neutral matter with its holiness and significance." He defines the "holy" as "inviolate" and as "somehow associated with the self (or soul). Therefore, he who defiles the holy, kills a part of the self."

After reviewing various viewpoints that pit spirit against the physical world (the views that the world is contamination, burden, or reminder of original sin), Muffs concludes that in Judaism, the world is viewed as the creation of the beneficent God. God plans His world with the Law, so that human freedom can be properly utilized. Death is the "inbuilt protection against man's latent tendencies to proclaim his own divinity."

Judaism, according to Muffs, teaches the "humanity of God." Biblical characters like King David are quite human, with human faults. They point to a God who appears to man in the garb of human emotions. Man is told that by imitating God he can become more human. Muffs quotes various Rabbinic sources that speak of God's "human" activities. Yet these are not to be taken literally, for God is "still more than man."

XIV

God and the World: A Jewish View

YOCHANAN MUFFS

IN THE PAST, most religions considered the dimension of the secular—the world with its pain and imperfection, its pleasures and seductions—as an impediment to the attainment of godliness. In our day, as a reaction to this anti-worldliness, there has been an equally unhealthy tendency for many religionists to lose themselves almost totally in the world and in worldliness. Others, however—among them many raised on the Jewish tradition—believe that the world is neither enemy nor end-in-itself, but the necessary, and potentially holy, milieu in which the spirit realizes itself, in which it takes form. However, even for these people, the inescapability of pain and death, the finiteness of our intelligence, the conflicts of our inner life—are inexplicable and perplexing phenomena which often outrage our deepest sensibilities. Even for them, the physical world poses a grave problem.

Furthermore, it is not only the physical world that poses a problem for religion. The social world with its independent—and often inimical—cultural values, science and aesthetics, often presents an equally formidable challenge. The spirit not only has to defend itself from the attacks of the scientific mind and the aesthetic sensibility, it also has to justify their existence within the divine economy. If the mind destroys faith—and even the belief in the self—why was it created? Why does the "beautiful" co-exist with the "good" as a possible—and idolatrous—object of man's ultimate loyalties? To put it simply: "worldliness" is often as great a problem to religion as the "world." This is especially true of the religious Jew, who may, on occasion, make his peace with the

170

physical world, but has rarely done so with the cultural values of non-Jewish society.

In the following study the painful—but often creative—conflict between religion and the world, between the holy and the profane, the spiritual order and the secular one—whatever particular antinomy is preferred—will be considered from a Judaic point of view. By Judaic we mean: an approach, necessarily eclectic and not identified with any specific branch of tradition, that suggests itself to a modern Jew on the basis of a long involvement with the full range of the Jewish historical experience.[1]

A word of caution. The religious types described in the following section are to some degree universal, i.e., they are not necessarily limited to any one religion, although most often they find their classical expression in one of the "great" religious traditions. Each religion usually comprises within its historical experience a wide range of types, some reflecting inner polarities such as Halakha and Aggada in Judaism; others reflecting outside influences such as Greek philosophy and various forms of Gnosticism on the three monotheistic religions. It is our awareness of the extraordinary richness and spiritual variety which is characteristic of almost all the so-called "higher" religions which prompts us to talk in phenomenological rather than in purely historical terms in the following section.

What is presented here are idealized types which find their most radical crystalization in an important branch of a given religion at a particular period of its development. The historical problem of unity within religions, which presents us with such a conflicting richness of experience, will be discussed elsewhere. In the meantime, suffice it to say that each religion, when studied from the inside in all its historical complexity, may appear to the outsider as many religions. Quite often, it is only when a particular religion, with all its complexities and contradictions is studied from the vantage point of an alien religion, that its distinctive characteristics emerge more clearly and definitively.

With these observations in mind, let us begin by briefly summarizing some of the ways men have devised for conceiving and coping with the relationship of the spirit and the world of imperfection.

I. THE SPIRIT AND THE PHYSICAL WORLD

a. Humanism, Ancient And Modern

This viewpoint takes an essentially optimistic attitude towards existence: the world is basically a good place to live in; order, not chaos, prevails; goodwill exceeds malice. Most of the evils of the world are the products of man's folly or self indulgence. Most evils, therefore, can be eliminated by the use of common sense, and by the application of science to the problems of human existence. Education and rationality are the hallmarks of this approach, and man is considered, rightly or wrongly, a highly educable creature.

This attitude is most attractive to many Jews. Certainly, our tradition has never deprecated the application of common sense to human problems, the activation of the rational faculties of man, or the importance of education. Nor has Judaism, at least in its biblical manifestation,[2] considered the world to be an essentially bad place to live in: at least, as it emerged from the hands of the Creator, it was "very good" indeed.

These obvious virtues of the humanist view should not blind us to its faults—its failure to take into account much of the intractable evil of this world—especially the evil that is not the immediate consequence of man's error and ignorance. It gives little or no attention to death, or to the impotence of our intelligence to give meaning to much of life, or to the perversity of men, who, though sensitive in the arts and learned in the sciences, are nevertheless failures as human beings. The slogan: "more rationality" simply does not answer these phenomena. And above all, the inexplicable nature of existence—if you will, its mysterious quality—is evaded. One does not have to be Freudian to realize that evasion is the result of fear: All of us fear death, fear the unknown; some face fear and the unknown with resignation; others simply deny their existence.

b. The Spiritual Radical: Reality Is Not Real

Polar to the humanists there are those who are intensely aware of the imperfection of existence. For them, the very act of living is a kind of mistake: It is shot through and through with pain, with the ache of fulfilled desire and the frustration of unfulfilled desire, by the transience of life and the meaningless repetitiousness of existence—and above all, by the fallibility of our senses. In fact, all unredeemed men—that is most of mankind—must suffer the material world and their material, sensible bodies as they would a disease. The enlightened believe that the world of birth and death is but a deception of the senses, a mask which has to be shed to secure for man a life of blessedness. We suffer evil only because we believe in the reality of our individual and differentiated personalities. As discrete human entities, we suffer the anxieties of desire, of jealousy and pain. However, once we overcome the misleading differentiation of persons, of the I and the Thou, and attempt to become one with Being itself, we experience the blessedness of non-

Being—a state of existence free from evil and immune from pain—and devoid of choice, volition and responsibility.

In this system, evil is so deeply experienced, that for life to go on, reality itself has to be redefined. One can reject this attitude for its lack of realism, yet one can only be moved by the human ache which motivates it, by its inner calm, and by its attempt to conquer the pain of existence through the application of mind—however unreal this application may seem. For the Jew, however, such a system, in its radical denial of reality, is the antithesis of biblical faith.

c. The Spiritual Rebel: Existence Is Evil But Real;
The Spirit Is Real But Hidden

Like the spiritual radical, there are others who are acutely aware of the problem of existence, but refuse to deny its reality. Evil is real in all its concrete immediacy. It is so real that it cannot be dismissed quietly as a disease of perception to be cured by self-enlightenment. This world in all its fleshy reality, with all its inner rules and limitations, with all its imperfection, is so totally perverse, so much the quintessence of all evil that only a demon or a maniac bent on causing unending suffering for mankind could have conceived the grotesque plan of creating a world so totally devoid of true spirituality, of holiness and good. A demon—often identified with the biblical creator—is the true creator of this world. The god of true spirituality has nothing to do with the world of flesh, form and reality; he is in hiding and only faint rays of his presence are occasionally felt by the illuminated.

In place of intellectual calm and repose, historically identified with some sort of Buddhism, this system—usually called Gnosticism—is possessed by an almost Promethean anger, a profound resentment against the cosmic status-quo. At times, one is tempted to admit that its description of reality fits the facts better than any other system. It is this seeming correctness which has engendered the Gnostic attitude in all sorts of places and periods: in Persia, in medieval France, and in the very heart of Judaism.

However, if the Gnostic analysis of reality seems correct, one can only shudder at its solution. Since chaotic reality is real and not a delusion, it cannot be read away by the mind: It must be shattered by an eruption of equally chaotic spirituality. If there is a god—and the Gnostics believe that there is—he must be hiding in the realm of pure spirit, unfettered by the limits of time and space, and the limitations of law and existence. Man wants to become one with the spirit. Anything connected with reality fetters man's spirit: law, structure, distinctions of good and evil, rationality, measure, the self as it presently exists—all of these must go;

all of them are the prison of the spirit that must be shattered to free the soul to return to its source. Only nihilistic and antinomian acts of rebellion against the inherent laws of reality can break open the prison. The realities of matter and the flesh are killed by the Gnostic in two ways: (a) by an extreme asceticism which kills the self by mortification; (b) an extreme orgiastic license: fight fire by fire; feed the devil with his own evil till his belly bursts.[3]

While the Buddhist solves the problem of reality by thinking it and himself out of existence, the Gnostic solves the problem by destroying reality and himself by acts of spiritual violence.

d. Reality Is Tainted But Grace Intervenes

Buddhism and Gnosticism face the evil of existence and, each in its own uncompromising way, attempts to abandon existence. There were others, mostly Christians, who were unable to accept the simple and terminal solution of a demon-created world and a spirit unsullied. They faced the horrible paradox of a good God who created the world in His goodness and a man corrupt and, by himself, incapable of redemption. It is as if Judaism and Gnosticism fight over the soul of Christianity. Like Gnosticism, Christianity is acutely aware of the pain that pervades the world and the weak and sinful nature that pervades man's will. The Jewish elements in Christianity prevented the latter from adopting the dualistic solution of the paradox of a benign god hidden in his absolute transcendence and an evil creator of the world—none other than the God of the Hebrew Bible. But Christianity is so aware of the pain of the world, the sinful heart of man and even the good deeds stemming from that heart, that the denial of the existence of Satan, the Evil One, is tantamount to denying the existence of God. Even though a good God created the world, the world cannot be that good if one has to die unto the world to be reborn in the crucified God. Hope and salvation are in a world beyond this world. If it were not for the freely-given, underserved condescension of a God who came into this world incarnate to save man from his condition, all would be lost. It is not man's love for God that counts but His love for man.[4]

Paradoxically, the Jew who suffered pain and death and expulsion more than any Christian, finds it difficult to understand the Christian's preoccupation with sin and salvation, death, all the existential evils of the world, man's basic depravity, and especially the worthlessness of man's deeds to redeem himself. Although Jews and Christians share the idea of the divine initiative in the God-human situation (i.e., it is God who turns toward man, not man to God), Jews and Christians part company when it comes to the reasons for this initiative. For Christians, God condescends to save man from his worthlessness. One can almost say with Marcion: The more worthless the recipient of the divine grace, the more loving the divine donor.

For the Jews, God enters the world to form a contractual relationship with man—one could almost say a partnership: "I hereby give you My law-book, filled with My commandments. I in My love will give you the necessary intelligence to study the book and translate My commandments into an earthly reality." The rabbis who were no mean students of the Bible, knew of man's sinfulness, but they also knew that they were sons of the King and partners with Him in creating a moral world through the instrumentality of the Law. In one religion, God comes down to save: The greater the depravity of the sinner, the greater the power and arbitrariness of His love. In the other religion, He comes down as a law-giver and a teacher. His greatest joy is independent students who so master inner-workings of the Law, that on occasion they can actually master the teacher at His own game. (Cf. Babylonian Talmud, Pesahim 119.)

In spite of the Jews' reservations about Christianity's anti-worldliness, its seeming obsession with sin and salvation, its lack of emphasis on man's creative partnership with God, or the absence of the mind-expanding joy in the study of the Torah—nevertheless, no sensitive person can deny the nobility and bravery of the Christian who is able to live with two true but conflicting realities: the goodness of God and the evil of the world. Many may be outraged at the central moment of Christianity: the drama of the crucified God. But even the outraged can only marvel at the great religious power released by this drama, and by the unique catharsis of all the raw experiences of existence—birth, pain and death—effected, and thus somewhat relieved, by the celebration of this aweful and awesome drama.

Empirically speaking, the simple fact that some people do actually survive the evils of this world and miraculously preserve their humanity can only be explained as the gift of divine grace, bestowed by a God, incarnate or not. The Jew may not like the term "grace," but no other word describes the fact more correctly.

II. SOME PHILOSOPHICAL REFLECTIONS

Before we approach the heart of our investigation—a Judaic approach to the conflict between the spirit and the world—a more precise definition of these polar terms is in order. This is especially true of the term "spirit" which, in the preceding section, has often been used as a virtual synonym for the terms "soul," "the holy," and even for "God."

It is assumed here that man is more than his body; that he has an objective psychic life. Furthermore, that his psychic life is at least as structured as his physical life; that one area of this life of the psyche is what traditional religion calls the soul. The term is not used here in the manner of psychologists, religionists, or philosophers, but in the common-sense fashion often employed by writers and artists. We all know what is meant by the expression "he has *soul.*" It is an objective personality trait; a certain kind of sensitivity, an openness to people and things, an awareness of certain dimensions of life—especially of the holy and the spiritual. As if it were possible to hypostatize this quality of soul and to give it special reality, we talk about *"the* soul." Metaphorically speaking, it is one organ of the psychic mechanism. It is an organ attuned to several dimensions of reality—the holy and the spiritual: attuned to, and, in need of. Thus defined, the soul is the subject of the religious life.

The spirit is that creative potential in man—and according to some, in nature as well—that makes for self-transcendence. It is the process which makes creations more than the sum of their parts, symphonies more than the totality of their notes, which allows us to say that it is the mind and its categories that "creates" reality, not vice versa. Because of the workings of the spirit, sound becomes language, individuals create and participate in collective patterns of culture, ideas are born and find expression in the symbolic forms of art, religion and philosophy. The spirit is a power which is in itself transcendent (it seems not to be derived from any prior category of existence) and which makes for self-transcendence in man. When we say that the creation is sometimes greater than the creator, or, that the creator through the creative act becomes more than he was, creates himself anew—we are confronted with a manifestation of the spirit, i.e., of self-transcendence. One does not have to posit the divine origins of the spirit—or its virtual identification with God—to feel the efficacy of the spirit in the experiential world. Most people sensitized to creativity would affirm the spirit as a concrete datum of our psychic life, as a constitutive element of the human reality. Many sense its inexplicability in scientific categories, and may even be in awe of its mysterious quality. Some even experience the psychological dimension of the spirit so intensely that they are willing to posit its ontological transcendence as well. For many such people, God and the Spirit are virtually identical.

The holy, unlike the soul, is not the subject of the religious. Nor is it, like the spirit, that power of soul which expresses self-transcendence in creative acts. The holy is an oblique way of talking about God. To say that things are holy is tantamount to saying that somehow God is in them. For some, this means that divinity and the substance of the object are one: Divinity is imminent in nature; holiness is physical-magical. For others, God's holiness is not to be seen as the eternal nature of certain things (e.g., it is the nature of fire to burn and water to be wet). Rather, it is God's sovereign power and will which invests neutral matter with its holiness and significance. Thus, for the Jew, the land and people of Israel are not holy from the beginning, but only become so at a moment in history, when God, by an act of selection, touched them with His presence, endowing them with the aura of His personhood.

Now if the holy is virtually synonymous with God, why do so many prefer to talk about the experience of the holy, rather than directly affirming the experience of God or the belief in Him? For many, especially those with a sense of delicacy in such matters, the use of the more oblique term preserves the privacy of the experience: One does not talk about God—or love—publicly or too directly. For others, the use of the term "holy" rather than God resolves a serious philosophical problem. While their empiricism prevents them from talking about the ontological reality of God, their experience of certain things and situations is so profoundly "religious," that a word is needed to express the intensity of this reality, a word which will adequately reflect the tension between their feelings and their thoughts. For them, to talk about the experience of the holy rather than about the knowledge of God is such a resolution.

But just how is the holy experienced? For many, the holy is experienced as a quality inherent in certain manifestations of the spirit. At first, the reaction to the holy may be one of attraction, of aesthetic appreciation. Gradually, however, this feeling may turn into one of awe. But it is more than awe; it has a moral-personal dimension as well. The holy is associated with that elusive x-factor—intensely experienced but almost incapable of definition—which somehow redeems life from its radical emptiness, and, paradoxically, makes it worth dying for. The holy has something ultimate about it: ultimate in the ecstasy one feels when confronted with it; ultimate in the urgency and demand it places on us. The holy is inviolate and is somehow associated with the self (or the soul). Therefore, he who defiles the holy, kills a part of the self. Conversely, he who has a soul, knows on some level, the immediacy and *ananke* of the holy.

Thus, loosely speaking, the soul is that sector of the psychic life which senses in certain manifestations of the spirit the quality of holiness. The soul, the spirit, and the holy are considered—rightly or wrongly—as actual categories of man's psychological being. For some, the affirmation that such experienceable categories do exist is sufficient. Others, however, seem to need some ontological or metaphysical underpinning for these categories, which they seek in God, the locus—or even creator—of the soul, the spirit, and the holy. Others, sceptical of such non-verifiable entities, would consider the word "God" as the spirit's noble attempt to explain to itself the source of its own transcendence. It is an attempt to describe a reality in which soul, the spirit and the holy are one. Even though this attempt is doomed to failure, it does point out that the workings of the spirit are forever a mystery, even to itself, and that the God who is more than model or metaphor is somehow a part of that very mystery.

The descriptions of various reactions of the human spirit to the problem of the world and worldliness presented in the first section serve several functions. First of all, they provide a dramatic foil which helps us to highlight what is essential in a Judaic reaction to the world. Secondly, we are confronted by the fact that each of these reactions has its own virtues and limitations. None succeeds entirely, yet each sees a truth not seen by the other.

However, the humbling realization that any attempt to make complete sense of the world is as difficult as attempting to square the circle should not lead us to avoid completely the act of theologizing or to escape into valuationally neutral areas such as abstract mathematics, where the truth of the proposition is its beauty or, to more objective fields where facticity is at least an approachable goal.

Whether we like it or not, all of us philosophize (i.e., try to make some sense of the world): it seems to be our nature to do so. Those who say they don't, do so unconsciously—and more often than not, badly. However, those who consciously philosophize, should arm themselves with the fore-knowledge that they are engaged in a noble, but ultimately tragic activity—one in which they cannot win, but also one which they cannot cease therefrom.

Only God knows all. To make peace with the paradox of a God who gave us enough mind to ask ultimate questions, but not enough mind to answer them, is to be truly wise and truly human. In the following section we will describe one attempt of Judaism to make sense of and to resolve these paradoxes.

III. BIBLICAL REALISM

Most historical confrontations between the spirit and the physical world—with the notable exception of Humanism, ancient and modern—have seen the world as the enemy of the spirit. Few men have had the calm of the classical Greek religionist for whom the world was *kosmos*, "eternal order," reflected in the divine heavenly bodies moving in their time-honored paths according to their eternal and imminent laws. Many men were inclined to see the world as a temporary order imposed upon an intractable chaos which threatened to break forth at any moment (so ancient Mesopotamian man). Others went even further. The world—with all of its order, temporary or eternal—is a physical impediment to the achievement of spiritual liberation or religious perfection. It is a burden to be sloughed off, a contamination to be avoided, a deception of the senses to be cured, a plight requiring redemption. This attitude is especially true of the radical and rebel spiritualist—especially the Gnostic—for whom the law is in many ways the very symbol of unredeemed reality: It is the law of that nature, both physical and psychological, which he refuses to accept. Therefore, by Gnosis, law could be either transcended or broken. For the Christian—at least in some early formulations and in Luther—the law is the embarrassing reminder of man's basic sinfulness and of his impotence to overcome it. Law, therefore, had to be replaced by Grace initiated not by man but from above.

IV. THE WORLD AS NECESSARY GROUND OF ACTION

Judaism—at least in some of its biblical and rabbinic manifestations—orients itself in a different manner. Instead of resenting the world, it accepts it as the creation of a beneficent God. For the radical spiritualist, such an idea is inconceivable, even impious. How could the spirit willfully contaminate itself by direct contact with the physical world? How could it build into the world the very laws of reality which inhibit man's spiritual quest? For God to seek some sort of fulfillment in the world, to use it as the stage for the workings of the spirit, seems to the radical spiritualist the very antithesis of true faith. Yet this is what much of the Jewish tradition seems to be saying.

Let us clarify this point by an analogy. A gifted dramatist has finally put himself down on paper. His play—the essence of his dreams and efforts—lies inertly on his desk. The dramatist, unfortunately, is held captive in the blueprint of his play until live actors realize his intentions on an actual stage. If he were a painter or a sculptor, his own creative efforts would be sufficient. However, as a dramatist or composer he needs the participation of performers to translate the score into reality. The performers however are also faced with their own problem: how to remain true to their own feelings without being disloyal to the dramatist's intentions. If they simply read their lines without projecting their own feelings, they kill the spirit of the play—if they make up new lines, they subvert its inner form. Everything depends on their balance and delicacy, empathy and control.

The realities symbolized by this analogy are clear. The Torah is God's play—the blueprint of a moral world waiting to be realized. The physical world with its water and dry land, and its necessary imperfection, is the stage on which the drama will unfold. This world—existence, reality, matter—is, in a poetic sense, a divine necessity. It is the raw material in which the creative urge is satisfied and finds form. To deny the world is to deny the God who created it.

The radical spiritualist is appalled by this drama because it affirms and glorifies all that he most fears and hates. It implies that God, although free from the physical limitations of time and space, magic and coercion, nevertheless acts as if motivated by a spiritual "need": the need to realize a moral order. It implies that He who is most free from the limitations of the world, is nevertheless limited in his "dependence" on a human partner, the actual builder of the moral world.

There are dangers in this situation. For man to be a partner, he must be free. But freedom without the potential of rebellion and sin is no freedom at all. Yet rebellion destroys creation and the possibility of partnership. However, the inner dialectic of God's plan requires a free human being, armed with intelligence and the potential of rebellion. An automaton devoid of impulses, a being like the angels, would lack the capacity to create. Unfortunately, it is this very creative factor that often subverts the plan.

According to the Talmud, God was well aware of this difficulty: He was torn between His desire to realize the Torah and His knowledge that a man armed with freedom could create chaos and destroy the world. But in an act of divine "bravery" He created man.

This often tragic tension in the divine mind—between realism and love—is beautifully reflected in the following midrash.[5] When God was about to create the world, He said to his angelic council: "Shall we create man in our image?" A group of angels stepped forward and offered this advice: "Lord of the Universe! Consider man's potential for evil: he will lie, murder, commit adultery, and create weapons to destroy your world. Don't go through with the plan." However, the divine urge to create a human partner was so great that no argument, however realistic, was tolerated. The Lord stretched forth His little finger, let loose a surge of energy, and burned the angels—the heavenly realists— to a crisp. Other groups made similar suggestions and were treated in a similar fashion, until the angels acquiesced to the divine desire and gave their approval saying: "Lord, the world is yours. Do with it as you see fit."

The predictions of the angels came true in full measure. One does not have to record all of the mishaps that followed the divine declaration: "Behold it is very good." Adam was given one commandment and broke it. Eve was tempted by the serpent. Cain murdered his brother, and his not-so-distant relative made weapons of iron to kill more men. The angels became overly interested in the daughters of men—all of which, together with the general corruption of man, brought on the flood. But even after this chastisement, the man "who was just in his generation" had nothing better to do after escaping the wrath of the waters than to drown himself in wine. And then came the Tower of Babel . . . after which, according to the midrash, the angels came before the Lord and said in a tone of not-so-gentle admonition: "The first group of angels were not so wrong after all."

The rabbis of the midrash realized that without human freedom and all that it implies—instinctual urges and the capacity to destroy as well as to create[6]—the law would be irrelevant. When the angels suggested that the Torah be given to them, instead of to man, God replied: "Do you lie, do you steal, do you have an evil *yeser?*" Without man, the law is irrelevant; without freedom and instinct man is not human.

It is related[7] that after the Men of the Great Assembly had abolished the *yeser hara* of idolatry, they decided to get rid of its partner, the overall *yeser:* the source of all instinct. They offered a petition to the divine court and their request was granted. The *yeser* was incarcerated; no longer would it stimulate the world. However, three days went by when someone went out to look for a fresh egg to cure a sick person—lo and behold!—there were no fresh eggs to be found. The generative processes had come to a full stop. Because of the inactivity of the *yeser*, the chickens were not laying eggs and the work of creation began to disintegrate. The Men of the Great Assembly were faced with a grave problem: To let the *yeser* loose was to court danger; to fetter it completely, was to destroy the world. They came to the following solution: Let it loose but put a pair of blinders on its eyes; regulate its excitations but do not get rid of them. The *yeser* is the yeast of creation. It makes the bread rise and stimulates man to struggle with his fellow man, thereby creating a society of people engaged in what was known as *yishuvo shel olam*. Like some vital nutriments before adequate preparation[8] the *yeser hara* in its raw state is dangerous and destructive. However, when processed by the Torah and sublimated by the rationality of the law, it becomes a vital and indispensable element in human life—the very impetus of the world of creation. As energy in the raw, it destroys; structured and chanelled it creates a new world.

Law is not merely God's dream, the plan of a new world, but also the instrument which humanifies man sufficiently to participate in the fulfillment of this drama. Man is created in the divine image; but as image, it is an unrealized potential. Only by becoming human under the guidance of the law, does man actualize this potential.

The Law, Death and Knowledge. Law is by essence a limit and a boundary. Our biological being is subject to the law of death; our intellectual grasp is limited by the law of the senses. Religions of radical spiritually rebel against these limits and in their hubris, create intellectual Towers of Babel to storm the heights of the spirit: By Gnosis, knowledge, enlightenment, man can transcend his biological finiteness, become one with infinite and eternal spirit and achieve immortality, in short, to become like the gods.

Judaism is not a religion of radical spirituality but one of law and limit. God created the world with these limitations; since He knew what He was doing, man must humbly accept them and make peace with them. For man to believe that through knowledge he can transcend the limit of death and become eternal is to deny that God is truly the Lord. The midrash states this insight with typical poetic breadth. "God anticipated that Nebuchadnezzar and Hiram king of Tyre would someday, in their hubris, declare that they were divine. Therefore, as a preventative measure, He decreed death for Adam and for all mankind."[9] Death, according to monotheism, is the inbuilt protection against man's latent tendencies to proclaim his own divinity.

In cultures where man thought he could become like a god and live forever, knowledge—either in the form of a secret or a philosophical discipline—was often considered as the key to eternal life: Gilgamesh comes to Utnapishtim[10] and men joined mystery religions—all in search of knowledge which made men like gods, immortal. However, in Israel, where the gap between man and God was absolute, nothing—not even knowledge—could bring about such a transformation. As long as biblical man accepts the authority of God, he is forced to make peace with his mortality and use his mind, not for the purpose of becoming like God, but simply to listen to His commands to live justly in an imperfect world.

The Humanity of God. The ultimate principles of most religions are the stumbling blocks of their believers. This is especially true of the faiths of radical spirituality. A God who is presented as absolute perfection, spirituality, non-involvement, self-sufficiency, omniscience, etc. is not a viable model for human behavior. Yet all religions set as the ultimate goal of their faith the imitation of the divine. Such a model is a stumbling-block for two segments of the population. The spiritual aristocrats will say in their arrogance, "If the divine is perfect, all-knowing, and above the fetters and limitations of reality, I will attain the same attributes; I too can achieve liberation from reality." These holy spirits, however, usually collapse in their attempt to transcend their creatureliness, the limits of reality inherent in their bodies and souls. The rest of humanity will find such an ideal totally unrealistic and will not even attempt an approximation. In fact, the radical perfection of the image may only discourage them and lead them into greater inhumanity.

The rabbis in their wisdom tell us all of the sins of the saints; in this they follow the Bible. They even add sins that the Bible does not tell us about. All of this is done with the intuitive genius of the master pedagogue. An educational model has to be capable of imitation; one cannot imitate perfection since there is little personal empathy between the sinner and the saint.

However, if David, the great and noble king, sinned and yet was able to repent, every man is already capable of empathy. David is human yet humane and this is why he can serve as a model. This principle can be extended mythically—that is seriously but not literally—to the divine. God in His infinite wisdom knew that if He revealed His true—i.e., transcendent—nature to man He would cause great human havoc. Therefore, He donned a human persona: He appeared before man as a human personality; fallible, human yet noble, warm and humane. He created a world, entered into a contractual relationship with man; became involved in the human condition, experienced exasperation over the hardness of their hearts, regretted that He had ever created man; was moved by the intercession of Moses and other prophets; broke out into fits of rage over the sinfulness of His people; was so involved in Israel, that in spite of their sinfulness, He actually re-espoused them after having delivered them the bill of divorcement. God appears in the garb of all the human emotions: love, anger, involvement, indignation, regret, sadness, etc. By so doing, God has given the seal of divinity to the very essence of our humanity. He implicitly says to man: "You cannot know what is above and what is below, but you can know what is in your hearts and in the world. These feelings and reactions and emotions which make up human existence, if illumined by faith and rationality, are all the divinity you can hope for. To be humane is to be divine: As I am holy, so you shall be holy; as I am merciful so you shall be merciful." Thus, there is only one kind of knowledge that is open to man—the knowledge of God's humanity:

> Let not the wise man boast of his wisdom,
> Nor let the strong man boast of his strength,
> Nor the rich man boast of his riches!
> Rather it is in this that a man should take pride:
> That he knows and attends Me
> That I, the Lord, am He who practices kindness,
> Justice, and righteousness on Earth;
> For in these things I delight. (Jer. 9, 22-23)

Neither the secrets of the universe nor the Gnosis that transcends death, but obedience to those human attributes in which the Lord, in His divine wisdom, clothes Himself to serve as the model of human behavior. This is the deeper meaning of the statement that the Torah speaks in human language.

The purpose of much of the rabbinic Aggada is to humanize the image of God, and by doing so, to humanize men created in this image. I end this section with a Midrash.[12]

How does God spend his time? During the first third of the day, as divine judge and cosmic administrator He recites this prayer: "May it be My will that My love for humanity will overcome My exasperation with them!" During the second third of the day, He takes out the Torah and studies. And during the third part of the day, He is the cosmic *shadchan* who brings man and wife together.[13]

Here is the quintessence of humanity and spiritual realism. It is as if to say that God has an inner life of prayer, an intellectual life of study, and a life of loving social responsibility; these are the really divine traits. He is the powerful administrator of the world. As an administrator, He faces all the problems that the human power-holder faces. If He did not love humanity, He would have never created men; nevertheless, they are exasperating. He prays that He has the strength to stand this inner tension. He also is constantly studying, and if you should say, "I know it all," consider the Lord and see that even He, at least poetically speaking, does not know it all; therefore, study!

And yet, it must always be borne in mind that all these statements, with all their power and beauty, are not to be taken literally: God is still more than man, and the midrash is still Aggada.

NOTES

1. Thus, for example, nomistic Judaism had room not merely for what Kadushin has called "normal mysticism," but for all sorts of real mystical phenomena: from the vision of the divine body and the hearing of the angelic chorus, to the Gnosticism of Lurianic Kabbalah and its antinomian transmutation in Sabbatarianism; from the positive attitude toward sexuality found in many rabbinic statements, to an attitude of absolute morbidity in many medieval pietistic works and, believe it or not, right in the heart of seemingly "healthy" Hassidism (cf. Heschel's study of the Kotzker Rebbi); from an aristocratic piety based on the centrality of learning, to a seemingly more popular piety based on the adoration of the charismatic leader and his theurgic powers.

2. While Judaism, unlike Gnosticism, does not see the *world* as evil, at least one of the biblical sources (Genesis 8:21) does see *man* as such. The realistic optimism that has been presented above, is but one strand in biblical thinking. Clearly, Jeremiah's vision of the new heart (Jer. 31:31ff.) represents a divine loss-of-nerve vis-a-vis man's educability. God no longer believes that man can be taught to be good under the guidance of the Torah. Yet, in spite of the divine exasperation with the old educational dispensation based on the belief that man can independently assimilate the message being taught, God keeps on trying new methods. If older methods based on freedom do not work, a kind of

"Skinnerian programming" is contemplated: God will write the Torah—not on books—but directly on the heart. So programmed, the "pretaped heart" should automatically lead man to an instinctive performance of the commandments, and thus lead him to the ultimate felicity where men shall not have to teach each other the word of the Lord, but shall perform it instinctively.

To cite a modern example, it was Heschel himself, whose whole corpus of writing breathed a positive, optimistic, almost humanistic spirit, who spent the last year of his life investigating the life and teachings of the Kotzker Rebbi—a morbid, relentlessly honest investigator of man's sinfulness, and a passionate hater of the world and wordliness. One of the first lectures Heschel gave upon arriving in America was his Yiddish "Kotzk and Kierkegaard" which finally took shape in English as *A Passion for Truth* (N.Y., Farrar, Straus, Giroux, 1973).

A friend of mine, upon leaving a famous East European yeshiva, was given the following parting blessing by his former teacher: "Sir—I know from now on you will not be a good Jew; I also know that having been with us, you will never fully enjoy the fleshly pleasures of the world."

3. Cf. G. Scholem, *Major Trends in Jewish Mysticism,* and H. Jonas, *Gnostic Religion.*

4. For better or for worse, much of my understanding of Christianity has been influenced by Kierkegaard, and especially by Nygren's *Eros and Agape.* My presentation may thus not do justice to more Catholic positions, which, in their stressing of Natural Law, may be less extreme and relatively more viable. Furthermore, contemporary Christianity's understandable, but violent repudiation of its traditional resentment against the world and worldliness, is hardly reflected in the above statement. The author may more correctly reflect the tradition against which many modernists are reacting, rather than Christianity as it is actually lived with its new appreciation of the world of the senses and its new concern with the world of communal responsibility.

5. Freely adopted after the Babylonian Talmud, Sanhedrin 38. While the ontological reality of angels in rabbinic literature cannot be totally denied, more often than not, angels often seem to be used as nothing more than literary devices—as dramatic projections of one of two opposing moods in the conflicted divine mind. Thus, in our midrash, God "plays out" divine love, and the angels externalize the opposing mood of God—divine anger or realism. Furthermore, the rather abstract value concepts of *din* and *rahamim* find a more dramatic—and pedagogically more effective—expression and concretization.

6. Cf. Genesis Rabba, 9:7. This and all following citations from the midrashic literature are free renditions rather than literal translations.

7. Cf., Babylonian Talmud, Yoma, 60 b. For more literature, cf. E.E. Urbach, *The Sages: Their Concepts and Beliefs* (Jerusalem, 1969) p. 418, note 9 (in Hebrew).

8. Midrash Tanhuma, Genesis, 7 and following.

9. Genesis Rabba 9:5. For more details, cf. Urbach, *The Sages, op. cit.,* p. 378.

10. Cf. Speiser's translation of the Gilgamesh Epic, in Pritchard, *Ancient New Eastern Texts,* 2nd Ed., p. 72ff.

11. Cf. I. Heinemann, *The Methods of the Aggadah* (Jerusalem, 1949) pp. 49ff. (in Hebrew).

12. The author will be forgiven the poetic license of fusing elements derived from different midrashim all dealing with the same theme: the divine work-day after the first six days of creation. The themes of divine study and judging/administrating are found in the Babylonian Talmud, Abodah Zarah, 3b.

13. The theme of the divine match-maker is found in Genesis Rabba 68:4 and in many other places.

DAVID NOVAK maintains that while the three classical proofs of the existence of God (ontological, teleological, and cosmological) may not be philosophically convincing, they *can* be theologically meaningful.

The ontological argument for God's existence maintains that creation implies a Creator. Novak declares that while the God-man relationship may not classify as empirical discovery or invention, it can, as personal communion, qualify as an "ontological interpretation" of the world, providing that one affirms the convenant as the "context of this relationship." The ontological argument as the "constitution of the direct God/man relationship" must precede the teleological argument, "which sees God's presence *through* the value of the world," and the cosmological argument, "which sees God's presence *through* the structure of the world."

The teleological argument for God, which maintains that "man can fulfill his values because he exists in a *valuable* world," must best be reinterpreted as stating that "God's relation to the world and man's relation to the world must complement the convenant and not mitigate against it." One must view the world as a product of God's providence, as the means for man to "observe the Torah with full physical, mental, and emotional attention."

The cosmological argument states, as Novak succinctly phrases it, that "the world requires a first cause." Reinterpreted in the context of covenant theology, this argument assumes an important psychological role. It provides "recognition of the transcendence of nature" as a "constant reminder to man that God's presence is not limited to His covenant with man."

XV.

Are Philosophical Proofs of the Existence of God Theologically Meaningful?*

DAVID NOVAK

PROOFS OF THE EXISTENCE of God have comprised the border area between philosophy and theology. They combine philosophy's concern for certainty with theology's concern for God. However, this border status of the proofs has made them troublesome for both philosophers and theologians. Many philosophers have regarded these proofs as asserting too much, as drawing conclusions unsupported by the premises whence they have been drawn. Many theologians have regarded these proofs as asserting too little, as being inadequate to the richness of God who presented Himself in revelation. Yet despite the efforts of some philosophers to deny the philosophical relevance of this question by making it an issue for dogmatic theology, it has, nevertheless, reappeared in contemporary philosophical discussion.[1] On the other hand, despite the efforts of some theologians to deny the theological relevance of this question by making it an issue for scholastic philosophy, it has, nevertheless, reappeared in contemporary theological discourse.[2]

As a theologian, I shall attempt to show in this paper how the three proofs of the existence of God (ontological, teleological, cosmological), outlined by Kant in the *Critique of Pure Reason*,[3] are theologically mean-

* This paper was originally delivered at the Philosophy of Religion section of the American Academy of Religion, November 1979.
My thanks are due to my colleague in the Philosophy department of Old Dominion University, Dr. William Brenner, for his insightful suggestions which led to the revision of this paper.

ingful statements if one reinterprets them within the context of theology and abandons the hope that they are or can ever be philosophically convincing. In other words, rejection of the philosophical claims made by some of their proponents does not make these statements about God themselves theologically meaningless.

I have purposely chosen Kant's outline of these three proofs for two reasons. (1) His outline has become so commonplace that it is quickly recognizable, even though I use it differently than he did. (2) By using his outline of the proofs I attempt to answer his charge that they have no necessary connection with our understanding of experience. I shall attempt to show that if one takes revelation to be a distinct type of experience, then the three proofs can be constituted as having a necessary connection with that experience: the ontological proof as a condition and the teleological and cosmological proofs as postulates. To borrow from the Psalmist, "The stone which the builders have rejected has become the cornerstone" (Psalms 118:22).

PRESENTATION AND PROOFS

In order to understand the meaning of a proof of the existence of God, theologically or otherwise, one has to understand what happens when something is "proven."

It would seem that "proof" is either logical or ontological. Logical proof is essentially formal, that is, it does not refer to real referents but, rather, makes such reference possible. Thus Wittgenstein noted, "A proposition that has sense states something (*Der sinnvolle Satz sagt etwas aus*), which is shown by its proof (*Beweis*) to be so. In Logic every proposition is the form of a proof."[4] Since proofs of the existence of God all intend a real referent, one cannot classify them as essentially logical.

Ontologically, proof is a type of presentation or re-presentation; that is, a method designed to make an entity which is now absent present. It thus constitutes a relation between a knowing subject and a knowable object. The object should determine the method of presentation. As Heidegger well noted,

> Every inquiry is a seeking (*Suchen*). Every seeking gets guided beforehand by what is sought. Inquiry is a cognizant seeking for an entity both with regard to the fact that it is and with regard to its Being as it is (*in seinem Dass-und Sosein*).[5]

DISCOVERY

There are three types of such ontological presentation. The most familiar type of such ontological presentation is empirical discovery. Here an inquiring subject, motivated by curiosity, seeks to discover an object, that is, seeks to make it appear to his senses. Experimentation is the device whereby this discovery is described, that is, made repeatable in public; in a word, *proven*. It should be clear that this type of presentation is meaningless when applied to the presence of God in revelation.

Now some medieval theologians rejected such an empirical approach because it presupposes the corporeality of God, a point they regard as blasphemous.[6] However, this is not where elimination of this empirical model of presentation should begin, because the incorporeality of God is an inference from revelation, not a datum of it. Although in the Torah God makes many statements about Himself—for example, "I am the Lord your God" (Exodus 20:2); "I am the first and I am the last" (Isaiah 44:6)—nowhere does He declare, "I am incorporeal."[7]

There is a more convincing theological rejection of this type of presentation, namely, it contradicts the dynamism of the relationship between God and man which is *the* datum of revelation. It is a contradiction because it makes God the passive object of discovery and man the active discoverer. In the Torah it is God who seeks man and it is man who either responds or hides. "And the Lord God called to man and He said. 'Where are you?' " (Genesis 3:9).[8] God is thus the seeking subject, man the responding subject, and neither of them is at all passive. Moreover, the moments of the God/man encounter are unpredictable and do not admit of experimental representation. "Do not hide Your presence from me" (Psalms 27:9). Because of this, one should drop the specific term "proof" when speaking of the religious quest for God. As a mode of ontological presentation it only has meaning in the context of empirical confirmability. The relationship of God and man cannot be constituted in this context. The primary reason for this elimination, then, is not the metaphysical inference that God is incorporeal but, rather, the phenomenological insight that objective passivity cannot be constituted as an essential component of this relationship. Also, both the freedom of God and the freedom of man made the moments of mutual encounter unpredictable events.[9] One relates differently to God than one does to the world. The purely aesthetic appreciation of nature, which is the beginning of scientific observation, is not the beginning of man's response to the revelation of God.

INVENTION

The Torah itself explicitly rejects from the God/man relationship the second type of ontological presentation, namely, invention. In this type of presentation man *qua homo faber* invents a thing for his own use. The criterion of invention is pragmatic. However, not only can man not invent God, he cannot even invent the method whereby God's presence can be controlled or conjured up. Thus the same logic which is used to reject idolatry, as the substitution of something else for God, is used to reject any attempts to make God's presence controllable by human *technē*. "Behold the very heavens do not contain You, can this house which I have built?" (I Kings 8:27).

PERSONAL COMMUNION

It is in the context of the third type of ontological presentation, namely, personal communion, that talk of the God/man relationship is meaningful. In this type of presentation the primary data are persons rather than objects or things, as in the first and second types of presentation respectively. The inappropriate features of the first two types of presentation, namely, passivity, predictability and manipulation, are absent from this type. Neither God nor man is passive. Their encounters are surprises to man, and although God commands man, that very commandment carries with it a recognition of human freedom and responsibility. In the context of the covenant and the commandments it entails, God does not manipulate man as a thing.[10] Furthermore, although the direct confrontations between God and man are unpredictable events, they are not amorphous. They have a structure and that structure is normative. God's revelation to man makes demands. "I am the Lord your God who brought you out of the land of Egypt . . . you shall have no other gods in My presence" (Exodus 20:2).[11] Moreover, man is given the right to insist that God's authority not function in a capricious, unjust way. "Shall the judge of the whole earth not do justice?" (Genesis 18:25). Now, this being the case, the type of certainty sought in the philosophical proofs of the existence of God is to be found in a satisfactory constitution of God's commanding presence[12] rather than in the constitution of His intelligibility or His accommodation to human *technē*.

At this point we can see how the so-called "ontological argument" is the necessary condition for the constitution of the authority of God. This argument—if it can be called that anymore than a "proof"—was presented most famously by Anselm, Archbishop of Canterbury, in the form of a prayer. That fact in and of itself should force us to abandon once and for all the designation "proof" or even "argument" for Anselm's quest. Any proof or argument that presupposes what it is trying to prove is nonsense.

Note what Anselm states:

And so, Lord, may You who give understanding to faith, give me, so far as You know it to be profitable, to understand that You are as we believe . . . And, indeed we believe that You are a being than which nothing greater can be conceived *(id quo maius cogitari non potest).*[13]

Thus we see that the ultimate greatness of God is already accepted by faith's positive response to God's revelation. Understanding then is insight into the necessary conditions of faith. The most necessary condition of faith is that there is no authority beyond God. This ontological condition can only be seen in the direct relationship between God and man in which faith is man's participation. Therefore, at this direct level it would be inappropriate to refer to any other relationship in which either God or man is involved, for reference to any other relationship would bring mediation into that relationship between God and man which is unmediated. Thus, both the teleological argument, which sees God's presence *through* the value of the world, and the cosmological argument, which sees God's presence *through* the structure of the world, must constitute the world before constituting the relationship between God and man.[14] That is why Anselm cannot formulate an approach to God which simply reiterates what philosophers have stated before outside the context of revelation and faith. The methodological rigor of his approach might well be philosophical, but the formulation itself must be theological to be authentic.

As a theologian, I can appreciate Anselm's insight better when comparing it with the too easy identification of the philosophical and theological quests made by Thomas Aquinas. Thomas Aquinas, at the beginning of his *Summa Theologica* presented five proofs of the existence of God, all based on inferences from our experience of the world. After each of these proofs, he added a remark like, "and this is what we say is God *(et hoc dicimus Deum)* . . ."[15] However, are any of the five proofs that Aquinas brings truly descriptive of the God to whom the faithful respond? Is not this relationship with God direct because of revelation? In all five proofs, conversely, all of which have philosophical antecedents, the apprehension of God's presence is necessarily subsequent to the constitution of the world. Thus the world mediates between God and man. But revelation, as God's direct presentation to man, must be constituted before God's relationship with man through the world, or His relation to the world itself. If this is not the case, then man's relation to the world will compete with revelation. Either revelation will become an act of knowing in the world, that is, a form of worldly wisdom, or the world will disappear in the face of some sort of *unio mystica* of God and man. Neither alternative, although having its respective adherents in the history of theology (Jewish, Christian and Islamic), is based on the Torah. Concerning the uniqueness of man's apprehension of God in revelation we read, "Has a people ever heard the voice of God speaking from the midst of fire as you have heard and lived?" (Deuteronomy 4:33). Concerning the reality of the world we read, "Thus says the Lord: the heaven is My throne and the earth My footstool . . . all of these things My hand has made and all of these things have come to be . . ." (Isaiah 66: 1-2). Anselm's approach, unlike that of Aquinas, avoids these inevitable theological dilemmas.

The theological meaning of Anselm's ontological presentation was best brought out by Karl Barth.

> All that the formula says about this object is, as far as I can see, this one thing, this one negative: *nothing greater than it can be imagined that in any respect whatsoever could or would outdo it* . . . It remains to be said: We are dealing with a concept of strict noetic content which Anselm describes here as a concept of God.[16]

In other words, Anselm is saying that *given* the revealed God who is affirmed by faith, such an affirmation, involving as it does man's total commitment, is inconceivable if man does not immediately deny the possibility that anything greater than He can be conceived. Thus the ontological interpretation of God's revealed presence is essentially a *via negativa*, that is, it negates anything that could be presented as a competitor with God's greatness.

It would seem that the religious doctrine of *creatio ex nihilo* begins to become intelligible in the context of the theological statement of the ontological argument. The doctrine of *creatio ex nihilo* should not be confused with the cosmological argument. This latter argument (as we shall soon see) infers a Supreme Orderer from the structure of the world. The doctrine of *creatio ex nihilo* however, is much more radical. Whereas a Supreme Orderer can be immanent in the world, a *Creator ex nihilo* transcends the world. Thus, if man attempts to religiously constitute the world *before* his relationship with God, the world becomes nothing, it has no real independence *(ex nihilo fit)*.[17] Thus the world can in no way compete with the greatness of God, which is the exact point made by the theological statement of the ontological argument.[18]

Anselm is not altogether explicit about what he means by the greatness of God. However, if I am correct about revelation providing the only meaningful context for such statements, then we can only understand God's greatness normatively, namely, no authority surpasses (or equals), or is able to surpass (or equal) the authority of God. Talk of God's greatness as the Maker of the natural order or the value of the world is certainly to be found in the Torah. "The heavens declare the glory of God and the firmament tells of the work of His hands" (Psalms

19:2). "He opens His hand satisfying every living being with favor" (Psalms 145:16). Nevertheless, God's existence is not inferred from these observations but is, rather, presupposed by them. It is the prior normative relationship with God that makes these observations possible. "Who is for me in heaven and besides You; I have none upon earth . . . the nearness of God is my good" (Psalms 73:25, 28). Man might admire God *through* vision of His handiwork, he might appreciate God *through* use of His bounty, but his direct relationship with God is first and foremost his obedience to His commandments which are authoritative because of God's most intimate and concerned knowledge of man and his needs.[19] "And God saw the children of Israel and God knew" (Exodus 2:25). Understanding God's causality is secondary to understanding His revealed authority. The covenant, not nature, is the context of this relationship. And, whereas in theologies not based on revelation nature *includes* both God and man and is thus prior to them,[20] in theologies based on revelation the covenant is what comprises the relationship *between* God and man and gives it duration. The covenant is thus subsequent to them both.

The use of the "ontological interpretation," as I now prefer to call it, is the initial part of theology's critical function, an area where philosophical method is still the most important *ancilla theologiae*. Theological inquiry must deepen its understanding of the meaning of faith's assertions about the God/man relationship. On the a *priori* level it must understand what conditions are required for these assertions to have meaning. On this level philosophy functions methodologically, offering no independent religious assertions of its own, because it has no realm of independent experience. It would seem, then, that both the analytical and phenomenological philosophical approaches offer the theologian invaluable critical tools he should neither neglect nor overestimate.

THE TELEOLOGICAL ARGUMENT

In reinterpreting the ontological argument we have seen that the constitution of the direct God/man relationship must not be subsequent to the constitution of either God's relation to the world or man's relation to the world. However, these relations are themselves components in revelation, as we have just seen, and must, therefore, be adequately constituted by philosophically critical theology. Understanding their apodictic sequence enables this constitution to be successful.

Man relates to the world as either a realm of things (culture) or as a realm of objects (nature). The former realm is constituted technologically, the latter scientifically. If interpersonal relationships are primary in the development of human consciousness, or, theologically speaking, if man's covenantal status is primary, then it would seem that man's consciousness first extends into the world of things before it extends into the world of objects. Things are defined in terms of their *personal* value.[21]

Man *qua homo faber* relates to the world as a realm of things either in his use or as something potentially ready for such use. The philosophical version of the teleological argument infers from man's experience of the *usefulness* of the world, the conclusion that the world has been so ordered by a supernatural benevolent Intelligence. It is not the crude anthropocentric notion that the world is made for man but, rather, that man can fulfill his values because he exists in a *valuable* world.[22] Teleology provides the ontological context for the concept of value.[23]

The theologian cannot accept this argument as primarily descriptive of the God/man relationship because it constitutes a fundamental mediator between man and God. However, once the direct God/man relationship in revelation is adequately constituted, this teleological assertion becomes an important postulate of that relationship. For we can now reinterpret this assertion to state that God's relation to the world and man's relation to the world must complement the covenant and not mitigate against it.

If man's technological relation to the world is not for the sake of the covenant, then his dominion over the world will inevitably lead to disobedience of God. "And you will say in your heart: my strength and the might of my hand have made for me all this wealth" (Deuteronomy 8:17). Therefore, man must include all the results of his labor in the relationship with God. This would explain the importance of sacrifice in the act of worship. This emphasis requires that man look upon his technological success as caused by God for the sake of the covenant, "And you shall remember the Lord your God that it is He who gives you strength to make wealth in order to uphold His covenant" (Deuteronomy 8:18).

This recognition is a postulate of the primary relationship we have been discussing all along. As Kant noted, "Postulates are not theoretical dogmas but presuppositions of necessarily practical import."[24] In our case here we are required to affirm God's benevolent causality because without such an affirmation man's practical relation to the world of things would continually conflict with his obedience to God's commandments. The world on the practical level must be viewed as the product of God's providence. This affirmation enables us to see biblical promises of tangible values not as *quid pro quo* rewards but, rather, as the necessary certitude that God will allow the things of the world to be included in the covenant by being useful for man's obedience to God. Thus the twelfth century Jewish theologian, Maimonides, wrote,

We have been assured in the Torah that if we observe it in joy . . . that He will remove from us all those things which prevent us from observing it, such as sickness, war, famine and the like.[25]

In other words, the Torah is not viewed as the means to the end of technological success with the world but, rather, the world is now looked upon as the means for man to observe the Torah with full physical, mental and emotional attention. The Torah is not for the sake of the world, but the world is for the sake of the Torah.

The teleological argument is helpful in formulating this postulate of revelation because it is the result of viewing the world as *valuable*. The reformulation of this argument constitutes God's relation to this valuable world in a way that permits an ontological foundation for man's practical use of the world in his covenantal response to God. This is exactly how the postulates of pure practical reason functioned for Kant. The logic is the same, but the fundamental practical reality is essentially different, for covenantal man is essentially different from morally autonomous man.[26] However, in both systems human *praxis* requires the cooperation of the non-human world. The cooperation is first required so that man *qua* covenantal participant and man *qua homo faber* do not mutually exclude each other thus making for a paralyzing human tension.

THE COSMOLOGICAL ARGUMENT

The cosmological argument states that the world requires a first cause. Kant saw it as the ontological argument in inverse order.[27] In other words, whereas the ontological argument moves from the concept of a Supreme Being (*ens realissimum*) to absolute existence in relation to contingent existence, the cosmological argument moves from the experience of the contingent existence of the world (*a contingentia mundi*) to the concept of a Supreme Being and His absolute existence. However, what Kant failed to realize is that the cosmological argument as presented by such philosophers as Aristotle and Aquinas, presupposes that we are already experiencing the world as ordered in some sort of linear hierarchy.[28] Without this presupposition the search for a *first* cause makes no sense because causality, as opposed to creation, is constituted *serially*, that is, as a process rather than an event. For the theologian *creatio ex nihilo* is an event rather than a process. Now, if, as we have seen earlier, the ontological argument really expresses God's radical transcendence of the world, which is the meaning of the doctrine of *creatio ex nihilo*, then the cosmological argument is not reducible to the ontological argument. A Creator is essentially different from a First

Cause.[29] This observation does not, however, make the cosmological argument any more convincing philosophically because one can argue whether our experience of a structured world in and of itself requires such a remote first cause, or, indeed, a concept of linear causality at all.[30]

Theological interest in the cosmological argument is motivated by an opposite concern than that which motivated its interest in the teleological argument. Interest in the teleological argument was motivated by a concern to constitute the world of things as immanent in the God/man relationship. This is where teleology is crucial. For if the end of human life is to be obedient to God, then the end of the world under man's actual or potential control is to function as the physical means which intends a state of active being included in that end; that is, it is immanent.[31]

The cosmological argument, on the other hand, constitutes the world as transcendent to man. It views the causal structure of the world as essentially independent of actual or potential human use. It does not assign any purpose to the causal structure of the world. That structure simply depends on a process of efficient causality of which God is the first member. Man's presence in that world is wholly irrelevant. Man's relation to the world of objects, motivated by his curiosity, is impersonal. He attempts to view it as it is, making his own subjective viewing as inconspicuous as possible. This interest follows from man's recognition of his finitude, for his recognition of the world of objects, which essentially transcends the interpersonal realm, saves him from the dangerous illusion of anthropocentricity. The natural world of objects reminds man of his essential limitation by showing an order far more complex and impressive than the world of man's own making. Nature transcends culture. For theology such a recognition of the transcendence of nature is expressed by the constant reminder to man that God's presence is not limited to His covenant with man. The relationship between them is not a symbiosis. As such man sees nature as a realm subject to a Divine authority in which he is not a participant but only a spectator. Both man and nature are subject to God's authority, but they are subject to it in radically different ways. Thus nature is not in essence simply a potential field waiting for man's technological control. On the other hand, because man is covenantally related to God, nature is not the medium of that relationship. Man is a participant in the covenant before he can admire God through viewing nature. Nevertheless, this very respect for the inner structure of nature reminds man that he cannot reduce God's presence to his own limited experience of it. "Then the Lord answered Job out of the whirlwind, saying . . . I will question you and you may inform Me. Where were you when I laid the foundations of the earth? Tell me if you have any understanding" (Job 38:1,3).

This theological use of the cosmological interpretation saves man's relation to the created order of nature from becoming either anthropocentric or cosmocentric. As such it performs a necessary philosophical service for theology.

CONCLUSION

The classical proofs of the existence of God are theologically meaningful if they are understood as statements of the ontological conditions and postulates of revelation. By not having their meaning constituted outside the realm of revelation, the "proofs," now regarded as *modes of presentation*, strengthen theology's critical function with philosophical tools.

At the beginning of this paper I delineated three types of ontological presentation: personal communion, invention and discovery. We can now see how the three quests which motivated these three respective types of presentation reappear in the modes of Divine presentation. The quest for personal communion is the motivation for the ontological mode; the quest for value (invention) is the motivation for the teleological mode; the quest for structure (discovery) is the motivation for the cosmological mode. A philosophically critical theology can constitute these respective modes of presentation in an apodictic order within the context of revelation.

We can thus see a working relation between theology and philosophy which, at least from the vantage point of theology, is most fruitful. It would seem that the type of philosophy which lends itself to such a relation is either of the analytical or phenomenological variety. Philosophers of these schools, even if not interested in theological inquiry into revelation, should, nevertheless be pleased at the widening range of applicability of their methods. Theologians should be grateful for methods of intelligent inquiry which enable them to be more precise and lucid in their understanding of the Word of God: of what it presupposes and what it implies.[32]

NOTES

1. See for example, Norman Malcolm, "Anselm's Ontological Arguments" in *The Existence of God*, John Hick, ed. (New York: Macmillan Publishing Co., 1964), pp. 48ff.
2. See for example Hick, *ibid.*, pp. 253ff.; German Grisez, *Beyond the New Theism: A Philosophy of Religion* (Notre Dame: University of Notre Dame Press, 1975), pp. 36ff.
3. B612ff.
4. *Tractatus Logico-Philosophicus*, 6.1264, D. F. Pears and B. F. McGuinness, trans. (London, 1961), pp. 130–131 (italic mine). See 2.221, 2.222, 3.142.

5. Martin Heidegger, *Being and Time, Intro.,* 1.2, John Macquarrie and Edward Robinson, trans. (New York: Harper and Row, 1962), p. 24.

6. See Maimonides, *Guide of the Perplexed,* 1.55.

7. For this reason Maimonides' chief theological critic, Abraham ben David Posquières, refused to accept his designation of anyone who believed in the incorporeality of God as a heretic. See gloss to *Mishneh Torah,* "Laws of Repentance," 3.7.

8. See A. J. Heschel, *Man Is Not Alone: A Philosophy of Religion* (New York: Jewish Publication Society, 1951), pp. 125ff.

9. My late revered teacher, Prof. Abraham Joshua Heschel wrote: "An event is a happening that cannot be reduced to a part of a process. It is something we can neither predict nor fully explain . . . the belief in revelation claims explicitly . . . that a voice of God *enters the world* which pleads with man to do His will." *God in Search of Man: A Philosophy of Judaism* (New York: Farrar, Straus, Cudahy, 1955), p. 210.

10. Maimonides, *Mishneh Torah,* "Laws of Repentance," 5.4.

11. See D. Novak, *Law and Theology in Judaism* 1 (New York: Ktav Publishing House, 1974), pp. 136ff.

12. See Emil Fackenheim, *God's Presence in History* (New York: New York University Press, 1970), pp. 14-19.

13. *Proslogion,* chap. 2. S. N. Deane, trans. in *The Ontological Argument,* Alvin Plantinga, ed. (Garden City, N.Y.: Anchor Books, 1965), pp. 3-4.

14. "In arguments for the existence of God the world is given and God is sought. Some characteristics of the world make the conclusion 'God' necessary. God is derived from the world." Paul Tillich, *Systematic Theology I* (Chicago: University of Chicago Press, 1951), p. 205.

15. *Summa Theologiae,* I, q.2, a.3. Cf. *Summa Contra Gentiles,* 1.13.

16. *Anselm: Fides Quarens Intellectum,* I. W. Robertson, trans. (London SCM Press, 1960), pp. 74-75. For the Augustinian background of this approach, see D. Novak, "The Origin and Meaning of *Credere ut Intelligam* in Augustinian Theology," *Journal of Religious Studies,* 6.2-7.1 (Fall 1978/Spring 1979), pp. 43-45.

17. For precisely this reason, viz., the denial of the "Selbstaendigkeit" of the world. Jean-Paul Sartre rejects this doctrine. See *Being and Nothingness,* Hazel Barnes, trans. (New York: The Philosophical Library, 1965), p. lxiv.

18. In his "Notes on Proofs of the Existence of God," *Hebrew Union College Annual* I (1924), pp. 185–186, the late Prof. H. A. Wolfson viewed the cosmological argument as a philosophical version of Gen. 1:1. However, the doctrine of *creatio ex nihilo,* which subsequent theology saw in Gen. 1:1, seems to be a theological version of the ontological argument because it states more about God than the mere cosmological assertion that He *made* the world. See also, L. Gilkey, *Maker of Heaven and Earth* (Garden City, N.Y.: Doubleday and Co., 1959), pp. 41ff.

19. See D. Novak, *Law and Theology in Judaism* II (New York: Ktav Publishing House, 1976), pp., 20-22.

20. See, e.g., A. N. Whitehead, *Process and Reality* (New York: Free Press, 1969), pp. 286, 410. Cf. Aristotle, *Metaphysics,* 1015a15.

21. A philosophical parallel to this scheme might be found in Heidegger's discussion of "Zuhanden" and "Vorhanden" in *Being and Time,* 1.3.16, pp. 102-106.

22. See Maimonides, *Guide of the Perplexed,* III.13. Cf. Saadiah Gaon, *The Book of Beliefs and Opinions,* IV, beg.

23. "The chief points of the physico-theological proof are as follows: (1) In the

world we everywhere find clear signs of an order in accordance with a determinate purpose . . ." Kant, *Critique of Pure Reason*, B654, Norman Kemp Smith, trans. (New York: St. Martin's Press, 1929), p. 521.

24. *Critique of Practical Reason*, I.2.6, Lewis White Beck, trans. (New York: Liberal Arts Press, 1956), p. 137.

25. *Mishneh Torah*, "Laws of Repentance," 9.1.

26. For the use of postulates in theology a là Kant, see D. Novak, *Suicide and Morality* (New York: Scholars Studies Press, 1975), pp. 126-127.

27. "The procedure of the cosmological proofs is artfully designed to enable us to escape having to prove the existence of a necessary being *a priori* through mere concepts . . . Accordingly, we take as the starting-point of our inference an actual existence (an experience in general), and advance, in such manner as we can, to some absolutely necessary condition of this existence." *Critique of Pure Reason*, B638, p. 512.

28. Re Aquinas see *infra*, n. 15; Aristotle, *Physics*, 241b24ff.: *Metaphysics*, 1072a25ff.

29. See Maimonides, *Guide of the Perplexed*, I.69.

30. See Bertrand Russell, *Mysticism and Logic* (Garden City, N.Y.: Doubleday and Co., 1957). p. 201.

31. See Aristotle, *Nicomachean Ethics*, 1098b10-15.

32. A similarly motivated approach can be seen in the following excerpt from the essay, "The Lonely Man of Faith" (*Tradition*, vol. 7, no. 2, [Summer 1965]) by the contemporary Jewish theologian. Dr. Joseph B. Soloveitchik. "While one may speak of the cosmic confrontation of man and God as an experiential reality, it is hard to speak of a cosmological experience. When God is apprehended *in* reality it is an experience; when God is comprehended *through* reality it is just an intellectual performance . . . The trouble with all rational demonstrations of the existence of God, with which the history of philosophy abounds, consists in their being exactly what they were meant to be by those who formulated them: abstract logical demonstrations divorced from the living primal experiences in which these demonstrations are rooted. For instance, the cosmic experience was transformed into a cosmological proof, the ontic experience into an ontological proof . . . the most elementary existential awareness as a subjective 'I exist' and an objective 'the world around me exists' awareness is unattainable as long as the ultimate reality of God is not part of this awareness . . ." (p. 32, note)

The role of Jewish education is, according to FRITZ A. ROTHSCHILD, "to convey knowledge of Jewish religious literature, culture, and history," and to "inculcate commitment to Jewish observances, Jewish ideas . . . and the Jewish people." In order to take these goals seriously, we must take God seriously, for His Name is central to Jewish religious literature. Since Judaism is a "theotropic" religion ("a religion in which the central subject is not man in isolation, but God in his relationship with man"), and since religious commitment in Judaism means "to understand life as lived in response to the divine command," the concept of God in Jewish education assumes even greater importance.

Natural theology affirms that man can attain knowledge of God through ordinary life experiences—especially through observation of nature. Revelational theology maintains that God is known only insofar as He makes Himself known. The former does not always lead to belief, however; and the latter is not always made relevant to human experience. Yet an "adequate view of God must combine the insight of natural and revelational theology, while avoiding their individual shortcomings."

Rather than indoctrinate belief, religious education must give the student a sense of wonder and human dependence, as well as of human responsibility. Rothschild then goes on to assert that one can be made aware of God through "five fundamental experiences": "change, dependence, order, value, and imperfection."

Rothschild concludes by dividing religious literature into two types of faith: the ontological-sacramental-or-cosmological, in which the Holy is felt as present; and the moral-or-utopian, in which the Holy is experienced as what-ought-to-be. He then introduces a third type of theology, the "quasi-mystical type," in which man "looks within his own depths," and "becomes aware that he is rooted in something greater than his own individual self."

The goal of Jewish education is, according to Rothschild, to inspire a sense of responsibility for observance of the *mitzvot,* through which one presents himself to God, and responds to His reality.

XVI.

The Concept of God in Jewish Education

FRITZ A. ROTHSCHILD

To be religious is to seek God with all one's being; to be blessed is to find Him; to be theological is to make the search and its object evident in discourse.
Paul Weiss

DISCOURSE ABOUT GOD *(theo-logy)* is an ancient and honorable discipline, pursued since the days of Plato and Aristotle and acclaimed the queen of the sciences in the Middle Ages. At the present time a multitude of scholars lecture and write on systematic theology, philosophical theology, existentialist theology, historical theology and, *mirabile dictu*, even atheistic theology. The non-Jewish world seems to be undergoing a theological revival—perhaps even a theological renaissance.

It would seem, therefore, that no apology is needed for considering the concept of God in Jewish education and even for according it a central place in our curricula. But, as we know, the opposite is true: there is hesitancy (and even outright opposition) about dealing with the idea of God and the problem of God in a systematic manner. One must justify its legitimacy and centrality.

Opposition to the study of theology[1] in Jewish schools stems from various grounds. The aversion of some spokesmen of modern Orthodoxy to the treatment of the God-idea is based partly on the doctrinal view that *halakhah* is the sole fountainhead and embodiment of Judaism, and partly on the prudential wish to avoid the intellectual ferment, doubt and possible pluralism which may follow in the wake of theological and philosophical discussions.

Religious liberals (Conservative and Reform Jews) avoid theology for almost the opposite reason. Any attempt to make the God-idea central to Jewish studies would, they fear, lead inevitably to limitation of freedom of inquiry and attempts to circumscribe the area of "correct belief" *(orthedoxa)*. Once we start discussing the concept of God we shall become involved, they fear, in the kind of doctrinal strife which is bound to end with the winning faction imposing its own brand of theology on the rest.

Jewish secularists and folk-culturists, in turn, fear that the idea of God may prove embarrassing, since it may be a divisive concept. From their standpoint it becomes meaningful to assert that "secularism is the will of God."

The view that *halakhah* is the sole fountainhead of Judaism is tantamount to saying that theology is somehow "un-Jewish." Yet the vast literature of *agadah* deals with questions of theology in numerous places. G. Scholem has shown that proto-Kabbalistic treatment of such topics as *ma'aseh bereshit* (the esoteric doctrine of creation) and *ma'aseh merkavah* (the esoteric doctrine of God) goes back to Mishnaic times, and A. J. Heschel has demonstrated that a great part of *agadah* can no longer be said to represent merely "opinions and views uttered on the spur of the moment" or "creations of popular fancy." They are expressions of consistent and profoundly thought-out theological doctrines, which in the case of Rabbis Akiva and Ishmael, for example, influenced decisions in the realm of *halakhah*.

It may be true that certain topics were not discussed by our ancient sages, but this would be no reason why we should abstain from dealing with them. Ideas which were accepted without question and formed part of the climate of opinion of many generations have become questionable in our time. We cannot evade our religious problems on the ground they were not problematical to our ancestors in Pumbeditha, Worms and Wilna, or to some or our contemporaries in Williamsburg.

The fear that discussion of the God-idea will arouse doctrinal strife and lead to new forms of dogmatism and heresy-hunting implies that unity in matters of religion is desirable even at the cost of evading basic issues. This is a snare and a delusion. If our ideas about God make no difference to our life and conduct, there is something radically wrong with our ideas, or ourselves, or both. If they do make a difference, then we cannot afford to present them to our students as being unimportant. The problem of doctrinal strife will be solved, not by avoiding the God-idea, but by dealing with it in a way that will produce neither cynical unconcern nor narrow-minded fanaticism.

A frank and continuing discussion of the God-idea among the various factions of contemporary Jewry might disclose that we have to face certain theological differences and live with them as mature and reasonable men. On the other hand, it is conceivable that as a result of such a continuing discussion we might discover an underlying consensus beneath the differences of emphasis and theological methods, thus restoring the idea of God as the core of our common faith and the source of our religious commitment. We do, after all, have differing views of the meaning of many rituals, and they do not necessarily lead to doctrinal strife.

Thus, to some Jews, the *seder* ritual means the fulfillment of a divine commandment from the God who slew the Egyptian first-born and took our forefathers out of slavery to become an exclusive and chosen kingdom of priests. To the Israeli secularist it may be a symbol of Israel's declaration of political independence. To many Conservative and Reform synagogue members it signifies the triumph of freedom over tyranny. Similarly, *mitzvot* are observed as divine commandments, as historically conditioned cultural forms of expressing man's response to the Divine, as folkways maintaining the coherence of the Jewish people, or as customs adding color and excitement to the workaday world and contributing dignity and structure to the *rites de passage*, from cradle to grave.

Pedagogical considerations are also cited as a reason for the exclusion of theology from the curriculum of Jewish schools. Two separate questions are raised by those who hesitate to teach about God in our schools.

The first question is: Should knowledge about the idea of God be taught?

The second question (which arises only when the first one has been answered in the affirmative) is: Should the idea of God be taught as a separate, special and distinct topic?

I have the impression that many teachers opposed to "teaching about God," really oppose introduction of the subject in a formal and scholastic manner reminiscent of Christian catechism lessons. They would be quite willing to deal with the topic in their regular classes wherever theological problems arise naturally out of the text and stories studied. This is as it should be. It is properly the teacher's decision where and when such matters should be taught. However, I am reasonably sure that they would agree it is desirable that the idea of God be a central aspect of Jewish education.

A COMMON PURPOSE AND A COMMON FAITH

Apart from some institutions concerned with higher learning for its own sake, the conscious aim of all Jewish religious education is: (1) to convey knowledge of Jewish religious literature, culture and history; and (2) to inculcate commitment to Jewish observance, Jewish ideals (religious and moral) and the Jewish people ("the Community of Israel").

Neither of these goals can be achieved or even attempted competently, unless the idea of God is afforded a central place. The reason is clear. In the chief classic of our literature, the Bible, God plays a conspicuous and central role. Since He is also central in the prayer-book and the teaching of religious observances *(mitzvot)*, we frequently pronounce His name. Unless we take *Him* seriously, we take His name in vain.

Addressing myself to the two-fold aims of Jewish education enumerated above, it seems to me that the following points are of the utmost importance. (1) Judaism is a theotropic religion; more precisely, a religion in which the central subject is not man in isolation, but God in His relationship with man. A clear and full exposition of this idea is a necessary condition for even an elementary understanding of Jewish literature, culture and history. (2) To inculcate *religious* commitment to Jewish observance and values means to understand life as lived in response to the divine demand.

I am fully aware that a wide range of opinions exists about how much is *divine* and how much is *human* in Jewish tradition. But all these opinions share the view that the Jewish religion is acted out not by men alone but with a divine partner, a partner to whom men react and whose commands and demands they try to understand and to heed. No matter how much faith or doubt, no matter how much pious acceptance or critical rejection a Jew brings to his heritage, if he considers himself to be within the *religious* tradition of Judaism, he accepts as a minimum commitment (1) the awareness that life is lived in the presence of Him who is the Ground and Creator of all reality; and (2) that our tradition embodies in some way the voice and demand of God, and not merely the projections of our needs, drives and aspirations.

The philosopher will complain that in all the above the key terms lack precision. His complaint is legitimate; it points to the dilemma which no theologian can hope to avoid. "He cannot define God in a way to satisfy the strict canons of logical proof, yet he *must* define God sufficiently to guide 'man's attempt to find his way in the world.' "[2] And this problem is closely connected with a second one. God is controversial; the truth about Him cannot be demonstrated. It is even doubtful exactly what one means by "truth" in this field. As Whitehead has pointed out, what is unsettled and doubtful is usually unimportant, and we postpone decision and action in regard to it. But unlike some abstruse and unsettled topics the question of God is of the highest importance, and the answer one gives determines one's life and character. It cannot be evaded or postponed indefinitely. "Your character is developed according to your faith. This is the primarily religious truth from which no one can escape."[3]

Thus the modernist cannot be spared the "religious test" of accepting the minimum commitment, if he wants to be accepted as a *bona fide* member of *religious* Jewry. By a *bona fide* member I mean one who claims to represent the tradition, whose views, though not necessarily acceptable to all, are listened to as those of an "insider"—a member of the convenantal circle. Thus, *bona fide* membership is not restricted to the traditionalist, and the latter is warned not to reject the "good faith" *(bonam fidem)* of those who accept as divine less of the tradition than he does. After all, there is hardly anyone who does not exercise his right to distinguish between the eternal and the temporal, the divine and its embodiments conditioned by human limitations and distortions, the revelation coming from beyond and the human records of its reception and appropriation. He who is committed to faith in God and a life lived in response to His demands, and who finds the *locus* of these demands in the classical sources of Judaism and the historic experiences of Jewry, draws his religious substance from the basic roots of our faith and cannot be said to be *kofer ba'ikkar.*

Because Judaism is conviction which affects attitudes and actions, the circle of its authentic representatives must exclude those who do not share this conviction. Yet, since no one can lay down precise specifications as to what this conviction implies and what it excludes, we cannot presume to draw the circle of membership in such a way that only those who stand with us are within it. And because no single discourse can adequately define or even evoke the inexhaustible reality of Judaism, we cannot hope to arrive at a definite *theo-logy.*

It follows that teaching about God in Jewish education must draw on the *variety* of formulations and approaches which have emerged in the history of Israel's religion.

Even an exhaustive treatment of Judaism's teachings on the nature of God will avail us little, unless we become aware of the questions which these teachings are attempting to answer. The author of Genesis, for example, assumed that the reader has entertained some such questions as: How did the world come into being? Was it always the way it is now? If not, what was it like in the beginning, and who made or generated it? Is the world the outcome of accidental happenings, of cosmic conflicts among gods and monsters, or was it planned and intended for a purpose?

The statements about God in Jewish documents must be seen as answers to questions, as solutions to problems. "The primary task of religious thinking is to rediscover the questions to which religion is an answer, to develop a degree of sensitivity to the ultimate questions which its ideas and acts are trying to answer."[4] It follows that religion and the knowledge of God are not the result of man's flight or with-drawal from the world, but of a more discriminating attention to reality, and an openness toward certain aspects of experience which are commonly overlooked or taken for granted.

The facts of life and death, of ideals achieved and hopes disappointed, generate the problems of religion. These experiences pose the questions and point to possible answers. They do not, however, *determine* these answers in a definite way. It is important to insist on this distinction, since it touches upon a basic issue in religious thought, the issue of *natural* versus *revelational* theology.

GOD'S WORK AND GOD'S WORD

The adherents of *natural* theology maintain that man can attain knowledge of God through the ordinary experiences of life, especially through the contemplation of the visible processes of nature: "If you want to know Him through whose word the Universe came into being, observe His works."[5]

The proponents of *revelational* theology have insisted that man can never attain knowledge of God's being or of His demands except through divine self-disclosure in revelation. The way to God cannot be discovered through His Works, but must be disclosed through His Word.

Both these views present difficulties which make them unacceptable to us.

The claim of *natural* theology that God can be adequately known through the contemplation of reality is refuted by the fact that such experience has led people to a bewildering variety of contradictory religious, irreligious and agnostic views. The variegated facts of nature do not supply unambiguous answers to the questions which they raise. Nature has been described as morally neutral by those who have pointed to examples of exquisite adaptation of means to ends as well as of colossal waste. Depending on the context and the principle of selection, nature can be seen as indifferent to man and his interests, or as the nurse and fostermother of the race. Facts no more teach a definitive theology, than tools teach their own use. "The heavens declare the glory of God; and the firmament sheweth His handiwork" only to the Psalmist who believes that "the *Torah* of the Lord is perfect."

The exclusive claim of *revelational* theology encounters equally formidable obstacles. It asserts a radical split between the divine and human, and denies that ordinary experience is conducive to the understanding of God. But surely such a sundering of the two elements makes revelation impossible or ineffectual. God's message may be eternal, but its reception requires that it address itself to the questions and problems of human existence. Thus man's experience and the knowledge of God cannot be totally disparate. Revelation which is unrelated to human concerns and modes of understanding is neither meaningful nor illuminating for men. A world and humanity which do not reflect the divine or intimate it in some way can hardly be said to represent God's creation and His image. If human existence is utterly irrelevant to the awareness of God, then a supernatural revelation of God must be irrelevant to man.

An adequate view of God must combine the insights of natural and revelational theology while avoiding their individual shortcomings. This can be achieved by the *method of correlation*[6] in which the questions originate in human existence, but the answers must be drawn not only from existence but also from divine revelation and sacred tradition. This is the case because the questions do not concern the facts of existence, but their meaning and value as directions to life. The answers require an act of personal commitment and faith, which need not be "blind," since it may or may not prove relevant to the basic problems of human existence. Neither is it "rational" in the sense that it can be deduced from the empirical facts which it imbues with meaning and direction. It follows that every man, except the cynic, the skeptic or the person who goes along with the values and directions of his environment without having any convictions of his own, has (implicitly or explicitly) a *theology* of sorts.

If we seek to avoid both the fallacy of confusing God with the conditions that instigate our quest for Him, and the absurdity of adding to God's glory by proclaiming the radical irrelevance and worthlessness of His creation, two important consequences follow for Jewish educational theory and practices. The nature of God must be taught by posing relevant questions; and Jewish theology must stress the characteristic affirmations of Jewish experience.

One cannot teach about God and religion through indoctrination, where the answers of the tradition are presented and advocated by the teacher. Since answers can only make sense in terms of the questions to which they are addressed, such teaching would be putting the cart before the horse. Religious education has to present the facts of human existence (which the pupil studies in secular schools and experiences in his personal life) in a new manner. The role of the teacher is to draw attention to aspects of ordinary reality which the student is likely to overlook or which he does not take seriously, in order to show him which tensions, problems and evocations of the transcendent challenge us and point to the Divine.

The phenomenon of *change* is known to everyone, although few of us realize its import. An awareness that each blade of grass, each human being and each situation, although conforming to the general laws of nature, is unprecedented and in some respect unique, points up the marvel and miracle of "continuous creation" and the preciousness of each being. Internalization of such awareness enhances the quality of man's life and opens his soul to consider the question of the source of all creativity.

Religious education should also develop a keen awareness that man is not self-sufficient and independent but the product and meeting place of forces beyond his control. Paradoxically, even our power of self-assertion, our refusal to accept our dependence on a higher power, are *dependent* on something beyond ourselves. Such awareness makes one receptive to the answer of Judaism which sees man as a creature of God the Creator.

And only when the pupil has been shown that *responsibility*, being answerable for one's actions, is a pervasive facet of human existence, can he understand the moral dimension of reality which points to the obligatoriness of life as an objective pre-condition of humanity. It will then make sense to teach the biblical message that there is One to whom we are responsible and that God's question to Adam, "Where art thou?" is not an ancient fable but an ever-present reality.

In addition to these universal aspects of existence, common to all civilized and moral people, Jewish theology must stress the basic affirmations unique to Judaism, as expressed in the classics of the Jewish faith. Thus, for example, it should be made clear to the student that the exodus from Egypt and its aftermath are *not* depicted in the Bible as just another struggle for national survival, freedom and independence by a downtrodden minority (though they were that too, of course!), but as the consecration of a people to the service of God and obedience to His commandments.

The shared and the unique aspects of Jewish faith cannot be separated, although they must be clearly distinguished by the teacher. The more skillfully their mutual relationship can be established, the more meaningful will our religious teaching be. To show that Bible, *halakhah* and *agadah* are relevant and are addressed to universal and ever-present challenges in the lives of men, will do more in the long run to create the necessary motivation for Jewish studies than superficial attempts to "modernize" the classical texts by transposing them into the current idioms of the latest literary or social fads.

THE EXPERIMENTAL MATRIX OF RELIGION

It has been said that "religion is for simple people, and so must itself be simple.[7] If that were true it would be easy for us to locate its sources in human experience. But unfortunately, seemingly simple things turn out to be complicated on closer analysis. One such deceptively simple fact is that religious consciousness is always characterized by *a profound dissatisfaction with reality as immediately given*. If man were but an ingenious robot photographing the visible and recording the audible aspects of his environment he would not develop religious problems. It is the unexpectedness of reality, the frequent failure of things to conform to our expectations, which is at the bottom of the quest for the Divine. Although we know ourselves to be *finite* we refuse to accept anything short of the Ultimate as *de-finite*. Man is a self-transcending being. In the cognitive realm perceptions refuse to stay isolated and drive us to more comprehensive knowledge, where general statements, laws and theories include and surpass single facts. In the realm of moral conduct, partially glimpsed values with competing claims impel us to search for ultimate meaning and purpose. The religious man "accepts" reality, but he never accepts it at *face value*.

Five fundamental experiences basic to the religious understanding of life are change, dependence, order, value and imperfection.[8]

(1) The fact of *change*, although sometimes neglected because that which is "real" is taken to be permanent and enduring, is ubiquitous. But change means something much more radical than difference, it means creation and destruction. Through memory and discrimination we can compare past and present experiences, and become aware of the appearance of the new and the disappearance of the old. The daily appearance of novelty confronts us with the problem of primordial Creation in an acute form. Anything that *begins* to exist confronts us with three alternatives: (a) We can dismiss the problem of where it came from as scientifically meaningless and limit ourselves to acceptance of change and attempts to discover the laws which describe and predict it. (b) We can accept the pre-existence of everything in the timeless Absolute which monistic religions such as Hindu mysticism teach; in this view the phenomenal world is the fall from the state of true and timeless reality. (c) We can accept God as the source of reality, whose creative activity is manifested in the origin and the sustenance of the world. The religious attitudes engendered by the awareness of change include a sense of mystery in the face of the inexhaustible character of reality, an expectancy based on the possibilities of the truly new and surprising, and the humility which comes with awareness of our limitations in the face of the mystery.

(2) The consciousness of *dependence* is the awareness that our life and our resources for growth and development are not of our own creation, but a gift. This points to the causal factor in existence and, more generally, to the relatedness of all beings. It poses the basic question:

What are the sources of being? The unearned gift of life is seen in Jewish faith as a sign of God's goodness and mercy. Man's stubborn assertion of his individual or group self-sufficiency is seen by biblical faith as the root of idolatry and arrogance. The sense of dependence leads to thankfulness, generosity, confidence and humility, as well as fear and awe. The realization that "He is God, He had made us, and not we ourselves"[9] assures us that "to Him we belong," of being accountable to God and of being sheltered and protected in His loving care.

(3) The experience of *order* reflects the fact that reality is not chaotic, but exhibits pattern, regularity and determinate structure. Order circumscribes the realm of the possible; even the new and unexpected happens within a framework of pattern and regularity. In biblical wisdom literature, the determinate structure and regularity of nature is a confirmation of God's beneficence and wisdom. The regularity of nature is closely related to its design and purpose.[10] In Rabbinic literature the pre-existent Torah, which is equated with wisdom, serves as the blueprint for the orderly structure of the world to be created. (*Gen. R., Proem.*)

The experience of order not only underlies the theological concept of divine wisdom but is closely connected with the structure and the consequences of human conduct as realized in the moral order. Law, whether ritual or moral, establishes modes of behavior, and by limiting possibilities creates a pattern which can be handed down, learned and imitated, thus preserving values and living up to expectations.

The relationship between order and pattern on the one hand and novelty and spontaneity on the other is of fundamental importance for the analysis of reality, for Jewish theology, religious life and observance.[11] The experience of order in natural phenomena gives rise to the confident expectation of the intelligibility of future events in terms of observed precedents. The order of man's duties toward God and fellow man as disclosed in the *mitzvot*, gives the Jew the assurance that, no matter how fallible and incomplete man's acts are, his efforts to fulfill God's will are not left entirely to his whims or intuitions, but can be discerned through the pattern of halakhic precepts and principles.

(4) Many people tend to denigrate *value* experiences as "subjective" and hence not valid, since they depend on the relativities of time, culture and society. Yet in morals and in science and art, values are pervasive not merely as personal decision but as reflections of objective structures and qualities that affect the valuer. Man does not invent values but finds or discovers them. In science, the "truth-value" of an idea depends on its congruence with the established body of science. In art, the esthetic value of a work is a function of many factors among which subject-matter, form and substance merge in a dynamic vision of

the artist's encounter with the world. In human conduct, "moral value" represents a congruence between the potentialities of the agent, the lure of the overarching aims issuing from the divine source of meanings, and the adaptation of means to ends in the given situation.

Values do not, of course, "prove" God any more than facts do. But seen from the standpoint of Jewish faith, they affirm the goodness and justice of God and the obligatory character of divine guidance for the achievement of the good. Creation, Revelation and Redemption—the three great concepts of our faith—speak meaningfully to the religious consciousness since they address themselves to universal experiences of value. The biblical account of Creation has as its refrain the words "And God saw that it was good," and its climax in the statement that it was *very good*. The central message of Revelation is expressed in the law of love (Deut. 6:5) and the exhortation of *imitatio Dei* (Lev. 19:2). The relevance of this injunction for the grounding of ethics in the divine identity was singled out by the Rabbis, who found it indicated in Deut. 32:4 that "all His ways are justice."[12] The ideal of Redemption is anticipated wherever men join together to give praise and thanks in common song: "O give thanks to the Lord, for *He is good*, for His steadfast love endures forever."[13]

The religious attitudes engendered by the experience of value include a sence of loyalty, a vivid apprehension of aims worth striving for, and a sensitivity to the potentialities of life.

(5) The sense of *imperfection* begins in the general recognition that things are almost always less than what they might be. Confronted with any state of affairs we can (and often do) envisage a better, more perfect one. Janus-like, imperfection points in two directions. It reflects the omnipresence of limitation, finiteness and partial failure in every situation, and it gazes equally at improvement, progress, evolution and a still unrealized perfection. If man were a godlike being he would not be imperfect; if he were an animal like all the others he would not be *aware* of his shortcomings. The sense of imperfection, then, is a manifestation of man's place as a rope stretched between the realm of "perfect" repetitive processes and that far shore of ever new, more ideal achievements and adventures. It is in the sense of imperfection that the possibility of scientific progress and social and moral advance are grounded.

Within the religious consciousness of Israel the sense of imperfection points to two aspects of reality. The inexhaustibility of existence, the ever-stirring surplus and richness of being, beyond any of its apprehended embodiments, prepares the Jew to accept God as the inexhaustible source of all which infinitely transcends His manifestations and works. It is in the awareness of imperfection that man is awakened to his kinship to the divine. The lure of higher values, aims and perfections prepares the Jew to accept God as an ever-active demand to surpass oneself and to reshape reality in the light of absolute standards of truth, goodness, beauty and justice which, though never finally attained or even clearly perceived, make possible whatever achievements fall to one's lot. Prophetic criticism in the name of the eternal God challenges every limited claim at final validity and drives man beyond all possible situations in the light of the divine and unconditional demand.

A PROGRAM FOR INSTRUCTION IN THEOLOGY

Teaching about God in a full and well-planned Jewish educational system must avoid the strait jacket of catechistic simplicity on the one hand, and the noncommittal looseness of a historical tour (where chronological succession is substituted for true tracing of the history of ideas) on the other.

As pointed out previously, the varied approaches of different periods and minds must be presented in all their richness, lest the student be led to believe that any one approach or doctrine "covers" the topic and that he can now label God in a final and satisfactory manner. And only by extracting from the underlying terms and categories the various "theologies" will the student acquire the conceptual tools to sort out, clarify— and thus to understand—the discipline of theology.

But before these complex and ambitious goals can be attempted in religious schools, a solid groundwork of teaching will have to be laid.

We can begin teaching about God by making use of two kinds of material. We can cull passages from world literature dealing with God, and we can start with passages from our own tradition. Each method presents unique opportunities and drawbacks. Our aim at this stage is not to present theologically formulated statements about God and His nature, but rather to present the experience of sensible and sensitive people who have testified to the presence and reality of God in their lives.

The advantages of drawing on a wide range of world literature are obvious; religious experience is not presented as the possession of the narrow specialist, but as something that belongs to mankind. The poets of the ages, the playwrights and novelists, the biographers and story-tellers can contribute to a broadening of experience, a deepening of sensitivity and the dislocation of normal consciousness, which enable us to perceive new things as well as to see old and familiar ones in a new perspective.

Yet the danger of this method is real. Even the most lyrical expression of direct and universal experience is usually framed in terms which reflect the theological convictions of its author. T. S. Eliot's *Choruses from The Rock* (especially sec. III) echo Ezekiel's accents as faithfully as Bialik, but the teacher who selects these pieces must also be attuned to the underlying Christian doctrines which are often inextricably commingled with the universal message.

A scholar who combines literary taste, deep Jewish commitment, and a nose for "strange" theologies, should prepare an anthology of this kind. The anthology need not shun expressions of view which differ from Judaism, *as long as they are clearly recognizable as such.* What is to be avoided is unrecognized smuggling in of strange *teraphim* under the cover of a harmless looking camel-saddle.

Wordsworth's quasi-pantheistic poems ought to be required reading: they illuminate a way of sensing the presence of the Divine through nature, which is important, although in Judaism it is balanced and countered by the equally important experience of the transcendent voice of demand and command. Rilke's poem on beholding an archaic torso of Apollo may be more valuable than all the drivel served up as "poetry" in many American books for Jewish children. And Holderlin's inimitable lines

> Nah ist
> Und schwer zu fassen der Gott.
> Wo aber Gefahr ist, wächst,
> Das Rettende auch,

are too true and important to be withheld from mature students, although they are the opening lines of "Patmos"—a poem with a Christian theme.

This kind of reading can achieve something that was taken for granted in almost every culture prior to our technological age, but that can no longer be taken for granted as part of our normal consciousness. I shall indicate it by a quotation from Bradley who, incidentally, was not even a theist:

> All of us, I presume, more or less, are led beyond the region of ordinary facts. Some in one way and some in others, we seem to touch and have communion with what is beyond the visible world. In various manners we find something higher, which both supports and humbles, both chastens and transports us. And with certain persons, the intellectual effort to understand the universe is a principal way of experiencing the Deity. No one, probably, who has not felt this, however differently he might describe it, has ever cared much for metaphysics.[14]

JEWISH MATERIAL

A much more significant method of teaching theology is to present material to the student from Jewish classical sources—although I suspect that the initiation ought not be systematic. Rather, the younger pupil ought to encounter statements about God as they arise in his ordinary classes in Bible, prayer, holidays, etc. These chance encounters can then be used to generate discussion in which the idea of God is explored.

This approach prepares the way for a subsequent more systematic study of representative texts dealing with the God idea. Although the vastness of the material (and the inaccessibility of much of it to anyone but the specialist) makes it impossible to deal with more than a limited number of texts, I believe that a "reader" on the idea of God in Judaism, containing a judicious selection of texts exemplifying different insights, emphases, symbolisms and conceptual methods, should be developed.[15] Such an anthology would explore some of the .contributions which each period of Jewish history has made to the understanding of God and His relation to man, and would introduce the student to mutually incompatible approaches to the concept of God, within the tradition of Jewish thought and faith.

The study of these representative texts will lead to the clarification of basic concepts and categories. Sometimes these basic terms can be extracted from the text itself; at other times modern conceptual tools will have to be used. When they are, we must be sure that connotations which do not apply to the original meaning of the text are not surreptitiously introduced (e.g., the Greek concept of perfection and changeless indifference, as applied to the anthropopathic God-idea of the Bible).

The God of the Bible who is passionately concerned with His creatures, who acts as Creator, Revealer of the Torah, and Redeemer of His people will be understood (not just "known") as the drama of the divine-human encounter is made the basis for an elucidation of biblical theology.[16]

The thought-world of Talmud and Midrash will have to be analyzed in terms of the polarities of *halakhah* and *agadah*, by an examination of the epithets applied to God and His attributes (*midat ha-rahamim, midat ha-din*, etc.) as shown in Dr. Max Kadushin's works. Abraham Heschel's studies of the consistently developed theological systems of Rabbi Akiva and Rabbi Yishmael will have a revolutionary impact on our understanding of Rabbinic theology.

The empiricist *fideism* of Judah Ha-levi and the intellectualism of Maimonides' *Guide* will have to be represented as well as the kabbalistic doctrines of the *Zohar*, Lurianic mysticism and Hasidism. And study of such representative modern Jewish thinkers as Buber, Rosenzweig,

Kaplan and Heschel will enable the student to understand the God-concepts of these men as their answer to the challenges of modern times, as well as their contribution toward achievement of a more adequate understanding of the traditional God-idea through the conceptual tools of modern philosophy.

ANALYSIS AND CLASSIFICATION

Important as it is to examine a representative selection of texts, to extract their basic terms and to understand their propositions, it is not enough. It is necessary also to compare and juxtapose the different theologies, to find out their logical and existential compatibilities and incompatibilities, the differences in their thought and their way of saying things.

Such a dialectical examination of each system would include attempts to translate the propositions and postulates of one system into the philosophical key of the other, and "experiments" to test whether partial truths or truth-claims of one approach can be made compatible or complementary to partial truths of another.

Despite the difficulty of such dialectical examination, some idea of the character of different theologies and of what they can achieve is necessary in the curriculum. Otherwise the student is left with a hodgepodge of alternative doctrines, rather than a sense of the inevitably ongoing character of the divine science.

We can also impose a certain order upon the variety of God-ideas, a typology, such as the one I shall briefly indicate now. (The scheme used here makes no claim to exclusive validity or eminence. It is merely presented as an example in classification.) The various approaches to God can be classified as belonging to one of three types, of which the extremes are the *ontological* and the *moral* type of faith.[17]

In the *ontological, sacramental* or *cosmological* type of faith, the Holy is felt as present. God, the source of holiness, manifests Himself in reality and hence the world, its structures and all beings reflect and manifest the divine. In biblical terminology we can say that *kevod hashem* (the glory of the Lord) stands for this manifestation. Thus, what *is* conveys the sacred provenance of its source. Holiness is here and now; God manifests Himself in nature and history. This type of faith tends to be *conservative* and accepting of things as they are, since reality reflects the divine.

In the *moral* or *utopian* type of faith, the Holy is not experienced as that which *is*, but rather as that which *ought to be*. God is manifested in the demand, the command, the call to change reality and to hallow it, or in biblical terminology, *devar ha-shem* (the word of the Lord). This results in God summoning the prophets to convey His demands, and in His revelation of the Torah through whose commandments reality is perfected. This type of faith tends to be *revolutionary*, and critical of the status quo.

Every theological statement in the religious literature of Israel and of all other religions (and secularized pseudo-religions) can be related to one of these two types of faith. We face reality with reverence and feel piety toward the sources of our being, acknowledging the sacred ground of all that exists; or we look for holiness and the divine beyond the here and now, in the fulfillment of the divine promise and the partnership of God and Israel in making the Kingdom a reality by responding to the divine command.

Although no actual religion ever displays either of these two types in a pure form, we can generally state which tendency is dominant in any theological system. In secularized versions of theology (nationalism or socialism), sacramental faith glorifies the status quo and justifies existing injustices and inequalities, while utopian faith condemns all existing institutions and exists only in expectation of the coming revolution which will bring the secular equivalent of the messianic age.[18]

The third type of theology combines elements of the other two types in a polar tension. For lack of a better name I shall call it the *quasi-mystical* type.[19]

As man looks within his own depths, he becomes aware that he is rooted in something greater than his own individual self. Although we are part of this greater reality, we also experience ourselves as free and responsible agents. Although we *are* like all other creatures, we are aware that we *ought* to be different. Man is the only being who is aware of what he is and at the same time knows that he faces the demand to change and make himself over in the light of divine demands and ethical norms. We realize that in our own soul *that which is* and *that which ought to be* meet and merge. We can sense the holiness of God as manifested in reality, yet we are driven to be dissatisfied with that which is, because we also feel the holiness of that which ought to be, but is not yet.

The quasi-mystical tension between our own independence and our rootedness in God is always in danger of moving toward one of two poles. (1) The man who experiences only the divine reality and loses his individuality, succumbs to the complete mysticism of Hindu faith in which the self is negated and dissolved in the Godhead. (2) The man who experiences only his individuality makes himself divine, because he thinks that what is called God is only embodied in man. As Feuerbach put it: *theology* (discourse about God) becomes *anthropology* (discourse about man).

The quasi-mystical approach of Judaism tries to avoid both these extremes. It is difficult to maintain a balance between sensing the goodness of reality, and judging it by the ideals of the eternal demand. In the words of R. Simhah Bunam of Przysucha, a hasidic master, every man should have two pockets, in each of which he ought to carry a slip of paper to be taken out and reread as the need arises. One was to contain the biblical verse: "I am but dust and ashes" (Gen. 18:27); the other was to bear the affirmation from the Mishnah: "For my sake was the world created" (*Sanhedrin* 4.5).

IMPLICATIONS FOR EDUCATION

In discussing the concept of God one may tend to forget that if God were nothing but a concept He would hardly deserve to be discussed. The religious person is acutely aware of the distinction between our changing ideas and fluctuating formulations of God, and the object of faith (which from the standpoint of the believer is the *Subject* of reality) whom our ideas can never adequately define or describe. Hence religious education cannot be limited to the conveying of theological information. Swimming instruction which provided only theory without actually getting the student to swim in water would be useless. Ethical education which turned out pupils who "knew" ethics but did not develop an instinct for decent conduct, would be a failure. Similarly, religious education must culminate in religious action and experience.

The relationship between theology and action, between religious knowledge and practice is one of mutual interdependence. Knowledge of God stimulates man to do His will; and only by actively doing His will can the knowledge of God be gained. In religion, knowledge cannot be acquired by study alone. Some of the central statements of faith do not disclose their meanings to the student who tries to analyze them objectively. It is only by acting out the pattern of practices prescribed by religion that one can slowly grasp what was meant by those statements. By *doing* we gain insight and intellectual illumination and through study our actions gain meaning and relevance. The Rabbis thought that the words "We shall do and we shall hear" (Ex. 24:7) revealed the "angelic" insight that only through doing can understanding be obtained.[20]

Acting religiously, fulfilling *mitzvot*, has a two-fold function in terms of man's relationship to God: (1) The religious act may represent one's attempt to approach God, to present oneself before Him and to gain an awareness of His reality. (2) Religious observance—whether "ceremonial" or "moral"—represents one's reaction or response to the experience of God's reality. For it is of the essence of God-awareness that it evokes a sense of *responsibility*. He who has been addressed, he who has heard the demand, cannot but respond.

These two functions of observance are not mutually exclusive. Very often they reinforce one another. A person prays to attain a sense of God's presence out of the despair of emptiness and the absence of the Divine. And the same person will pray again, once the despair and emptiness are gone.

The implications of these observations for the theory and practice of Jewish education are clear. If study and observance are mutually complementary, then we cannot plan them in isolation. We shall have to explore how *mitzvot* can be made more meaningful to students at different age levels. And we shall have to investigate how differences in the teaching about God affect the students' attitudes toward other aspects of life and their overt behavior pattern.[21]

If we accept that religious actions are either human attempts to approach God or human responses to the experience of the Divine, some important consequences for education result. We will have to conclude that mere study or action without the accompaniment of the appropriate feelings will not evoke the sense of the divine-human confrontation which is at the basis of all genuine faith.

Judaism can not be reduced to a form of knowledge conveyed through doctrines and symbols, nor is it solely and emotional experience or a system of ethical behavior. It is a total relationship between man and God, in which neither intellect nor action nor emotion are thwarted. The god of the philosophers is a necessary condition of reality; the God of religion is a transforming agent. The sense of humility and courage, the vivid experience of divine judgment and love, and the sense of the reality of the spirit, are qualities which may reward those who heed the call: "Seek you My face!" (Ps. 27:8).

NOTES

1. The term "theology" is commonly applied to the broad subject of religious doctrines dealing with "God and related matters." In this essay it is employed in the more limited sense of discourse dealing with the idea of God.

2. E. A. Aubrey, "Naturalism and Religious Thought," *Journal of Philosophy,* Vol. 48, No. 3, p. 76.

3. A. N. Whitehead, *Religion in the Making,* p. 15.

4. A. J. Heschel, *Between God and Man,* p. 35.

5. Quoted in the name of R. Meir in *Teshuvot haRambam,* ed. Freimann, p. 312.

6. The term was coined by Paul Tillich, *Systematic Theology,* Vol. I, pp. 59-66; Vol. II, pp. 13-16; *The Protestant Era,* Ch. VI. Cf. Heschel, *God in Search of Man,* Ch. I.

7. H. J. Paton, *The Modern Predicament,* New York: Collier Books, 1962, p. 70.

8. See Philip H. Phenix, *Intelligible Religion,* New York, 1954, pp. 29–92.

9. Psalm 100:3.

10. Cf. Ps. 104:24, Job 28:25, Ps. 148:15, Jer. 31:34, 35.

11. For the centrality of these polar concepts in Abraham Heschel's philoso-

phy of religion, see my introductory essay in *Between God and Man*, Free Press-Macmillan paperback edition.

12. See also, Deut. 8:6, 10:12, 11:22, 19:9, 26:17, 28:9, 30:16.

13. The interpretation of "good" as a key word of Creation and Redemption is found in Franz Rosenzweig, *Der Stern der Erlösung*, II, pp. 82-87, 185-186.

14. F. H. Bradley, *Appearance and Reality*, 1893, p. 5.

15. A first step toward such a source book is the collection of texts (in Hebrew) on God as Creator in Jewish thought, which I have compiled for the use of my students.

16. For simplicity's sake I have assumed the existence of an entity called "biblical theology," although the biblical scholar may well object and point out differences in various parts of biblical literature.

17. In the initial bifurcation of types, I follow Tillich. Cf. his *Dynamics of Faith*, where a full and lucid presentation of this typology is given in Chapter 4.

18. Cf. K. Mannheim, *Ideology and Utopia*, translated by L. Wirth and E. Shils, London and New York, 1952.

19. Cf. my remarks in *Between God and Man*, p. 16.

20. Cf. T. B. *Shabbat* 88a, Leviticus Rabbah 1:1. See also Heschel's views on the "leap of action" in *Between God and Man*, Ch. 12.

21. Henry Cohen's article, "The Idea of God in Jewish Education," *Judaism*, Vol. 12, No. 2 (Spring 1963), is an excellent contribution to this subject.

RICHARD L. RUBENSTEIN laments that after Auschwitz, "the old God of Jewish patriarchal monotheism" has been "dead beyond all hope of resurrection." Yet though the modern Jew has lost faith in the historical and theological justification of Judaism, the *psychological* value and truth of religion offers "the most fruitful path for a contemporary rationale for religious belief and practice." Thus, for example, the Kabbalistic myth of creation is valid because it "expresses a very concrete reality all can recognize. It is predicated on the image of man as a finite, alienated creature thrust into a world which cannot entirely satisfy him and in which he is separated from, and yet drawn to, the source of his true being." Ritual practices rooted in human need include *bar mitzvah* and other *rites de passage*. Also inherently valuable are rituals that dramatize ethical teachings and possess a definite survival value for the community. Jewish rituals even in such matters as death and mourning "cease to be meaningful unless they are appropriated in the shared life of the community," which, despite its human imperfections, nourishes Jewish identity.

As for God and the death of God, it is best to understand Him as the "focus of ultimate concern." God is "the infinite measure against which we can see our own limited lives in proper perspective." Prayer is no longer to be regarded as "dialogue with a personal God," but as "aspirations shared in depth by the religious community."

XVII.

The Symbols of Judaism and the Death of God

RICHARD L. RUBENSTEIN

THE GROWTH OF religious institutions and the decline in religious belief have been frequently observed phenomena in post-war America. This development has often puzzled students of religion. A number of scholars have commented especially on the tendency of suburban churches and synagogues to become primarily social institutions. Condemnations by clergymen of the growing religious indifference have been frequent. Yet belief continues to decline, while religious communities continue to expand.

The postwar decline in religious commitment has been very much in evidence in the prospering synagogues of America. While the decline in belief is largely a cultural phenomenon, it does reflect a theological problem which has been covertly understood in religious circles for several decades. The rise of scientific scholarship in the field of religion has been especially threatening to the believing Jew. As a result of the new insights, it has been impossible to accept at face value the myths concerning the authority of traditional Jewish belief and practice. Religious Jews have been compelled either to retreat to a fideistic dogmatism which ignores modern scholarship, or to seek a new rationale for their theological commitments. For many, the problem of finding a new rationale has been aggravated by the death of their personal God. After Auschwitz many Jews did not need Nietzsche to tell them that the old God of Jewish patriarchal monotheism was dead beyond all hope of resurrection.

At the heart of traditional Judaism there is the belief that God, the omnipotent creator of heaven and earth, gave the Jewish people the Torah at Mt. Sinai. This document contained the laws and disciplines by which Jews were obliged to conduct their lives. Traditional Jews believed that they were to fulfill the disciplines of their faith because God had commanded them so to do. Righteousness consisted in obedience to God's will as revealed in the Torah; sin was a want of conformity with His will. Basic to this perspective was the conviction that the Torah was a unitary document which expressed a harmonious point of view. There were some laws in the Torah which seemed to contradict others. The religious Jew believed that such contradictions could be resolved through recourse to the Oral Law, the rabbinic interpretation of the Torah. Since the Torah was a single document emanating from a single source, the discrepancies were more apparent than real. Guided by the interpretations of the rabbis, the religious Jew could rest secure in the knowledge that the conduct of his life was in accordance with God's will.

Biblical scholarship has proven far more threatening to traditional Judaism than to Christianity. The Christian believer is expected to affirm the centrality of the Christ-event for his destiny. Christian faith never rested its ultimate claim on the unitary authorship of the sacred documents of Christian religion. Judaism depended upon the belief in the historical authenticity and the literary unity of the Torah. This text was traditionally regarded as containing an accurate record of God's encounter with Moses. Its interpretation by the rabbis was thought to be faithfully in keeping with its original intent. As a result of modern scholarship, we now understand that the Torah is a collection of many documents with some internal discrepancies of age, environment, and point of view. The documentary hypothesis made it impossible to claim that the Torah was a unitary work containing the record of God's covenant with Israel without contradiction. The traditional believer did not have to face the problem of why he ought to fulfill religious commandments of doubtful origin and authority. We do. The traditional believer was convinced that in obeying the Torah he was fulfilling God's will. We no longer possess that assurance.

When one accepts the new situation, one is forced either to reject Jewish religious practice or to find a new rationale for continuing to fulfill that sector which remains meaningful. As Tillich has suggested, we live in an age of "broken symbols." The problem of the symbolic content of Judaism in our time is to find a viable basis for continuing to maintain Jewish religious practice after its traditional validations have become altogether transparent to us.

While it is no longer possible to accept the traditional justifications of the authority of Judaism, new insights, especially in the social sciences, have made it impossible to dismiss such rituals as entirely meaningless. Edward Gibbon could look upon Notre Dame in Paris as a towering monument to superstition and dismiss it with contempt. Today we see religion as far too deeply rooted in the realities of the human predicament so to reject it.

The insights of depth psychology have been especially helpful in offering us a new understanding of the significance of religion. A century ago the seemingly irrational aspects of religion were either accepted by the faithful without insight or dismissed by the sceptical as meaningless. Today we understand that irrational phenomena in religion, as in other spheres of human activity, are meaningful, purposeful, and goal-directed. They express some of the deepest and most important feelings we experience as human beings. The key to our new understanding lies in a distinction implicit in Freud's work on the interpretation of dreams. I refer to the distinction between the latent and the manifest content of fantasy productions. While the manifest content of dreams frequently lacks coherent meaning, an understanding of the associations the dream symbolism elicits usually reveals that its latent content expresses some unconscious fear or wish of the dreamer.

Freud's insights about dreams were quickly extended to other types of fantasy production, including myths, legends, and religious beliefs. While their manifest content frequently made little sense, their latent content was understood to give expression to unconscious feelings concerning our most significant life-experiences. Freud had spoken of religion as a group neurosis. He tended to regard religious belief as a group phenomenon which paralleled neurotic strivings in the life of the individual. At one level this disparaged religion; at another level, Freud's suggestion pointed to the degree to which religion reflected the deepest fears, aspirations, and yearnings of the individual and the group. As Ernest Jones has commented, although Freud ceased to believe in the *historical* truth of religion, he never ceased to believe in its *psychological* truth. The modern Jew has lost faith in the historical justification of his faith. The psychological justification offers the most fruitful path for a contemporary rationale for Jewish religious belief and practice.

An excellent example of the psychological truth of religious tradition can be seen in the mystical transformation of the Biblical doctrine of *creatio ex nihilo* in the Kabbalistic doctrine of R. Isaac Luria, a Palestinian mystic of the latter part of the sixteenth century. In the Biblical doctrine, God creates the world out of a nothingness *external* to His person. In the mystical doctrine, we find one of the most persistent of all myths, the myth of the separation of the world from a primordial sacred ground and the yearning of the separated world ultimately to return to its source. In Luria's myth, *creatio ex nihilo* is taken to mean creation out of the "no thing" which is the primordial Godhead. The primordial ground is understood as beyond substance, above all finitude, and incommensurate with the categories of human discursive reasoning. God in the original plenitude of His being is therefore no thing and, in a sense, nothing. The nothingness of God, in the mystical doctrine, is not the nothingness of absolute privation. It is the nothingness of the absence of all concreteness and "thinghood." God's original nothingness is the nothingness of a superfluity of being. At this stage, one cannot say that God exists. Discrete, quantifiable entities exist. As the distinguished contemporary Jewish mystic, Zalman Schacter, has paradoxically stated, "If there is a God, He doesn't exist." According to this doctrine, God can *exist* only when He becomes less than Himself and ceases to be no thing. This can only happen when God *gives birth to* the world out of His primordial ground. My emphasis on the image of giving birth, though hopelessly inadequate, is nevertheless deliberate.

This mystical doctrine of creation is an attempt to give mythic structure to the creation of the world through an analogy with the human womb-birth-tomb sequence. Just as the infant discovers its world through severance from its symbiotic relation with the mother, so too in the myth the primordial Godhead becomes God and the world through the self-division or self-diminution of the primal ground of being or *Urgrund*. In Lurianic Kabbalism this process is called *tsimtsum*, the creative self-diminution of the Godhead. The primal Godhead creates both the world and God out of its own no-thingness. The finite persons and things which constitute the created world consist of the divine sparks which have left their primordial source to wander about, only to be regathered at the end of time in the allness which is nothing. It is also of consequence in this doctrine that the first act of creation is a *fall* or an original catastrophe. The ultimate goal of the created world is the reparation of the catastrophe and a return of all things to God as He was in the beginning. Thomas Altizer has commented that non-Christian religions have as their ultimate goal the recollection of a primordial sacred beginning. His description fits Lurianic Kabbalism. Creation is a catastrophe; creatures are caught between a tendency toward self-maintenance and reabsorption into the primordial ground; the restoration of the original, undisturbed unity of all in God and God as the all-in-all is the final goal.

This is a myth. Nevertheless, it expresses a very concrete reality all can recognize. It is predicated upon the image of man as a finite, alienated creature thrust into existence in a world which cannot entirely satisfy him and in which he is separated from, yet drawn to, the source of his true being in the *Urgrund*. The myth can be read in two ways: In one, the separated and broken character of human finitude is stressed. In the other, man is seen as a fulcrum balancing the forces of life and death, love and hate, organic separateness and inorganic sameness, being and nothingness. The mystics stress the broken character of separated human existence. Freud in *Beyond the Pleasure Principle* stresses the fulcrum character of life which is inextricably bound to the dialectic tensions of *eros* and *thanatos,* and in which *thanatos* is ultimately victorious. There is one vital difference between the mystics and Freud. Freud, and in a sense all of the moderns, would say that the human predicament has "no exit" save death. For the mystic there is always hope for the ultimate reconciliation with God by a return to the ground of being. Nevertheless, the critique of life in the here and now is very much the same in the mystics and the moderns. Both see the human predicament as broken, alienated, and destined to terminate in the nothingness out of which it has arisen.

The same human reality is comprehended by Paul Tillich in *The Courage To Be* in which he describes two types of anxiety. Tillich refers to existential anxiety or *Urangst* and neurotic anxiety. Anxiety is the reaction of the organism to the possibility of loss. According to Tillich existential anxiety is man's ineradicable reaction to the possibility of loss which stems from his condition of finitude and creatureliness: the fact that man is born to grow, see himself decay, and be overwhelmed by an ultimate oblivion against which his own powers offer no hope of rescue. As Tillich uses anxiety, it has a cognitive aspect. It is the non-conceptual, unmediated awareness by man of his own finitude. Unlike neurotic anxiety, existential anxiety is ineradicable. The very condition of human existence makes man forever in danger of ultimate loss, the loss of his own selfhood in death.

Tillich's analysis of anxiety rests on Heidegger and, in the final analysis, on Kierkegaard. Kierkegaard stresses an aspect of anxiety which seems to anticipate Freud. Kierkagaard calls *Angst* a "sympathetic-antipathy," by which he means that we are drawn to the very condition we fear even as anxiety helps us to ward it off. Thus, *Urangst* is not only man's cognition and primordial reaction to his ultimate nothingness, it is also, as in Freud, man's primordial yearning for the same nothingness. The mystic yearning for a return to the Godhead, Tillich, Kierkegaard, and Freud all point to the same existential condition. Man's selfhood is a delicate fulcrum balancing those forces which would restore him to sameness with the cosmos and those forces which preserve his separate individual identity. The same critique of existence is implied in the mystical creation myth that is found in the modern writers. The theme is perennial. The religious myth may lack scientific warrant. Nevertheless, it is, psychologically speaking, very true. As a matter of fact, in its religio-mythic form it calls forth a far greater emotional response than when it is expressed conceptually in its non-religious forms. The unconscious was not invented by Freud. The basic responses of human beings to their condition were dealt with long before the twentieth century. Religious myth expresses many of the most abiding concerns of human beings in every generation in a form that can be understood by people of all levels of intellectual attainment. In all ages religion has addressed itself through myth and ritual to such questions as "What is my origin? What is my destiny? How can I be cleansed of my guilt? What are the meaning and purpose of life?" These are questions of ultimate concern. The fact that myth and religious symbol no longer are regarded as true at the manifest level is entirely irrelevant to their central function, which is to give profound expression to our feelings at the decisive times and crises of life.

It is almost a commonplace that religious myth is deeply congruent with human strivings in our psychologically-oriented culture. It may not be nearly so apparent that religious ritual is also congruent with the most important human strivings. I would not want to suggest that all religious rituals remain worthy of observance. Many have arisen out of obsessional needs which once understood diminish in usefulness. There remains, however, a body of ritual practices so authentically rooted in human need that they are unlikely ever to be dispensed with.

Bar Mitzvah is one such ritual. It is one of the most maligned and vulgarized Jewish religious ceremonies. As practiced in the United States, Bar Mitzvah is especially embarrassing to those who see ritual primarily as a pedagogic instrument through which ethical or moral principles can be dramatized. This embarrassment may be acute when a child, innocent of any knowledge of the Hebrew language, reads for his Bar Mitzvah ceremony a section in Hebrew from the Prophets which contains a bitter denunciation of mechanical ritual devoid of any inner meaning. When the young man is congratulated upon completion of the ceremony for his success in the rote reading of an incomprehensible text, there is a very strong temptation to question the value of the practice. Yet this ceremony continues to have an enormous hold over all denominations within the American Jewish community. Without it it is unlikely that American Jewish adolescents would be motivated to ac-quire even the modicum of religious training they do receive.

This ritual has a far greater significance than is apparent on the surface. Bar Mitzvah is a *rite de passage*. It allows a young man to formalize his passage from childhood to adolescence and incipient manhood. It confirms him in his newly acquired masculine role. The disappearance of such a ritual would diminish the extent to which the community compels recognition of the new stage the young man has reached in the timetable of life. Since there is something in all of us which would remain an infant if it could, the failure of society to provide ceremonies of passage such as Bar Mitzvah or confirmation can result in the prolongation beyond its time of relevance of the feelings and behavior of the child in the body of a man. There is renunciation of the infantile and acceptance of the reality of the passing of time in the ceremony. Bar Mitzvah reconciles the boy with his father through a reinforcement of identification. The boy passes through the same rite as his father did. He sees his father as encouraging his entrance into manhood rather than impeding it. Not only does the ceremony formalize the child's entry into manhood, it also is the occasion of the parents' entry into middle age. Parents are as much in need of a *rite de passage* as are children. They often "enjoy" Bar Mitzvah more than their children. In short, Bar Mitzvah is a puberty rite.

Sexual identity is one of the deepest sources of conflict and anxiety within American culture. It does not come automatically or with any degree of ease. One of the most effective ways of helping the Jewish male adolescent to achieve an appropriate sexual identity is through this puberty rite. There is much that is primitive and even archaic in the ritual. It is the one in which contemporary Judaism resembles primitive pagan cultures most completely. Here as elsewhere in Judaism the primitive and the archaic prove upon examination to be among the most meaningful aspects of religion. We err when we stress the distance we have traveled from the ways of primitive man. We have been far more successful in mastering the physical world than in dealing with the emotional crises arising out of the developing personalities of individuals in our culture. In such really important aspects of human experience as birth, adolescence, mating, guilt and death, our fundamental experiences tend to remain the same as those of primitive men. If anything, we are at a disadvantage in our secular culture. Primitive man never left the individual to face the crises of life unaided by meaningful myths and rituals as we do. The Bar Mitzvah ceremony is significant because it confirms the young man in his growing identity at a most appropriate time and in a setting of the greatest possible significance. Even without God, this ritual would remain emotionally indispensable for Jews.

Many religious ceremonies dramatize ethical teachings; others possess a definite survival value for the community. Nevertheless, neither the ethical nor the sociological justification of ritual, though entirely valid, is adequate in itself. Where such rationales are stressed, there is an unfortunate tendency to be rid of seemingly irrational rituals which actually play an enormously important role in the development of the personality. One is almost, but not quite, tempted to reassert the doctrine of the divine origin of ritual in that rituals were intuitively created by the community as an unconscious response to its deepest needs. In the time of the death of God, I suspect we need rituals to dramatize and celebrate the crises of life more than ever.

One of the problems which face today's radical theologians is that of formulating an adequate answer to the question, What shall we say of religion in a time of no God? Sooner or later Protestant radical theologians will have to formulate a doctrine of the church if their theology is to have any relevance for Christendom. Similarly, contemporary Jewish theology cannot ignore the question of the meaning of the synagogue in our times.

The synagogue is an extremely problematic institution. All of the tensions felt by Protestant theologians as they confront the conflict between Christianity and Christendom have their analogue in the discomfort felt by contemporary Jewish thinkers as they contemplate the American synagogue. I shall avoid a further rehearsal of the short-comings of the American synagogue. Enough has been said on that account to make such an effort unnecessary here. Nevertheless, Jewish thinkers know that this inadequate institution in which they can never entirely feel at home is indispensable for Jewish religious life. From Kierkegaard to Bonhoeffer and Cox, Protestant theologians have been fascinated with the problem of a Christianity without the church, a "religionless Christianity." There can be no such thing as a religionless Judaism, a Judaism without the synagogue.

We cannot rest content with asserting the psychological relevance of religious literature, myth and ritual. To do this would be to see these phenomena as no more significant humanly speaking than great literature such as *Antigone, Faust* or *The Brothers Karamazov.* Religion transcends this kind of relevance. Religious symbols cease to be meaningful unless they are appropriated in the shared life of a community. The synagogue is such a community for all of its obvious weaknesses and even vulgarities. It is the institution in which we share not only our inherited rituals and memories but also the human realities which are their ground and content. One need not plead the divine origin of Jewish symbols to understand their special appropriateness to the Jew and Jewish life. There is an interdependent relationship between Jewish identity, Jewish history, and Jewish traditions. Each has helped to create the other. To a very large extent men are the product of the way they bring their memories to bear on their present activities. This is also true of religious communities. History is a decisive determinant of identity in both the individual and the group. As Sartre has suggested, we are our acts. Jewish traditions mirror Jewish identity and Jewish history. No other body of tradition would be appropriate for us. It is part of the givenness of Jewish existence.

The synagogue and the Jewish community retain continuing centrality in Jewish religious life. There can be no Jewish "single one" who turns his back on the community and its traditions and seeks his path to God alone. The mutual need of the individual and the community are perhaps most strongly in evidence in the face of death. No Jew is permitted to mourn the loss of a family member alone. There are few periods in the life of a Jew when the religious community and its traditions mean more to him than at the *shivah* period, the seven days of mourning after the death of a close relative. Judaism possesses no myths of denial by which Jews can pretend that this time is other than tragic. No attempt is made to disguise the emotional impact of death. Every Jewish ritual at the time of mourning forces the Jew to acknowledge the stark reality of what has transpired. Death is not denied; it is affirmed so that the survivors can take up the task of living realistically when the time of healing begins. During the *shivah* period the mourners are not left to themselves. In that crisis in which the individual feels most bereft, the community offers him the presence of his peers to acknowledge and share his terrible burden. *Shivah* is one of the institutions through which Judaism transcends meaning and insight and becomes a sharing of ultimate concern. By use of a common and essentially fixed ritual, we tread a path which others have trod before us. In the face of death we share our predicament with both our peers and those who came before us. The repetition of a common crisis calls for a fixity of form in the rituals with which we confront the experience. This fixity of form is also important for the chain of the generations. It makes for the likelihood that those who follow us will also share with us.

Death, is, of course, the most radical of human necessities. Inevitably it calls forth our freest and most undisguised response to the human predicament. It is for this reason that the synagogue manifests itself here as the community of ultimate concern with the least ambiguity. It would be both untruthful and unhelpful to suggest that the synagogue is normally free of very real impediments to genuine sharing. Usually the need for existential honesty is far less strong. Nevertheless, before we dismiss the conception of the synagogue as the community of ultimate concern altogether, we must ask whether there is any other institution than the church or synagogue in which the existential crisis of birth, death, growth, joy, sorrow, pain and mutual support are more meaningfully shared. Both institutions are woefully inadequate because they are, after all, human institutions with very human failings. We possess no better instruments for sharing the decisive events in the timetable of life.

Finally, there is the problem of the God after the death of God. The focus of the synagogue upon the decisive events and seasons of life gives us a clue to the meaning of God in our times. At one level, it is certainly possible to understand God as the primal ground of being out of which we arise and to which we return. I believe such a God is inescapable in the time of the death of God. The God who is the ground of being is not the transcendent, theistic God of Jewish patriarchal monotheism. Though many still believe in that God, they do so ignoring the questions of God and human freedom and God and human evil. For those who face these issues, the Father-God is a dead God. Even the existentialist leap of faith cannot resurrect this dead God after Auschwitz.

Nevertheless, after the death of the Father-God, God remains the central reality against which all partial realities can be measured. I should like to suggest that God can be understood meaningfully not only as ground of being but also as the *focus of ultimate concern*. As such He is not the old theistic Father-God. Nor is He Reconstructionism's "power that makes for salvation in the world." He is the infinite measure against which we can see our own limited finite lives in proper perspective. Before God it is difficult for us to elevate the trivial to the central in our lives. The old Hebraic understanding of the meaning of idolatry is important for an understanding of the meaning of God as the focus of ultimate concern. Idolatry is the confusion of a limited aspect of things with the ground of the totality. This is not the occasion to catalogue the idolatries of our time. That task has been well done by others. If an awareness of God as the ground of being does nothing more than enable us to refrain from endowing a partial and limited concern with the dignity and status reserved for what is of ultimate concern, it will have served the most important of all tasks. The ancient Hebrews regarded idolatry as a special form of enslavement. Nothing in our contemporary idolatries makes them less enslaving than their archaic counterparts. God can truly make us free.

We live in a culture which tends to stress what we can do rather than what we can become. A few examples will suffice to illustrate the encouragements to idolatry and self-deception with which our culture abounds. We are forever encouraged to deny the passing of time in our overestimation of the importance of both being and looking young. One of our greatest needs is to acknowlege our temporality and mortality without illusion. By so doing, we are not defeated by time. We establish the precondition of our *human* mastery over it. As the focus of ultimate concern the timeless God reflects our seriousness before our human temporality.

Another decisive contemporary need is to learn how to dwell within our own bodies. That is not so easy as it may seem. Fewer capacities come harder to Americans than the capacity to dwell within their own bodies with grace, dignity, and gratification. We become caricatures of our human potentialities when we fail to acquire this wisdom. By coming to terms with the biological nature of the timetable of life, we experience an enormous liberation yet develop the capacity for equally great renunciations when necessary. In the presence of God as the focus of ultimate concern, we need no deceptive myths of an immortal soul. We are finite. He is eternal. We shall perish. He remains ever the same. Before Him we confront our human nakedness with truth and honesty. In this venture, our voyage of self-discovery is enormously aided by Judaism's insistence through ritual and tradition on our continuing awareness of where we are in the biological timetable of life. The ancient Gnostics disparaged the God of the Jews as the God of this world. They asserted that all of His commandments were concerned with the conduct of life in this perishing cosmos. They correctly understood Judaism in their hostility. Unlike Gnosticism, Judaism refused to turn the regard of Jews away from the only life they will ever know, the life of the flesh in this world. God as the focus of ultimate concern challenges us to be the only persons we realistically can be, our authentic, finite selves in all of the radical insecurity and potentiality the life of mortal man affords.

One cannot pray to such a God in the hope of achieving an I-Thou relationship. Such a God is not a person over against man. If God is the ground of being, He will not be found in the meeting of I and Thou but in self-discovery. That self-discovery is not necessarily introspective. The whole area of interpersonal relations is the matrix in which meaningful and insightful self-discovery can occur. Nor can the I-Thou relation between God and man be achieved through prayer. This does not do away with worship. It sets worship in proper perspective. Even Buber admits, in his discussion of the eclipse of God, the contemporary failure of personal prayer. While prayer as address and dialogue has ceased to be meaningful, the burden of this paper has been to suggest some of the ways in which religious ritual has retained its significance. Ritual is more important today than prayer save as prayer is interwoven with ritual. Our prayers can no longer be attempts at dialogue with a personal God. They become aspirations shared in depth by the religious community. As aspiration there is hardly a prayer in the liturgy of Judaism which has lost its meaning or its power. Worship is the sharing of ultimate concern by the community before God, the focus of ultimate concern.

Paradoxically God as ground does everything and nothing. He does nothing in that He is not the motive or active power which brings us to personal self-discovery or to the community of shared experience. Yet He does everything because He shatters and makes transparent the patent unreality of every false and inauthentic standard. God, as the ultimate measure of human truth and human potentiality, calls upon each man to face both the limitations and the opportunities of his finite predicament without disguise, illusion or hope.

There remains the question of whether the religion of God as the source and ground of being, the God after the death of God, is truly a religion. Can there be a religion without a belief in a theistic, creator God? Pagan religions have never celebrated such a God. As I have suggested elsewhere, in the time of the death of God a mystical paganism which utilizes the historic forms of Jewish religion offers the most promising approach to religion in our times.[1]

Judaism no longer insists on the affirmation of a special creed. It has long since ceased rejecting its communicants because of ritual neglect. This does not mean that Judaism had descended to the level of a tribal herd bound together by a primitive and externally enforced we-feeling. No religion can exist without a meaningful form of sacrifice. Though it is not always apparent, contemporary Judaism does have its form of sacrifice. It is just as meaningful and in some ways more demanding than the older forms. This form of sacrifice is peculiarly appropriate to our new understanding of the meaning of God and the power of symbols in contemporary Judaism. Our sacrifice is not philanthropy. Nor is it the renunciation of personal autonomy which some traditions demand. The sacrifice required of those who would participate in the community of ultimate concern is perhaps one of the most difficult in today's society. It is the sacrifice of that pride through which we see our individual roles, status, attainments, or sophistications as in any way more significant than that of any other human being with regard to the decisive events in the timetable of life. We share in the synagogue what we experience in common from birth to death. These events which we celebrate with the traditions of Judaism are the really decisive events. We can succeed in the world of affairs yet, humanly speaking, be wretched failures in the business of life if we fail to put a goodly measure of energy and attention on the decisive events. The traditions and ritual of the synagogue call upon us for this kind of concentration. That is why the sacrifice of pride in attainments which are not central to the business of life is so essential. I do not wish to disparage worldly attainment or professional competence; I want to suggest the wisdom of Judaism in insisting upon its essential emptiness when the business of life is ignored. Each of us before God as the focus of ultimate concern must regard the real challenges of his personal existence as essentially the same as those of any other human being. Whether we are intellectuals, merchants or laborers, we are born in the same way, need the same love, are capable of the same evil and will die the same death. Concentration on what is of genuine significance in the business of life is the contemporary form of the renunciation of idolatry.

The religious symbol and the God to whom the religious symbol points were never more meaningful than they are today. It is no accident that the twentieth century is characterized by theological excitement and renewal. Our myths and rituals have been stripped of their historic covering. No man can seriously pretend that the literal meanings given to our traditions before our time retain much authority today. Happily, in losing some of the old meanings we have also lost some of the old fears.

God stands before us no longer as the final censor but as the final reality before which and in terms of which all partial realities are to be measured.

The last paradox is that in the time of the death of God we have begun a voyage of discovery wherein we may, hopefully, find the true God.

NOTES

1. Richard Rubenstein, *After Auschwitz*, pp. 93-111.

HAROLD M. SCHULWEIS advocates "predicate theology" rather than "subject theology." The latter "rivets our attention upon the divine Subject." Yet Schulweis finds it more practical and sensible to regard "God" as a functinal, rather than as a subjective, noun. "It is not the attributes of a divine Ego," he argues, "but the divinity of the attributes which demands our allegiance." The problem with classical theology is that it must underplay the human aspects of the divine attributes of justice, mercy, etc., in order to avoid projecting human values on the divine Subject. Yet this is dangerous because "denial of the human comprehensibility of the moral attributes of God is accompanied by the denial of human competence to make moral judgment." Instead of attempting to explain how God allows suffering and death, it would be best to affirm that healing is divine. This leads to greater recognition of the human role in healing, and at the same time provides man with a more workable concept of divinity (elohut). Godliness is One in that it "unites and relates the godly attributes. . . . Intelligence, compassion, justice, peace, etc., are named divine when they serve ends which the community of faith judges to be good." One must therefore speak of "Godliness" rather than of "God."

XVIII.

From God to Godliness: Proposal for a Predicate Theology

HAROLD M. SCHULWEIS

IN A PAPER presented at the Rabbinical Assembly in June, 1909, Mordecai M. Kaplan set forth in Kantian fashion his "Copernican revolution." He argued there that a deeper understanding of Judaism, and a more effective way to deal with the challenges to Judaism, call for an inversion of the claim that the Jewish people exists for the sake of Judaism. To the contrary, Kaplan maintained, Judaism exists for the sake of the Jewish people. That proposal reveals both the descriptive and prescriptive elements of Kaplan's reconstructionism. Kaplan's new perception directs us to ask not simply what Judaism *is* but ask what Judaism ought to be.

THEOLOGY WITH A NEW PERCEPTION

In this paper I want to take advantage of Kaplan's methodological principle (and for Kaplan reconstructionism is more methodology than doctrine) by applying it to our understanding of God. To paraphrase Kaplan's inversionary principle, I will be arguing that, better to understand the God-idea and more effectively overcome the obstacles to the acceptance of God in our lives, we must view theology with a new perception. Elohut, Godliness, the divine predicates do not exist for the sake of Elohim, God, the Subject, but vice versa. It is not the attributes of a divine Ego, but the divinity of the attributes which demands our

236

allegiance. What I propose for consideration is adoption of a "Predicate Theology" as a viable alternative for those who are not persuaded by the arguments and claims of traditional "Subject Theology." I am convinced that for many who intellectually and temperamentally are blocked from expressing their religious sensibilities because of the formulations and presuppositions of Subject theology, Predicate theology offers a way to relate positively to divinity, and its celebration in prayer and ritual. My proposals differ from Kaplan's theological claims in a number of important areas, but I believe they are in consonance with his orientation. While Dr. Kaplan cannot be held responsible for my errors, he is responsible, in larger measure than he can know, for encouraging my own theological reconstruction.

TWO WAYS OF SEEING

God did not create theology. Men differ in temperament, in needs and wants and their theologies reflect those needs. This should not mean the denigration of theology, but it should introduce a necessary measure of theological modesty in our claims. I have argued the importance of the God-idea before many diverse groups, especially in college circles, and for many years. I have noted an interesting response to two different ways of formulating the God-idea. In one form I ask how many could subscribe to the belief that God is just, merciful and good; that it is He who uplifts the fallen, heals the sick and loosens the fetters of the bound. The question is generally met with reluctance, at best with agnostic reserve and frequently with strong denial.

The other formulation asks how many would affirm that justice, mercy and goodness are godly; that uplifting the fallen, healing the sick and loosening the fetters of the bound are divine. Here the response is largely positive and most often enthusiastic. What is the meaning of these different reactions? Is it a response to style or to religious substance? Is it the aim of the theologian to prove the existence of the Subject God or to convince others of the reality of the divine predicates? Does my religious interest lie in persuading others that the divine Subject possesses certain qualities, or is it to identify, exhibit and name those qualities as themselves divine? Is the theological task to encourage faith in the Subject or to elicit faith in the Predicates of divinity? Which is more important religiously, morally and liturgically—to endorse faith in the "who" or in the "what" of divinity, fidelity to Elohim or to Elohut? And what difference does there appear to be in the minds of those who are willing to affirm (a) that that which heals the sick is godly while denying (b) that it is God who heals the sick?

THE GRAMMAR OF SUBJECT THEOLOGY

Theological statements are traditionally expressed in terms of subject-predicate relations. However God is portrayed, whether as Person, Being, Power or Process, one speaks of Him as a Subject to which there is attached a number of qualities. Here Orthodox, Reform, Conservative and Reconstructionist prayer books alike follow the same subject-predicate formula: "Blessed art Thou, O Lord our God who. . . ." The very language of our theological and liturgical forms focuses attention upon the Subject who brings forth the bread from the earth, establishes peace in the heaven, reveals, rewards, punishes, judges and forgives. The language of Subject theology rivets our attention upon the divine Subject and frames the way we look for and at divinity.

The very grammar of our ordinary language is biased towards Subject theology. To say "God" is to use a concrete noun which insinuates the naming of some separate entity. George Berkeley long ago warned that it is only grammatical convention which makes us "apt to think every noun substantive stands for a distinctive idea that may be separated from all others: which hath occasioned infinite mistakes." Despite Berkeley's strictures against the ontologizing bewitchment of language, for most people, "God" is a concrete noun which suggests a corresponding substance, something or someone which underlies the predicates assigned to Him. The Subject is independent of the predicates as the noun is of its adjectives. Modern philosophers have noted that this grammatical prejudice played an analogous role in classical philosophy which favored substantives over verbs and prepositions. Bertrand Russell argues that such linguistic bias led to the erroneous notion that "every proposition can be regarded as attributing a property to a single thing, rather than as expressing a relation between two or more things." It is to avoid such theological limitations that Kaplan insists that God be considered as a functional, not a substantive noun, a correlative term which implies relationship, e.g., as teacher implies pupil and king implies subjects.

Yet, the inherited language of traditional theology and prayer reflects the dominance of the Subject. And it is the Subject, whether described through the categories of classic or modern metaphysics or the biblical notion of a divine Personality, which is regarded as alone unqualifiedly real, objective and independent, and worthy of worship.

THE DEPRESSION OF THE PREDICATES

What happens to the predicates of divinity within the systems of traditional theology? They live under the shadow of the Subject and at its mercy. Characteristically, theologians have qualified them out of their independent and affirmative meaning. They may be analyzed away as negative qualities, puns (homonyms), equivocal or essentially incomprehensible. All that is known for sure is that God is, or that God is He who is, i.e., that God is Subject. But as to His character, His attributes, these must be accepted with a grain of salt. The caution over ascribing literal meaning to the predicates of divinity derives from a sensitivity to the charge that in so doing we are projecting our own human values upon the Subject. Even the Biblical theologians, who will have nothing to do with the bloodless negative theology of the philosophers, tend to suppress the moral predicates of the living God. For they sense that to hold firmly to the moral connotation of the divine predicates, to cling to the positive and humanly comprehensible meaning of such attributes as goodness and justice and mercy is to risk playing havoc with the Subject.

THEODICIES DEFEND THE SUBJECT

Most especially when confronting the gnawing problem of evil and the suffering of innocence, the traditional theologian feels compelled to mute the original moral meaning of the predicates. To defend the Subject, and that is the core concern of all theodicies, the moral predicates must be rendered inapplicable to the Subject. Reciprocal divine human convenant or not, moral *imitatio dei* or not, confronted by the patent immorality of events, the theologian grows aware that the danger to the Subject comes from the moral predicates within. For the Jobian outrage with which the theological defenders of God must deal is based upon earlier belief in the moral predicates of divinity. Reluctantly but invariably the theodicies of Subject theology feel compelled to raise the divine Subject beyond the reach of the moral predicates. The underlying strategy of traditional theodicies is to render the Subject invulnerable from the internal attack of the moral predicates. The warm and full-blooded intimacy with a personal moral God must be cooled. The moral attributes originally ascribed to the divine Subject are now discovered to be *qualitatively* other than the same moral attributes ascribed to human conduct. The meaning of God's goodness is not simply "more than" human goodness, it is "wholly other," apart from the connotation it possesses in the domain of human affairs. Over and again, relief is found in the assertion that the Subject's ways are not the ways of man, nor Its thoughts ours. It is a costly defense. For the denial of the human comprehensibility of the moral attributes of God is accompanied by the denial of human competence to make moral judgment. If "good and evil" in the eyes of God are construed as qualitatively different from that understood by man, then man's judgment and emulation of God's moral traits are invalidated.

MORAL PREDICATES CHALLENGE THE SUBJECT

Karl Barth articulates the root case for Subject theology in bold fashion. "Strictly speaking" he asserts, "there is no divine predicate, no idea of God which can have as its special content *what* God is. There is strictly speaking only the Divine Subject as such and in Him the fitness of His divine predicates." While few Biblical theologians flaunt the absolute autonomy and independence of the divine Personality as openly as Barth does, in the last analysis, and particularly before the onslaught of innocent suffering, they too resort to the same argument. God's ultimate retort to the Jobian plaint draws upon the inscrutability and freedom of He who is. The moral predicates normally assigned to Him must fade away. For faith in the moral predicates would mean the right to challenge the Subject. But it is the Subject who judges the predicates and who assigns it meaning. The divine Subject's disclosures cannot be questioned or held to any single, constant meaning by the standards of the moral predicates.

With Subject theology, faith in God is faith in the Subject itself, independent of the attributes. The love of God is not justified by man's appreciation of His qualities, for that would set man above God and limit the freedom of God. The unconditional love of God is for the divine Ego, for the Personality. However God may appear to act, whatever moral contradictions may appear in His conduct, the height of faith demands acceptance of the Subject beyond the predicates.

THE SCHISM WITHIN DIVINITY

Inadvertently traditional theology is compelled to sever the Subject from the predicates of Divinity. For it, the proper subject of theology is the Subject. The moral predicates seem all too human. This separation of Subject and predicate is reflected in the growing tension between faith and morality, the divine and the human. In his *Meaning of God* and throughout his works, Kaplan expresses his sensitivity to the schism we have described by warning against the erroneous theological view which conceives of God and man as separate and distinct, "with man, on the one hand, enslaved by his physical self, by his fellow man, or by his own tools, and on the other hand, God completely transcendent, in Himself absolutely, free, dispensing the gift of freedom."

THE "WHY" AND THE "WHO"

The mind-set which allows the Divine personality to swallow up the moral predicates and frames God as the Subject, conditions the believer to see the world in a particular fashion, to raise certain questions and to accept only certain answers. To draw some of the implications of this orientation, let us examine a typical benediction informed by Subject theology. The prayer which proclaims "God heals the sick" entails a number of presuppositions. The liturgical language suggests a linear causal relationship between the Subject and the patient. In recovery, all praise is due the Subject. Should the patient fail to be healed or indeed die, theological explanation of the tragic event again must refer to the Subject alone. For however the competences of the physician and attendants may be involved in the cure or the failure, these are secondary factors which for satisfactory explanation must be traced to the sole agent who directly or obliquely heals or restrains the hands from healing. Which rabbi has not experienced the series of "whys" in such crises! "Why did he die?" "Why did he have to suffer?" "Why did it happen to him?" No explanation of the tragedy in terms of congenital or contagious disease, ignorance, neglect or accident is acceptable to the questioner. For these explanations are regarded as secular, naturalistic, human accounts which ignore the divine Subject who ultimately controls the destiny of men. "Why" questions are the consequence of "Who" formulations; and the latter legitimates only certain kinds of explanations.

THEODICY SUBJECT LEADS TO RELIGIOUS MASOCHISM

Only answers which refer to the will or design of the Subject may put an end to the limitless "whys." And, insofar as many of the events to be explained patently violate the moral expectations expressed in the moral attributes of divinity, the situation can be saved only by mind-reading the intention of the inscrutable God. Somehow we are to be persuaded that the affliction is not truly bad or else that it is deserved. Our predicates are not His, but whatever His are they must be good. It is not for naught that so much of the theodicies of Subject theology lend themselves to exercises or religious masochism.

As a consequence of such Subject theodicy, the identification of the "acts of God" with those phenomena which are unpredictable, uncontrollable and inimical to man is irresistible. For it is precisely where men are incompetent and impotent to act that God's hand appears to be unmistakably revealed. Hurricane, earthquake and whirlwind appear as the unambiguous bearers testifying to the divine Subject's free will.

Contrariwise, where men participate in the curative process, the acts of healing are merely human, at best derivative. The acts of God are not the acts of men, else we flirt dangerously with humanism.

THE PERCEPTION OF PREDICATE THEOLOGY

How different is it to invert the prayer that God heals so that it reflects the belief that that which heals is divine? The newer formulation directs our attention to the natural realm in which transactions between man and his environment take place in the process of healing the sick. The vertical relationship between Subject and patient is horizontalized. We no longer look for "Elohut" in the unknowable designs of a supra-moral personality, but in the activities whose qualities we experientially discover as sacred. We learn that healing is dependent upon the non-human givenness of energies, the potentially curative powers which remain dormant without the will, competence and moral purpose of men. We come to recognize that actualization of these potencies depends upon the training, skill and dedication of researchers, medical practitioners, nurses and the manner in which a society chooses to dispense these powers. These activities manifest qualities of intelligence, cooperation, and responsibility which are not dismissed casually as merely human or simply secular or only natural. They are the significant signs which are daily with us, morning, noon and evening, and testify to the reality of "Elohut."

GOOD AND EVIL NOT PERSONALIZED

In what sense are these signs of divinity? What makes them divine is not their lodging in some alleged Subject. They are sacred not because they inhere in any person or supraperson, but because they are instrumentally or intrinsically good. The discovered qualities of Godliness reside in no single thing but in relationships through which they exhibit their sacred character. Elohut or Godliness, then, describes the way the predicates of divinity are organized and coordinated. Sickness, suffering, death, according to the predicate view of divinity, are real but their origin stems neither from a benevolent or a malevolent Subject. Good and evil are not personalized in the form of a God or a Satan. They are neither rewards nor punishments visited upon us by a mysterious Subject. The painful reality of accident, negligence, greed are neither divinized nor demonized. Blame, responsibility, guilt are not foisted upon another realm wherein the Subject needs be either exonerated or condemned.

Suffering and evil, fault and responsibility are taken seriously by predicate theology; but the latter invites different expectations and demands different human responses from those which are generated by Subject theology. The Job of predicate theology is sensitive to the evils which beset man, but his questions are not directed towards a plotting, purposing, supra-human Ego nor are his friends raised in a theological atmosphere which prompts them to decipher the hidden motives of a morally remote Subject. The Job of predicate theology and his friends look elsewhere for explanation and for response. They would examine the "how" and "where" and "what" which brought forth the pain of the situation, in order to call upon the powers of Elohut in and between them and the environment so as to bind the bruises and to act so as to avoid repetition of the tragedy.

PREDICATE PRAYER

To reverse the Subject and Predicate of theology is no idle grammatical inversion. It proposes that we reflect upon the predicates of divinity as the proper subject of our theological concern. Not the attribute of the Divinity but the divinity of the attribute requires our attention. The form of our traditional Subject liturgy is focused upon an It or Thou or He. In the coin of the traditional benediction it is a "who" to whom all praise is due; a "who" brings forth the bread from the earth. Predicate liturgy would invert the formula so that religious attention and appreciation is directed to the givenness of earth and seed and sun and water, to the preparation of the soil, the weeding, ploughing and nurturing of the field, the reaping, winnowing, grinding of the wheat, the kneading, seasoning and baking of the dough and to the equitable distribution of bread to those in need. "Brukhah elohut hamotziah lehem min ha-aretz." Blessed is Elohut which brings forth bread from the earth. The prayer form celebrates the reverent acknowledgment of those values and qualities which through human effort unite to satisfy the needs of man.

These divine qualities are not invented but are discovered in society. They are revealed not by or through some hypostatized existence above or beyond or beneath the world in which we live, but in and through our transactions with each other. They are located in the this-worldly hyphenated realm of I-thou-we which Buber has called "betweenness." They are disclosed in the values discovered through the relationship "between" self and other, "between" self and community, "between" self and the environment. The discovered attributes are as real as living, as objective as our social agreement and our community's acceptance of the consequence of their use, as significant as love, justice and peace are for our lives. And because discovery and confirmation of divine attributes is an on-going process coterminous with the life of our people, Elohut is not fixed forever. As long as the community of faith is open to life, no predicates reign immutable, no set of predicates can exhaust the changing and expanding character of Godliness.

THE CATEGORY MISTAKE

But where is Godliness in all this discussion? Where is "Elohut" located? The question is itself inherited from the vertical view of Subject theology. On our analysis the question stems from what philosophers have termed a category mistake. Gilbert Ryle's questioner also sought to know where exactly the "university" is, even after being shown the faculties and facilities, the student-body and alumni. His query could not be answered, not because the "university" is not real or important or objective, but because "university" does not function logically like the term gymnasium which can be inventoried as an item alongside the laboratory. The university is not illusory, an imaginary, arbitrary invention. One can not point to the university because the university is simply not a thing among things but the way in which all that has been pointed out is organized and inter-related. The university is no mysterious entity beyond those events which have been exhibited. Analogously, Elohut or Godliness refers to the way the predicates a tradition discovers, accepts and names as divine are related. Elohut, like university, has a unitive function. Elohut, Godliness is One in that it unites and relates the godly attributes. Unlike Subject theology, the unity of the predicates is not maintained by virtue of their belonging to some independent Subject. The oneness of Elohut is found in the common relationship of all the predicates to goodness. Intelligence, compassion, justice, peace, etc., are named divine when they serve ends which the community of faith judges to be good.

PREDICATE THEOLOGY IN A POST-HOLOCAUSTAL WORLD

Predicate theology is not for all persons. Some may think it too prosaic, too natural, too human. Others may think it denies the mystique of the wholly other Subject. But for many others, living in a post-holocaustal world, the older consolations and mysteries of traditional theologies and theodicies take too high a moral toll. In this Nietzsche spoke for the modern consciousness: "To look upon nature as if it were proof of the goodness and care of a God; to interpret history in honor of a divine reason, as a constant testimony to a moral order in the world and a moral final purpose; to explain personal experiences as pious men have long enough explained them, as if everything were a dispensation or intimation of Providence, something planned and set on behalf of the salvation of the soul: all that is passed; it has conscience against it."

For too many the alternative to the traditional presuppositions and forms of Subject theology is simply the abandonment of the God-idea together with all of religious sensibilities. The twists and turns of traditional theology before the face of Auschwitz appear to them as desperate rationalizations, worse, as a betrayal of the moral stance. For them, to save God the Subject at the expense of faith in the moral attributes of divinity is to be left standing before a naked God. To have faith in the Subject alone strikes them as at least amoral. Feuerbach warned that devils too believe in God. What is important then is not faith in a Subject God but in the character of divinity which serves as a model for our own lives. The criterion of theological meaningfulness remains that of C. S. Peirce. The serious theologian must ask, "Suppose this proposition were true, what conceivable bearing might it have on the conduct of our lives?" After the traditional theodicies are over we are left with a God beyond morality. Belief in such a God, for many, makes no moral difference. Following Peirce's criterion, William James concluded "a difference that makes no difference is no difference." Predicate theology deserves to be considered by those who require a conceptualization of God which will reflect the primacy of a moral ideal respectful of man's moral capacities, one recognizing divinity in his creativity and demanding his responsibility. This is entailed in the shift from Subject to Predicate, from noun to adjectival characterization of divinity, from substantival entity to transactional process of the idea of God.

TWO DIFFICULTIES

Aside from the problems which some have in identifying divine qualities as real without some substantival base, there appear two ancillary blocks to predicate theology. One of these is apprehension over its emphasis upon the moral essence of divinity which seems to reduce religion to ethics. The other difficulty questions the legitimacy of employing such terms as godly, divine and godliness to describe what are primarily ethical qualities.

I would answer the first question by pointing out that, while ethical concern and behavior must lie at the heart of the God-idea and of religion, there is far more in belonging to a community of faith than belief in a moral deity. Judaism includes ritual and liturgical reflection, an entire gamut of affective, cognitive and celebratory activities and a central fidelity to the career and destiny of our world people. Our discussion of the God-idea in no way is meant to reduce the religious phenomenon to ethical culture or philosophy.

As far as the use of terms such as divinity, Elohut and godliness, these are chosen for three reasons.

(a) There is a commonality of interest and value between traditional and modern conceptions of divinity which is expressed by allegiance to certain sacred terms. Godliness, godly, Elohut express the nexus between my ancestors and myself. However critically different the many forms of Jewish theology may be, what they hold in common, and thus what is the essential core which unites them, are the moral predicates which are to be lived out in our lives. Analogously, the myths of the Bible, e.g., the Garden of Eden episode, the deluge and Tower of Babel, the miracles in Egypt, are differently interpreted by different generations. Although I may question their historical accuracy, they remain significant because the common moral intention of their telling can be translated in non-miraculous terms. Does a non-Orthodox interpretation of the Torah lose thereby its legitimation as a sacred text? The diverse theological forms in which the divine qualities are posited ought not eclipse the sanctity of the attributes which express our faith and direct our behavior.

FROM SECULAR TO SACRED

(b) The briefest rehearsal of the history of Jewish theology from Philo to Kaplan will offer evidence that each reflective thinker of Judaism has proposed conceptions of God quite other than that which is found in the Biblical text. Maimonides' reconstruction of the God-idea might have been, and indeed was challenged, on the grounds that his notions of an incorporeal deity and of negative attributes were foreign to the Scriptural text. To establish monopoly on the use of God-terms would serve only to arrest theological freedom. To submit to a monolithic semantics would stymie theological response to the intellectual and moral demands of our people and would put a halt to theological progress.

(c) Terms like godly or divine are emotionally charged. They are used to express the ultimate significance which a community of faith attaches to certain qualities. The identification and naming of such predicates as divine mean to raise them out of the ordinary, "merely" secular into the realm of the sacred. The incorporation of values into the realm of Elohut, into the liturgical vocabulary of our faith-language is no casual act. The naming acts which call "peace" or "justice" divine are critical in articulating the conscious spiritual tasks and purpose of a people.

In his haunting novel *The Accident*, Eli Wiesel portrays the tortured spirit of Sarah, the prostitute-saint of the death camp. His hero cries out that "whoever listens to Sarah and doesn't change, whoever enters

Sarah's world and does not invent new gods and new religions, deserves death and destruction."

Wiesel is a traditionalist, but he cannot endure the thought of theology and religion as usual after Auschwitz. Theological and liturgical sameness is not of itself a tribute to tradition, especially when that tradition records so much courage and audacity in propounding new ideas of God and new ways to commune with the divine.

Our proposals for predicate theology and predicate liturgy, despite the dispassionate and analytic character of its presentation, is one response to Wiesel's challenge. Its intention is to help those embittered by the absurdity of the Holocaust, and upset by the amoral tones of the defense of God after Auschwitz, to look again and differently at the face of Elohut. It is meant for those who cannot go home again using the old routes, but who may learn to believe and pray and celebrate again through another way. We are an old-new people and we require old-new ways to renew our connection with our ancestor's faith. From Elohim to Elohut is not a path away, but towards our spiritual renewal and reconciliation.

The experience of the Holocaust represents one of the watershed events in Jewish history. Its horror and intensity raise profound questions about the nature of a God who is both good and powerful. How could the horror have occurred?

SEYMOUR SIEGEL tries to cope with the theological problems raised by the Holocaust. He points out that theological reflection should yield viable approaches to those problems.

First, there ought to be an abandonment of the notion of the perfectability of human nature. In the real world the human being is capable of both the greatest self-sacrifice and the greatest inhumanity to his fellow. This is the eternal dual nature of the human spirit. "Utopian Man died at Auschwitz." Faith in God means believing in Him despite the trials and doubts that emerge from encountering radical evil. Faith, meaning "trust" *(emunah),* implies a relationship that endures even though there is tension, puzzlement, and questioning. Siegel calls attention to the profound doctrine of *hastarat panim,* the "hiding of the Face." This doctrine teaches that in history, when evil accumulates in gigantic quantities, the Divine Face is covered up: God withdraws from the affairs of men, awaiting a return. This doctrine offers a meaningful approach to the time of the Holocaust, a time of *hastarat panim.*

The very perverseness of the Holocust shows in an uncanny way that there is something special about the Jew. He is singled out for special suffering. Could this not be a sign of the chosenness of the people of Israel, who, because of their divine dimension, arouse the hatred and fury of those who are against God? Therefore, Siegel concludes, every Jew must live two lives: one for himself and one for those who perished. This is the peculiar and holy destiny of the Jew in the post-Holocaust age.

XIX.

Theological Reflections on the Destruction of European Jewry

SEYMOUR SIEGEL

IT IS WITH *d'hilu u-r'himu* that I begin to speak. The subject is too vast, the problems too agonizing for words. *L'kha dumiah tehilah.* But speak we must, otherwise we would not be forced to clarify our thoughts, and clarification of thinking is also part of divine worship.

The events we discuss this morning are among the most momentous events in Jewish history-perhaps in all history. They involve horrors that defy description and called forth heroism which seems to go beyond human limitations.

One of the most horrible paragraphs in all literature is the first sentence of a first-person account of the last days of the Warsaw Ghetto:

> The ghetto was burning—for days and nights it flamed, and the fire consumed house after house, entire streets. Nearby, on the other side of the wall, citizens of the capital strolled, played and enjoyed themselves.[1]

It is a damning criticism of our times that the events we commemorate here have not resulted in a radical revision of our thinking on the crucial problems of existence—both individual and Jewish—and that books on Judaism in the fifties and the sixties are not much different from those written in the thirties and forties.

The task I have been assigned is to point out some theological consequences which emerge from the contemplation of the tragedy we commemorate today. I cannot offer solutions to the agonizing question of how God could allow children to be cast into the gas ovens. To attempt to do so would be both presumptuous and foolish. I cannot— nor can any human being—offer an illustrated map of the mind of God.

I will, however, attempt to offer some reflections and suggestions as to the directions in which our thinking should move in the light of the European tragedy.

THE NATURE OF MAN

When we consider what has happened, and how it happened, and the reactions of the vast majority of those who were responsible for what has happened, one echoes the words of one of the survivors: *es iz gevehn a harpeh tzu leben*, it was shameful to be alive.[2]

Once and for all, we should put to rest all utopian views of man, all views which see human nature as perfectable, as basically rational. We should recognize the immense strength of the demonic forces which reside within the human breast—demonic forces which do not result from bad education or poverty but from the perversity of human nature which caused even God to regret the fact that He had created us. The evil inherent in human nature is not the result of the jungle which evolution eventually will conquer. It is not the result of a lack of evolution; its very ferocity is due to our enormous development. Our infinite imaginations, our awesome power and our need for security make almost anything possible.

We cannot, of course, yield to a corrosive pessimism. This would make existence too much to bear. Man seesaws in history between animality and divinity. "Like a pendulum, he swings to and fro." Man is potentially the most wicked of all beings, because spirit and animality are so curiously intertwined in our natures. Animals eat. Only men are gluttons. Animals have sex. Only men are lustful. Animals kill each other. Only men construct Dachaus. Man is also potentially the most exalted of all beings, for he is given the gift of freedom and the awesome responsibility of completing the work of creation—to guard the destiny of God in the world. To recognize both the misery and the grandeur of human nature is a task we must undertake.

In a world which has experienced Auschwitz, we must breach utopianism once and for all. We must abandon the dream that all problems are theoretically solvable, that we can perfect society through our own efforts.

The Torah is the antidote to the *yetzer hara*. But, alas, all too frequently the poison is stronger than the remedy. We are bidden to improve conditions, to fight for justice, for truth, for decency. But let us not underestimate our enemy, which possesses the power of the demonic and which has infiltrated every level of existence, including that of the Holy itself.

זמן נתן לעולם כמה שנים יעשה באפילה שכל זמן שיצר הרע בעולם אפל וצלמות בעולם
(בראשית רבה פא:א).

We cannot solve the problem of evil completely. But we are not exempt from dealing with evils. "At the end of days evil will be conquered by the one. In historic times, evils must be conquered one by one."[3] Great cities, millions of people, ideas, institutions, governments, dreams, and plans all lay in ruins at the end of the war. Utopian man died then, too.

THE NATURE OF PROVIDENCE

One question keeps repeating itself over and over again. How could God allow all of this to happen?

David Hume expressed the dilemma:

> If he is willing to prevent evil, but is not able,
> then he is impotent.
>
> If he is able, but not willing, then he is malevolent.
>
> If he is both able and willing, why then evil?[4]

The ancient problem of evil arises because three assertions are held to be true.

1. evil is real
2. God is good
3. God is omnipotent

Historically, solutions of the problem have tended to deny one of these propositions. Evil is not real (Oriental mysticism); God is not necessarily good (Islam) or He is not omnipotent (the "limited God" theory of Brightman). These solutions deny the heart of religion.

There have been other suggestions as well. It has been asserted that suffering chastens, that it enobles, that it tests a person's character. It has been pointed out that *tzohar* (brilliance) and *tzarah* (suffering) have the same letters, that *leid* leads to *mitleid*.

Inflict thy promises with each occasion of distress—that from our incoherence we may learn to put our trust in thee and brutal fact persuade us to adventure, art, and peace (W. H. Auden).

All of these assertions, part of the literature of religion, may make suffering palatable, but not understandable. They certainly have little relevance when we speak of suffering in the dimension of the European holocaust.

What can we say? Let me suggest some lines of consideration or meditation rather than explanation.

It is a major premise of our faith that God is all-powerful. Otherwise He would not be God. However, in the Jewish view, God may be understood to be limited, not by other divinities but by Himself. He is limited because He has given man freedom to choose, and He has given freedom to nature to operate according to natural law.

The price for this freedom is the possibility of suffering—a suffering which God Himself endures.

בשעה שאדם מצטער שכינה מה לשון אומרת, כביכול קלני מראשי קלני מזרועי (משנה
סנהדרין ו:ה).

If every time a man tried to stab his fellow the knife would become blunt, if every time he put his hand into the pocket of his neighbor he could not withdraw it, then the sheer impossibility of committing evil would propel men in the direction of the good, and there would be little or no merit in doing it.

Without the power to produce its sinners, mankind could not produce its saints. The ability to sin is man's greatest distinction. God is omnipotent. But He has given us the power to create history, and we cannot commit the folly of shifting the responsibility for our debacles to God. Providence is the potential power to control events, the power to shape evil events into good consequences.

אתם חשבתם עלי רעה, אלקים חשבה לטובה.

The evil remains evil, terribly evil. But the power of God working through men and through the contingencies of nature and history pushes events into good ends.

In understanding the events of our time we would do well to reconsider the ancient concept of *hastarat panim*. Man first hides from God. He disobeys Him. The will of God is to be with us, to be manifest. "But the doors of the world are slammed on Him, His truth is betrayed. He withdraws, leaving man to Himself."[5] Can this be a partial explanation for our tragedy?

It has been pointed out that, in our tradition, "God is a *hiding* God, not a *hidden* God."[6] He makes darkness His hiding place. History is now a mystery. We know only hints and guesses now. In the end, we will know the meaning of our anguish and our suffering.

דברים שהם מכוסים מכם בעולם הזה עתידים הם שיהיו גלוים להם (פסיקתא, פרה).

History yields only partial meanings. But when there is *hastarat panim*, we can pray with the Psalmist: "How long, O Lord, will You forget me forever, how long will You hide Your face from me?" (Psalms 13:2)

These notions do not pretend to be an answer. The mystery remains, the questions remain on our lips and in our hearts. But perhaps we can begin to understand.

THE NATURE OF FAITH

Much has been written about the nature of faith. Faith is not the acceptance of intellectual propositions alone. Faith involves a relationship which persists even though we cannot fully comprehend the ways of the One in Whom we have faith. Though we lack understanding, we have the certainty of relation, of concern for us. Though we cannot explain God, we can speak to Him. We can still ask ourselves to love the Lord with all our hearts, even though we live in the age of Auschwitz. This is the meaning of *emunah*. Two quotations from contemporary writers explain this eloquently.

In this our own time, one asks again and again: how is a Jewish life still possible after Oświęcim? I would like to frame this question more correctly: how is a life with God still possible in a time in which there is an Oświęcim? The estrangement has become too cruel, the hiddenness too deep. One can still "believe" in the God who allowed those things, but can one still speak to Him? Can one still hear His word? Can one still, as an individual and as a people, enter at all into a dialogic relationship with Him? Can one still call to Him? Dare we recommend to the survivors of Oświęcim, the Job of the gas chambers: "Call to Him, for He is kind, for His mercy endurest forever"?

But how about Job himself? He not only laments, but he charges that the "cruel" God has "removed his right" from him and thus that the judge of all the earth acts against justice. And he receives an answer from God. But what God says to him does not answer the charge; it does not even touch upon it. The true answer that Job receives is God's appearance only, only this that distance turns into nearness, that "his eye sees Him," that he knows Him again. Nothing is explained, nothing adjusted; wrong has not become right, nor cruelty kindness. Nothing has happened but that man again hears God's address.

The mystery has remained unsolved, but it has become his, it has become *man's*.

And we?

We—by that is meant all those who have not got over what happened and will not get over it. How is it with us? Do we stand overcome before the hidden face of God as the tragic hero of the Greeks before faceless fate? No, rather even now we contend, we too, with God, even with Him, the Lord of Being, Whom we once, we here, chose for our Lord. We do not put up with earthly being, we struggle for its redemption, and struggling we appeal to the help of our Lord, Who is again and still a hiding one. In such a state we await His voice, whether it come out of the storm or out of a stillness which follows it. Though His coming appearance resemble no earlier one, we shall recognize again our cruel and merciful Lord.[7]

I have said that I do not know what the meaning is of this desert of thick darkness that shuts us in. But by means of this religious approach I find myself facing in the positive direction, and not the reverse. It is as though two men were together standing on a narrow, obscure path. This path is the pessimism common to both. Then the one turns with all his might in the direction of No, and there he remains standing, while the other turns with all his might in the direction of Yes—yes, there is a meaning to all this.

Thus turned, this man cannot stand still. He has started on a long weary road. He wants with all his will to be among those who seek the Face and pursue righteousness. But from that man God hides His face. An opaque screen holds him asunder from the living God. For all his trying to come nearer and to touch the outer fringe, he cannot. It will not be given him to appear before the presence, to hear the voice or to understand the meaning of these massacrings, this wanton butchery. Yet, he can do no other than to persist in his quest to the last, to keep on inquiring, struggling, challenging. He will not be granted tranquillity of soul. But if it be given him to renew the forces of his being day by day and constantly to be among the seekers, the rebellious—that is the crown of his life and the height of his desire.

It is said of Rabbi Isaac Levi of Berdichev that he spoke thus:

I do not ask, Lord of the world, to reveal to me the secrets of *Thy* ways—I could not comprehend them. I do not ask to know why I suffer, but only this: Do I suffer for *Thy* sake?

For us, too, it would be enough to ask, not *what* is the meaning of this anguish, but that it *have* a meaning; and that our need of asking be so sincere that it becomes a prayer.

Teach us only this: Does man suffer for *Thy* sake, O Lord?[8]

It is only with this faith that we who have witnessed so much death can live.

THE NATURE OF JEWISH EXISTENCE

We must bring our minds and our hearts to again contemplate what it means to be a Jew. We are challenged, threatened, persecuted. "It is either tragic or holy to be a Jew." The very fury of the events which we speak of this day, their very irrationality betrays to us that there is something mysterious, something unique about Jewish existence. Being a Jew is not merely a natural phenomenon. In a curious, uncanny, and tragic way, anti-Semitism is the other side of the coin of chosen-ness. The violent enmity against the Jew of totalitarians of all stripes, shows that the Jew by his very being is an affront to those who would enslave man and claim sovereignty over the whole person. This is the tragic yet awesome quality of Jewishness. The natural inclination is to sacrifice chosen-ness:

אל חנון

קלייב אויס אן אנדער פאָלק

דערוויייל

מיהר זיינען מיד פון שטאָרבען

מיהר האָבן קיין תפילות מעהר

קלייב אויס אן אנדער פאָלק

דערוויייל

מיהר האבן ניט קיין בלוט מעהר

אויף צו זיין אַ קרבן

אל חנון

גיב פּראָסטע בגדים אונז

פון פאסטעכער פון שאָף

פון שמידן ביי דער האמער

און נאָך איין חסד טו אונדז

נעם פון אונז דיין שכינה.[9]

Merciful God
Choose another people
We are exhausted of dying
We have no prayers left
Choose another people

We have no blood left
To be a sacrifice
Merciful God
Give us coarse clothes
Of shepherds of sheep
Of smiths by the hammer
And do us one more kindness
Take away your Presence from us.

However, in the light of all that has happened, can we give up the essence of our Jewishness? To be a Jew is a high destiny, to witness to the Almighty. This witness all too often arouses fury and hatred. We dare not give up our destiny.

THE NATURE OF OUR RESPONSIBILITIES

One final thought comes to mind. We cannot explain how all that happened was possible. But we can understand what we must do, because it has happened. We can rededicate ourselves to the belief that without Torah we will be overwhelmed by the evil which is part of our natures. We must realize that every hour we fight on a spiritual battlefield where millions have already perished. We must commit ourselves to the fight for human betterment with realism, dedication and devotion.

We cannot forget those that perished. Nor can we forget that being a Jew is a high destiny, that the values of Judaism are precious and not to be lightly sacrificed for the sake of embracing Western culture, which— let us repeat it daily—created Auschwitz. Let us not forsake the moral and intellectual values created within Jewish life. The West, with all its great institutions, has proven to be a tragic failure. If nothing else, it is incumbent upon those of us who have survived to take the place of those who have perished. We must teach it diligently to our children when we sit down and when we go in the way and put it on the doorposts of our houses: this is a people which bears the awesome badge of suffering, suffering brought about not by accidents of nature but through the demonic forces which so often take possession of man.

More than that, each of us has to live two lives, one for ourself and one in proxy for a life that has been destroyed.

Who can fathom God's ways? His thoughts are not our thoughts. But we must believe that in some way the suffering of our people has brought the redemption of mankind closer. I once thought this last statement to be callous and presumptuous. But then I read a collection of poems, statements, stories and songs composed by victims of the *Shoah*. I should like to close with reading a page from that book.

טויזענטער מענשען, לעבעדיקע, געזונטע, לעבענס־וויליקע געהען צו דער שחיטה. מען
שפּרייזט מיט אָפּגעלאָזענע שריט אפּאַטיש גלייכגילטיק. דער שאָטן פֿון טויט ליגט שוין אויף
אונז אַלע. לעבען מיהר שטיילט זיך אויס פֿון דער מאַסע אַ געשטאַלט אַ הויכער עלטערער איד
מיט אַ פּאַטריאַכעלער גרויער באָרד . . . עהר טראָגט טלית און תפילין אונטערן אָרעם ניט
מעהר. זיצט מען אַזוי אין צרות און יאוש. פֿלוצלינג גיט זיך דער אַלטער איד מיטן טלית און
תפילין אַ שטעל אויף האַסטיק און גיט אַ גיט אַ זעג מיט אַ שטאַרקער און זיכערער שטים — אידען
זייט ניט צוטראַגען זייט ניט מרה ניט שחורה'דיק וואָס זיצט איהר אַזוי? נאָר ניט אין עצבות חס
ושלום נאָר ניט אין יאוש וואָלט איך געהאַט בראָנפּען וואָלט איך לחיים געטרונקען לחיים אידען
לחיים זעט איהר דען ניט ווי מיר געהען משיח'ן אַנטקעגען.

Thousands of people, living, healthy, life-loving, go to the slaughter, marching with shuffling feet, apathetic, indifferent. The shadow of death already hovers over all of us. Near me there stands out a figure of a tall, old Jew with a patriarchal, grey beard. . . . He carries his *talis* and *tephillin* under his arm. Nothing more. . . . Thus we were in tribulation and despair. Suddenly, the old Jew with the *talis* and *tephillin* jumps up and speaks with a strong and confident voice. Jews, do not be troubled! Do not be melancholy! Why do you sit thus! Not in sadness, God forbid. If I would only have something to drink, I would propose a *lechayim. Lechayim*, Jews, *Lechayim*. Do you not see how we are going to greet the messiah?[10]

NOTES

1. Ziviah Lubetkin, *The Last Days of the Warsaw Ghetto, Commentary*, May, 1947, Vol. III, No. 5, p. 401.

2. Quoted in *Kiddush Hashem*, ed. S. Niger, (*Cyco Bicher-Farlag*, 1948), p. 27.

3. A. J. Heschel, *God in Search of Man*, p. 377.

4. *Dialogues Concerning Natural Religion*, quoted from C. W. Hendel, *Hume Selections*, (New York: Scribners, 1927), p. 365.

5. A. J. Heschel, *Man is Not Alone*, p. 153.

6. *Ibid.*

7. Martin Buber, *At the Turning*, (New York: Farrar Straus and Young, 1952), pp. 61-62.

8. Judah Magnes, *In The Perplexity of The Times*, (Jerusalem: The Hebrew University, 1946), pp. 77-78.

9. Kadya Maladovska, *Der Melekh David Iz Alein Gebliben*, pp.3-9.

10. *Kiddush Hashem*, op. cit., pp.27-28.

According to MILTON STEINBERG, intelligence or common sense leads to affirmation of God. The "disquiet of the spirit" which spurs man on to preoccupation with the God-faith stems both from "straight curiosity" and from an "unquenchable hope of the human heart." A decision must be made, however, with regard to faith. One must decide because one's idea of the cosmos will affect his character. One must also make a decision because life puts one into situations where decisions must be made.

Arguments against the origin of religious institutions are in no way relevant to the God-faith, since the value of an idea or practice depends not on its origins but on its ultimate validity for thought and action. Science cannot provide ultimate meaning because it deals only with tangible phenomena, offering description and not interpretation, and because each science deals with only a limited aspect of reality. Yet religion deals with the "known" as much as science does. God is, according to Steinberg, the "only tenable" explanation for what we know about the universe: its organic unity, its dynamism, its creativity, its rationality, its purposiveness and consciousness. These indicate the value of the God-faith even given the problem of evil. Steinberg asserts that man also needs to believe in God in order to live "joyously, hopefully, healthfully." On a purely practical level, such a positive view of the world cannot but elevate the quality of life. Hence, the God-faith is essential to human morality, as well. Without it, there is no real ground for human idealism and self-sacrifice. (See Simon Greenberg's essay for an elaboration of this last theme.)

After discussing the differences between immoral religionists and moral atheists, Steinberg points out that eventually the "contradiction between theory and practice must reveal itself." The former will have to yield to the pressures of doctrine; the latter, to rework his thinking. Jews have an added impetus to struggle toward the God-faith because of the uniqueness of their history.

XX.

The Common Sense of Religious Faith

MILTON STEINBERG

I

I. THE IMPORTANCE OF RELIGIOUS FAITH

DOES BELIEVING IN God make sense? Or is religious faith something for the ignorant, the muddleheaded, those too wishful, lazy, or cowardly to think the matter through?

This essay answers these questions in favor of religion. It argues that not only is intelligence no enemy to the affirmation of God, but that if a man will but think long enough, hard enough, broadly and freely enough, he will almost inevitably come to such an affirmation.

The case to be made will be all the way an appeal to reason and experience. At no time will the reader be asked to accept any proposition on any other ground. He is, of course, free to take recourse to authority or revelation if he feels the desire or need to do so. Neither figures in any fashion in the discussion that follows. . . .

Being in fact greater than creed alone, a religion is experienced and acquired in more ways than through reason. To one man, it will be primarily a matter of intuition and feeling, to another of tradition, to a third of morality or of esthetics, or of group solidarity, and to still another of some combination of all these. Indeed, a person may be intensely devout and yet be but little occupied with theology.

On the other hand, the religion of some people is basically intellectual. Philosophical reflection is, in many instances, the beginning of piety. . . .

The thesis of this essay, that common sense supports faith, must not be misunderstood. It does not mean that religion is intellectually a matter of common sense only. Religion among other things is an awareness of mystery and poetry, of that which is too deep or too subtle or too vast or too grand for human comprehension. Religion is furthermore a sensitivity to the realms beyond realms of possibility, in which, as Ibn Gabirol put it, "our thoughts weary themselves to find a stopping place." The "sense" of religion, in other words, is *uncommon* as well as *common*. But—and this is the crux of the matter—it is always *sense*. It may and should transcend reason, it must never run contrary to it.

One more preliminary observation. Every communion, as has already been indicated, propounds a *Weltanschauung*, a view of things. In some religions, Confucianism, for example, or early Buddhism, that view is nontheistic, being indifferent to the idea of God. Conceivably a church might be organized which would be actively atheistic, propagating a theory of reality which explicitly denied God. Jewish religion, on the other hand, and the faiths which derive from it are committed to theism, that is to say, they construe the universe in terms of a God, such a construction being essential to them. If the words "religious outlook" do not invariably connote theism, that is their usual meaning for us, and it is so that we shall understand them in the ensuing discussion.

II

Religion sets a philosophy of reality and life before men. But are they in need of it? Or is it something without which they can get along quite well?

Undeniably, some people can. These are the persons whom William James once characterized as "tough-minded." To them all abstract and nonpractical issues seem remote and artificial. They require no metaphysics, whether theistic, nontheistic, or atheistic.

Most men, however, would seem to belong to the "tender-minded," James's other class. The riddle of the universe haunts them. They are forever restless, aching to search out why things are as they are, what meaning they may have, what may be the good for which mankind exists, and why it is the good.

Whence comes this preoccupation, this disquiet of the spirit? Part of it is straight curiosity, a yearning to understand the awesome pageant which is the cosmos and the baffling experience which is life. That part is of one piece psychologically with the impulse that moves science. Another part expresses a deep and unquenchable hope of the human heart, that there may be an intelligible scheme to things, one sympathetic to man's ideals, so that his career may possess significance and his aspirations validity beyond himself and his brief span. The last motivation is practical. Men are ever being called on to decide between alternative courses of action. But what is right or wise as to conduct depends, at least partially, on the nature of reality and life. Given a cosmos of one character, one code of conduct may be indicated. In another sort of world another ethic may be appropriate. Willy-nilly then, the riddle of the universe keeps forcing itself on men.

That is why so much of mankind, including many of its keenest minds and noblest spirits, has always been so mightily exercised over theology. In it they have seen their classic opportunity, perhaps the sole one, to understand reality, find it congenial, and know how to deal with it and themselves.

Now too we can perceive why agnosticism, a permanent suspension of judgment, is inadequate, and all but impossible, for most men. It leaves the curiosity of the intellect unanswered, the hungers of the heart unsatisfied, the soul aquest after goodness unilluminated and uninspired. Worst of all, it leaves the hand undirected. Whatever else may be true about agnosticism, this much is certain: no one can practice it. Life forbids. Life is forever putting men into situations in which they *must* turn one way or the other, in which they *must* make up their minds, for the purpose of action if for nothing else, as to what is true and what false, what good and what evil. They may talk indecision to their heart's content, they must live decisively. To cap the climax, it is not true, as the agnostic claims, that only *his* position is consistent with intellectual integrity. For, as we shall soon discover, the evidences for the religious outlook are more than adequate to justify a decision in its favor. Mental honesty is no monopoly of anyone, let alone of those who refuse to make up their minds.

III

This discussion of the motivations behind faith should help to dispel the widespread misconception that religion has its origins in, and panders to, disreputable human interests. It was the fashion among eighteenth-century rationalists to account for it as the handiwork of witch doctors and priests eager to make a "good thing for themselves" of human credulity. Marxists habitually deprecate religion as the "opiate of the masses." Some of the advocates of the new dynamic psychology maintain that the beginnings of religion are to be sought in fear, or in the quest of a father substitute or in what not else.

Were all this completely true, it would be of only academic relevance, since the value of an idea or practice depends not on its origins but on the validity it eventually attains for thought and action. It would be as silly to condemn present day religion because of its supposed beginnings, as to reject chemistry because of its involvement, in ages gone by, with alchemy.

The truth is, however, that this argument against religion is only fractionally true in sober fact. No doubt fear, superstition, social manipulation, and class interest have had and continue to have a share in the rise and course of religion. Certainly religion, like all other human pursuits and institutions, has at times been perverted to the service of obscurantist or wicked causes. But that is neither the whole story nor even its larger part. Most fundamentally, religion is the expression of a thirst for understanding, a hope of meaning, a quest for goodness, and a sanction for it. These motivate religion on its deepest level. They make the cultivation of it a fascinating, unavoidable, and thoroughly legitimate enterprise.

But why religion for the fashioning of world outlooks? Why not science? Given its precise methods and careful disciplines, is it not a more reliable guide?

Science can help us in framing a philosophy of the universe. Indeed, we must look to it for most of the materials we use to that purpose. But it cannot itself do the job for us—and that for three reasons:

First, every science deals with some single and limited aspect of reality. This is the nature of a science, this the goal of its techniques and skills: to explore a particular category of things. Yet men are vitally interested not only in limited classes of things but in the nature of "things as a whole," and for "things as a whole" there is and can be no science. Here metaphysics, whether religious or not, must step in.

Second, science deals with phenomena, with that which can be weighed, measured, counted—in sum, with those objects and forces which can be grasped through sense perception or inferred from it. Beyond these, however, are vast areas of human concern with which science does not deal: the nature of the beautiful, of the good, of the ultimate reality, if there be one, of which phenomena are an outward manifestation. These are respectively the domain of aesthetics, ethics, philosophy, and theology.

Third, the function of a science is *description*, that of a world outlook *interpretation*. Every science describes some aspect of reality, rendering an account of *what* composes it and *how* it behaves. Even when science asks *why*, thus giving the appearance of engaging in interpretation, its question is always intended to evoke an answer in terms of cause and effect. Its very *why*, in other words, is really a *how*, a demand for a *description* of the fashion in which things come to be as they are. On the other hand, a world outlook, whether religious or not, has for its subject matter not the *what* and *how*, but *of what worth* and *to what end*, that is to say, issues of value and purpose. And when *it* inquires *why*, it is not with reference to cause and effect but to some possible ultimate reality in the light of which all else is illumined.

Religion and science operate then in different spheres. Not, as some have suggested, because science deals with the known and religion with the unknown. Both deal with the known, and from it leap to the unknown. The materials are the same; it is the purposes which are different. One confines itself to parts, the other to the whole. One busies itself with the quantitative and the phenomenal, the other with whatever may be outside and beyond these categories. One is devoted to description even when it seems to interpret and evaluate, the other entirely to interpretation and evaluation even when it appears to describe.

In sum, science is, as it were, a camera which furnishes schematic photographs of reality, whereas religion uses these photographs—and those supplied by other forms of human experience—to arrive at a judgment of the character of reality, whether it be sane or insane, purposeful or blind, good or evil. Whence it follows that religion has every reason to hail scientific progress, since the better the camera, the clearer and more trustworthy the pictures available for interpretative and evaluative purposes.

But if so, why the protracted and bitter conflict between religion and science?

Most of the fault for this unhappy condition rests with religion, but some with science also.

Religion has been guilty of invading areas where it has no business, of trying to tell the scientist what the facts of the world are: how old it is, for example, or how man came into being, or whether natural laws are suspendible. Even graver, it has at times advocated authoritarianism, seeking to limit freedom of inquiry or to dictate its results in advance.

In other words, religion is not necessarily or invariably a good thing. The popular saying that it doesn't matter what a man's religion may be so long as he has one is sheer poppycock. It makes as much sense as would the assertion that it makes no difference what a man's character may be so long as he has one. Insofar as a religion supports exploitation, resists social and moral progress, and engenders more of hostility than of good will among men, it is evil, not good. And it is no less a curse when, in the fashion we have just indicated, it infringes on scientific inquiry or seeks to limit its freedom.

But if much of the blame for the conflict between religion and science is assignable to the former, no slight part must be charged against the latter. Whether in reaction to the tyranny of churchmen or in expression of an intolerance of their own, many scientists have displayed disinterest or impatience with the quest after a religious interpretation of reality, and indeed, in some extreme instances, with all interpretative and evaluative efforts. On either side, the attitude has too frequently been, to paraphrase Job: "We are the people, and all wisdom will die with us."

Fortunately, conflict between the two sides has rarely been total; at no time has it been really necessary; it can be avoided with especial ease these days when so much of religion is liberal and science has been so sobered. All that is required is that either camp recognizes the limitations of its own pursuit and the legitimacy of the other. Let religionists leave to science the enterprise of photographing reality. Let scientists admit that even when their job is finished, another task awaits doing, that of construing and evaluating.

II. THE REASONS FOR RELIGIOUS FAITH

Religion's world outlook centers about God.

Before attempting to indicate what we mean by that word, let us first make clear what we do not mean.

"God" does not denote an old man on a throne somewhere up in the sky. That notion is in part a survival of the infancy of the human race, in part a hangover from our personal childhood, from those days when, having first heard about God and possessing only limited intellectual resources, we pictorialized Him according to our naïveté. However the conception is come by, it is far less innocent than is generally supposed. It impels many a person to regard himself as an atheist, simply because he does not believe that there really is an old man in the heavens. On the other hand, it condemns individuals capable of ripe spirituality to the stuntedness, perhaps lifelong, of puerile, unsatisfying, and undignified convictions.

To believe in God, maturely, intelligently, is to believe that reality did not just "happen," that it is no accident, no pointless interplay of matter and energy. It is to insist rather that things, including man's life, make sense, that they add up to something. It is to hold that the universe, physical and moral, is a cosmos, not an anarchy—made a cosmos instead of an anarchy, meaningful rather than mad, because it is the manifestation of a creating, sustaining, animating, design-lending Spirit, a Mind-will, or to use the oldest, most familiar and best word, a God.

Here at last we come to the crux of our investigation. Are there any reasons for maintaining that the world is of this character rather than that, that Deity rather than Nullity moves behind and through it?

There are such reasons, not one but a number, all good, indeed compelling.

I

God is the only tenable explanation for the universe.

Here we are, creatures of a day, in the midst of a vast, awesome world. Sometimes it strikes us as a big, blooming tumult. But through the seeming confusion some traits persist, constant and all-pervading.

Thus, the universe is *one*, an organic unity, subject everywhere to the same law, knitted together with interdependence.

Again, it is *dynamic*, pulsating with energy, movement, life.

It is *creative*, forever calling new things into being, from stars and solar systems to new breeds of animals, new ideas in the minds of men, new pictures on the artist's canvas.

It is *rational* in the sense that everything in it behaves according to law! Electrons and protons according to the rules of their being, plants in harmony with their nature, animals after the patterns of their respective kinds, and man in consonance with the mandates not only of chemistry, physics, and biology but of psychology and the moral order as well. Everywhere: form, design, predictable recurrence, law.

The universe, furthermore, is *purposive;* at least it is in some of its phases. An insect laying its eggs in a place where the larvae yet to be born will be assured of food as they will require it; a spider weaving its web, a bird building a nest, an engineer designing a bridge, a young man charting his career, a government drawing up a policy, a prophet blueprinting a perfected mankind—all these are instances, rudimentary or advanced, conscious or instinctual, of planning ahead. Purposiveness is indisputably an aspect of reality, and no theory can be said to explain the latter if it does not account for the former as well.

The universe further contains *consciousness*. It has produced man. At least in him it discloses intelligence, a thirst for truth, sensitivity to beauty, a desire for goodness. And man is a component of reality. Whence it follows that no explanation of the entirety can be acceptable if it does not illumine the existence and nature of this most complex, challenging and mysterious of its components.

This then is the world in which we live: one, dynamic, creative, rational, and inclusive of elements of purpose, consciousness, and goodness. For such a universe the religious theory is by far the best "fit." Only *it* accounts at all adequately for the striking features just enumerated. That is why men of all eras, cultures, and capacities, including most of the world's great philosophers, have tended so generally to arrive, no matter what their point of departure, at some kind of God-faith. For, once one begins to reflect on the nature of things, this is the only plausible explanation for them.

But what about the evil of the world? Can the God-idea account for *that?* Not entirely, and not to anyone's complete satisfaction. This fact unquestionably counts against faith. On the other hand, there are many interpretations of evil from the religious viewpoint whereby its existence can be reconciled, partially if not thoroughly, with the existence of God.

But even if evil were a total mystery on which theology could not make so much as a dent, the God-faith would still be indicated. For, at the worst, it leaves less unexplained than does its alternative. If the believer has his troubles with evil, the atheist has more and graver difficulties to contend with. Reality stumps him altogether, leaving him baffled not by one consideration but by many, from the existence of natural law through the instinctual cunning of the insect to the brain of the genius and heart of the prophet.

This then is the intellectual reason for believing in God: that, though this belief is not free from difficulties, it stands out, head and shoulders, as the best answer to the riddle of the universe.

II

The second reason for belief in God is that man cannot live joyously, hopefully, healthily, perhaps not at all, without it.

Consider what the universe and man look like under the assumption of atheism.

Reality appears totally devoid of point or purpose. Like everything else, man is seen as a by-product of a blind machine, his history a goalless eddy in an equally directionless whirlpool, his ideals random sparks thrown off by physiochemical reaction in the colloidal solution, compounded by chance, which is his brain. Everything adds up in the end to exactly nothing.

What is the consequence of such a view for man and society? Can it be other than discouragement, demoralization, despair? What else shall one say of it except that "that way madness lies."

Now consider what face the universe takes on once God is assumed.

Because there is Intelligence behind it, its countenance is now intelligible, not vacant. The things that exist both within and without ourselves cease to be capricious, irrational, and isolated episodes. To the contrary, they are bound together into unity, reasonableness, and pattern by the Mind and Being before which, by virtue of which, they exist.

The spectacle unfolding before our eyes, this awesome pageant which has for its actors stars and atoms, plants, animals, and men, our private worlds of thought and feeling—this is a pageant after all, executing a design, spelling out a message.

What is more, it is a friendly visage which, given God, the universe turns upon us. The suns flaming in space are not altogether alien to us; trees, blades of grass, and beasts are all our kin, near or remote; and we humans, for all our differences and contentions, are brothers one to another by virtue of the Father we share.

As the God-faith transforms the cosmic countenance, so it illumines the darkness within ourselves. It dispels the misgiving lest our strivings serve no purpose, lest our ideals be mere idiosyncrasies, without validity beyond ourselves and hence doomed to extinction with us. Instead, our aspirations come to be seen as refractions of God's purpose, our struggles as elements in the working out of the divine scheme. Before us opens an exit from our human impasse. Frail and short-lived though we be, we can still transcend our limitations by serving God's will, advancing His design and so partaking, by identification, of His infinity and eternity. Finally, the God-faith sends us into the battle for the good in ourselves and society with heightened morale. We know, as we join issue with the forces of evil, that we do not fight alone. In the face of seemingly insuperable odds we can reassure ourselves with the words of the prophet: "Fear not; for they that are with us are more than they that are with them" (II Kings 6:16).

Such are the emotional states distilled respectively by denial of God and by the affirmation of Him. Between them, who can hesitate?

III

Man's moral life requires belief in God.

Under atheism, as we have just seen, all ideals depreciate in value. Regarded as the creations of cosmic chance, if not indeed as the expression of mere human preference, they lose in validity and authority, until, in the end, the reasonableness of their continued observance comes under question. Men begin to ask themselves what logic there may be to devotion and self-sacrifice on behalf of ethical principles and human welfare, if these principles are as rootless and man's career as pointless as the atheist position implies.

That this is the upshot can be seen from Bertrand Russell's *The Free Man's Worship*, one of the noblest and most thoughtful statements of irreligion ever penned. Mr. Russell is a rare atheist; he is a thorough enough logician to follow his premise to its consequences, and is too earnest to prettify them once he has discovered their true character. He grants point blank that from his point of view there is neither basis nor sanction for moral ideals.

These, he concedes, are altogether alien and inappropriate in a blind world machine. Nevertheless, Mr. Russell concludes, he will cling to them. Not that he has any foundation or logic to justify them. He accepts them, as he is frank to admit, arbitrarily, capriciously, in part because, thanks to indoctrination and habit, he has come to love them; in part *zu l'hachis*, as it were, to defy and spite an uncomprehending and soulless universe. All of which is noble, if a bit theatrical, of Mr. Russell. But it is far from constituting an adequate basis for ethics. And it leaves unanswered the question of what Mr. Russell would have to say to persons who insist on logic to their morality and who wait for arguments more convincing than a dramatic gesture before they will be persuaded to dedicate their lives to the classic ethical code.

The very origin of our higher moral aspirations supports the thesis immediately before us, that a close connection exists between them and religion. Ethical conceptions such as the worth of the individual, human brotherhood, the future regeneration of mankind are not self-evident. None of the great, ancient civilizations, not even the Greek or Roman, attained to them. Even in our time acceptance of them is far from universal.

These principles were first formulated by the prophets of Israel, in association with their God-faith and, in part at least, as inferences from it. Not that the prophets first framed their theology and then proceeded systematically to deduce a morality from it. History is never that precisely logical. As a matter of fact, the faith of the prophets and their ideals evolved pretty much side by side, with now one element, now the second, ahead of the other and stimulating it, now both being prodded by social circumstances. But the special theology of the prophets, their doctrine of a God, who is a universal Spirit, just, merciful, holy, was an ever-active agent in the development of the Jewish conception of the good life.

From the theology the morality flows directly, unswervingly, irresistibly. If every person incarnates God, then every person is sacred, too precious to be oppressed or degraded. Because every man embodies the Divine uniquely, he is entitled to an opportunity for the expression of his individuality. Since all men manifest God, they are brothers, owing each other the duties of brotherhood. Since God is good and rational, the present world order, marred by evil and irrationality, cannot be His final work. Some day it must yield to another, more truly reflective of His nature, a perfected society of perfected men, the Kingdom of God.

In other words, the ideals we take for granted are not self-generating. In historical actuality, they came into being in relation to a particular God-faith, in which to find their theoretical justification to this day. Whether they can long endure without it is, as the instance of Bertrand Russell has suggested, profoundly questionable.

Ideals, be it remembered, demand self-sacrifice, and self-sacrifice has to appear justified or it will not be undertaken. A man may give up his comfort or lay down his life for something that seems to him to be worth the cost. But who will do either for what is regarded as of superficial value or of none at all? Yet, in the light of atheism, ideals can be no more than the phosphorescence emitted by physiochemical process within the organic compound which is man. And as for mankind, in the eyes of an irreligionist, it must appear as only a bigger accident than he is. And it is for such as these that a man may reasonably call on himself to suffer and perhaps to die?

But is this fair to atheists? Have not some of them been among the most unselfish and self-forgetting of mortals? And on the other hand, are not many of the most bestial and least idealistic of human beings religionists?

No, what we have just said, had it been said of atheists, would have been grossly unfair. But it does no injustice whatsoever to atheism, the inescapable effects of which are to trivialize ideals, to present the human enterprise as a futility, and so to undermine the classic ethic of justice, mercy, and self-negation on behalf of moral principle and human welfare.

But, if so, how is one to account for the goodness of so many irreligionists? Very simply. Men often behave better than their philosophy. Only they cannot be expected to persist in doing so. In the end, how a man thinks must affect how he acts; atheism must finally, if not in one generation then in several, remake the conduct of atheists in the light of its own logic.

The fact of the matter is that most irreligionists, Bertrand Russell included, are living by the Judeo-Christian morality which follows from Judeo-Christian theism. At the same time, they profess a world outlook which in all its implications denies the code to which they conform. Eventually the contradiction between theory and practice must reveal itself. Then one or the other will give way. Either disbelievers will yield to the pressure of their doctrine and begin to act on its implications, or, refusing to accept the implications, will have to work back to a philosophy which sanctions the morality by which they desire to live, by which alone society can endure.

It is just such a crisis in choice on a mass scale through which mankind seems to be passing right now.

For several centuries irreligion has advanced steadily, all, it seemed, without appreciable effect on human behavior. The bulk of men continued, it appeared, to be about as good or as bad as they had ever been. And then suddenly new moral cults emerged. In ever-increasing numbers, men began openly to deny the worth of the human personality. (They had always acted in denial of this principle, but this was the first time in two thousand years that they repudiated it publicly.) They preached the glorification of violence and conquest. They deprecated justice and mercy. They rejected overtly the notion of the brotherhood of man.

What had been happening, all unobserved, within the human spirit? What, except that having adopted irreligion, men were beginning to be in earnest about its thoroughly unmistakable directives for conduct?

When the props beneath an edifice rot away, it does not fall immediately. The decay is likely to be gradual, and slower in some areas than in others. Again, the building may hold together by inertia and the interweaving of its parts. But ultimately a collapse must come. This, there is reason to believe, is what we are now undergoing: a moral breakdown consequent on the disintegration in modern man of religious faith.

The belief in God then is necessary to morality. For, without it, moral values turn arbitrary, even trivial; self-sacrifice for an ideal becomes irrational; the life of the individual loses all direction except, of course, that of self-interest; society suffers and may in the end be ruined. Only on the faith which gave them birth do ethical values retain their vitality.

Two objections may remain in the reader's mind to the thesis just propounded, that the classic moral code is ultimately dependent on the classic religious outlook.

The first of these is: What is the religious immoralist? What of the man who professes all the correct doctrines and performs all the prescribed rituals, and then behaves like a beast of prey? What of pious tyrants like Francisco Franco, and devout exploiters like Judge Elbert Gary, and religious racialists whose number is too great for telling?

Yes, they exist, men of this ugly stripe. If people are often better than their philosophy, they are, alas, often worse. They may refuse to draw the inferences of their doctrine, or, having drawn them and found them unwelcome, may suppress, pervert, and corrupt them.

The point, however, is that the religious immoralist is acting contrary to his convictions, is either consciously or unconsciously a hypocrite, whereas the irreligious immoralist is thoroughly consistent with his creed.

In other words, a man's world outlook exerts a steady pressure on his conduct. That pressure may be diverted or resisted for a time, perhaps for a long time, but in the end it must make itself felt.

The second question which may be present in the reader's mind is this: Cannot self-interest and fear be relied on to keep men in line, regardless of their philosophies? Suppose it be true that the religious position leads to one pattern of behavior and the irreligious to another, what difference does that fact make when men know that no one can be secure unless everyone behaves himself, when they are aware in addition that society has weapons with which to punish deviations from its codes?

Unquestionably, some respect for law derives from considerations of this sort. Some, but never enough. First, the policeman is not always at hand. Indeed, just when he is most needed, in the hour of social crisis, he is likely not to be on the job at all.

Besides, it would be a sorry morality which is no more nor better than the law requires and the policeman can enforce.

As to the argument from self-interest, let us not be naïve. True, the classic morality is essential to the health and survival of society. But the convinced immoralist knows perfectly well that he can rely on the good citizenship of his fellows. No matter then what his own sins, society will keep on running, dispensing its benefits and securities not only on the righteous, who have earned them, but (so long as he continues to avoid detection) also on a sinner like himself.

To be sure, once enough people begin to play fast and loose with ethical principles, society will suffer. It may even fall apart in the end. But not at once. "*Après moi,*" the immoralist admits, "*le déluge.*" But it will be long after, and by the time it breaks he will long since have shuffled off this mortal coil. Finally, there are some situations in which both fear and self-interest work against morality, when a man will be safe if he violates ethical principle and most certainly in peril if he stands by it, and when the policeman, the state, indeed all organized society are aligned not for but against the right. What becomes then of honesty in the hands of those who urge on its behalf only that it is the best policy?

No, there is no trustworthy basis for the ethical life in either advantage or fright. These factors may co-operate with the angels; they cannot be counted to do so always, or at all adequately. Human virtue admittedly does not rest on one foundation only; it has many props and shorings. Among these, however, the strongest and ultimately the most indispensable is the knowledge that reality is of such a nature as first to commend the good and then to support and sanction it.

IV

Man learns of God from history, from the directions in which it persists in moving.

Look back over the weary way mankind has traveled down the ages. Consider how, though with frequent and heartbreaking retreats and deviations, a line of progress can be drawn from points of departure toward goals—from insensibility toward consciousness and knowledge, from servitude toward freedom, from brutality and ruthlessness toward compassion and conscience.

Is such a movement, so insistent and cumulative, likely to be no more than a chance eddy in a reasonless flow? Or is it more probably the consequence of a great propulsion working through man and driving him?

Or consider the pattern of human affairs: how falsehood, having no legs, cannot stand; how evil tends to destroy itself; how every tyranny has eventually invoked its own doom. Now set against this the staying power of truth and righteousness. Could the contrast be so sharp unless something in the scheme of things discouraged evil and favored the good?

If all history bespeaks God, that of Israel testifies to Him with especial eloquence and clarity. For this is the people which first discerned His true nature, earliest identified itself with Him, and has longest sought to do His will.

And Israel is alive this day.

The nations it knew in its youth and first maturity are memories. Not so this people. Consigned to an iron destiny, armed against it only with faith, it has survived the ages and their rigors. What is more, its influence has with extraordinary consistency been exerted on behalf of justice, compassion, freedom, and truth. And it has been creative far beyond its size and opportunities.

Jewish history demonstrates that the God-faith is life-giving, humanizing.

But it is likely that a belief will evoke such echoes from reality unless it is in tune with it?

V

Among all peoples and in all times some men have made the claim of contact with God, insisting that in an intuition transcending sensation or thought they have had firsthand experience of Him. The Prophets of Scripture brought such testimony, as did a variety of others; among Jews, numerous rabbis of the Talmudic era, Kabbalists, and Hasidim; in the classical pagan world, Plato, Aristotle, and Plotinus; among Christians, Augustine, the two Theresas, and Jacob Boehme; and in the East a great company of Brahmans, Taoists, and Moslems.

Now, these men and women, who are the world's mystics, have been of the most widely diverse backgrounds and temperaments. Yet, despite the many differences among them, they all report having undergone substantially the same spiritual episodes: an awareness, derived not from the senses or the mind but from some faculty beyond them, of the immediate presence of Ultimate Reality, a conviction of its goodness, so potent as to fill the soul with a feeling of illumination, purity, and redemption. It is on such spiritual events, personally undergone, that mystics rest their doctrines concerning God, His nature, and the good.

In the development of Judaism specifically, the role of mystics, though far from decisive, has been larger than is generally perceived. They had a hand in the making of the prophetic faith and morality. From time to time, they have rekindled the Jewish religion with their own fervor into incandescence. They are responsible for no slight part of its dynamism to this day.

Most of us, however, have never met with mystical adventures. What the mystic relates comes to us at second hand, on the word of someone else. We would be well advised therefore to credit it, if at all, with reservations.

Yet, even for incorrigible nonmystics, mystical evidences should carry some weight—about that which one would allow to some stubborn, widely diffused, and self-consistent rumor. Being hearsay and hence inadmissible as formal testimony, no case may be built on it. Yet a reasonable person will reckon with it in his calculations. And if the judgment arrived at on other grounds happens to account for this also— so much the better, both for the judgment and it.

III. THE NATURE OF RELIGIOUS FAITH

I

In the foregoing discussion the logic of the theistic position has been presented. The nature of the world, the course of history and, for the mystic at least, the evidences of mysticism argue for God. The needs of human morale and morality make the God-faith desirable, even pragmatically necessary. But "argue for," "desirable," "pragmatically necessary" are not *proof*. And it is not proof which men want?

If the reader is asking for an indisputable case for God's existence, he will not find it here. Neither theism nor atheism is susceptible to final and unquestionable demonstration.

But then, nothing is. There is not a single proposition of any sort which can be established beyond challenge. The intellect never leads to absolute certainty.

From modern philosophy we have learned that the reality of the physical world cannot be verified, nor, if it exists, that it conforms to our notions of it. The deductive sciences—logic and mathematics, for instance—begin with axioms and postulates, so that any conclusions they reach are contingent ultimately on assumptions. That is why Euclid's geometry is no "truer" than any of the non-Euclidian systems, since all alike begin with intellectual "acts of faith."

And as for the physical sciences, from physics to sociology, these are of hypothesis all compact. They posit the knowability of nature, its uniformity, and innumerable more limited postulates. They take for granted concepts such as causality, matter, energy, time and space, ideas which are shot through with unresolved enigmas. And then, after all these assumptions, the empirical sciences achieve at best, as the scientist will be the first to admit, not certainty, but probability, more or less high.

In a word, intellectual finality exists nowhere, not even in the most exact of sciences. Nothing can be so proved as to be beyond dispute.

What then remains for men? They must do as best they can with what they have. Whether they be ordinary folk trying to make up their minds about some simple issue, or scientists weighing alternative theories, or all of us hesitating between religion and irreligion, they cannot do other than look at the various possibilities, select the best, and take that for the truth.

Such is the procedure of the scientist. Knowing that no absolute demonstration is attainable, he does not waste himself trying to achieve one. Instead he frames a *hypothesis*. That is to say, he studies his facts, considers the theories which apply, and posits as true the one which covers the facts best, works out best, and is the simplest.

Which, in a different field, is exactly what we have done. Confronted by a choice between the theistic and atheistic views, we have adopted the former.

It fits better.

It works better, both for morale and morality.

It is simplest; with one concept it unifies reality and makes it intelligible.

Or, to restate the point in formal, philosophical language: Religious faith is a hypothesis interpreting reality and posited on the same grounds as any valid hypothesis, viz., superior congruity with the facts, greater practicality, and maximal conceptual economy.

Does this sound awesome and far removed from religion as we know it? Let us not be dismayed. All we are doing is to put into technical terms what all religionists have always said: that religion is in the end a matter of faith, and that that faith, far from being blind, arbitrary, or merely wishful, is indicated by compelling reasons, intellectual, practical, emotional.

This is not to say that theology is intellectually as exact or certain as is science, even if both are arrived at by the same general common sense.

(For that matter a scientific theory in turn is less sure than the sense data it is devised to account for.) The hazards increase as one mounts upward in the edifice of the intellect, for at any level there will be present the risks of error implicit in that level plus all those in the levels below. The higher one climbs, the further he may fall. But then the view is almost certain to be better, the climate more healthful, and directions more clearly discernible.

The possibility remains however—and every religious person must face up to it—that, despite the preponderance of evidence in its favor, the theistic conclusion may be mistaken. One takes a chance with God. But, if so, it is a chance that has to be taken for the sake of head, heart, life itself.

Besides, who ever said that religion was something tame or safe? To the contrary, it is the greatest adventure of the human spirit, the boldest leap the soul can make; it is a man betting his life, with the evidences in his favor to be sure, but still betting his life, that things—the universe, ideals, the very life he is wagering—make sense and good sense to boot.

II

But if there is an admitted risk to faith, what about solidity of convictions? Is the religious person condemned to an everlasting tentativeness about what he believes?

Not at all. Firmness of opinion is attainable. Not on the basis of logic unaided, since, as we have already seen, argument is never definitive. But confidence fortunately comes from the heart rather than the head; it is an emotion rather than a proposition. It can be induced.

First, a man must purify his belief of logical and factual impossibilities, making it the most plausible belief available to him. For, if constancy in conviction is not to be fashioned in the intellect alone, it most certainly cannot be won, at least not by thinking moderns, without it, let alone in opposition to it.

Next, he must make up his mind. He commits himself, saying: "In view of the evidences and my needs, this is the position I adopt."

Then he lives by his decision. Only as he lives by it is sureness distilled within him. The view he has accepted becomes habitual with him; it is imprinted ever deeper on his consciousness by familiarity and, more effectively, by the cumulative evidences of its adequacy and value—until, in the end, though he can envisage other possibilities and though, as is inevitable, his moods go up and down, this emerges as the only position for him.

Acquiring faith, in other words, is only in part like proving a proposition in geometry. Equally, perhaps more, it is like falling in love. First the mind must assent; the fervor, however, wells from the heart, and the certainty, whether in marriage or religion, is the final upshot of the mind's assent, the heart's fervor, all confirmed and deepened to immovability by the testimony of the years.

III

The Jewish tradition makes no attempt to enforce a particular conception of God. Within Judaism, God has been envisaged as a Mind apart from and contemplating the world; or as a Spirit within it, as both, or in any number of other guises. In this respect, each Jew is left to his own needs and preferences.

And yet the reader who has followed our argument to this point may, especially if he be a stranger to religious speculation, lack the materials and skill to fashion a God-conception for himself. Conceivably, it would be helpful to him were some typical God-idea to be put before him, if only as an object of study. To this purpose, let me submit the particular envisagement I know best and most intimately, my own.

To me, whatever *is* is the outer shell of a Spirit. That spirit is the essence and ground of all things, sustaining and animating them, yet not exhausted by their totality.

Very often, I think of the world in relation to God in a parable. I imagine a mighty river with currents, waves, ripples, bubbles. Each current, wave, ripple, bubble, I recognize, has an independent existence. Yet each is but part of the stream and carried along by it in its course. What is more, there is more to the river, depths below depths, than is visible to my eyes.

As are the waves, ripples, bubbles to the river, so all things stand vis-à-vis God. Each has its individual identity. Yet each is but a manifestation of Him, pervaded by Him, existing only by virtue of Him, moving with His purposes. Touch anything and you may say: He is here. Yet add all things together and you will not have Him, for He is more than the world.

When I describe God as Spirit, I mean that He is not only a Power but a "Mind." His nature, in other words, is akin to our own. He is rational, which is why the universe is law-abiding. He is conscious with a consciousness like, though infinitely greater than, ours. Indeed He is the source of human consciousness, our private minds being individualizations of Him, sparks as it were of His fire.

When I speak of God as Spirit, I mean further that He is purposive. Whatever the case elsewhere in space, on our planet He has worked through inorganic nature to the plant, thence to the animal, thence to man, through whom He is now driving toward every increasing freedom, justice, and mercy, or, to use a good old theological phrase, toward the Kingdom of Heaven.

And man, how do I picture his role in this design? Man, I believe with the ancient rabbis, is a "partner with the Holy One, blessed be He," laboring with the God he incarnates toward ever increasing truth and goodness, toward, in sum, the realization of the cosmic design.

Of my specimen God-idea it should be observed that, without violating in the least the scientific description of the world, it yet satisfies all the needs for which a God-faith is posited to begin with. It accounts for the universe in its most challenging traits: the unity, dynamism, rationality, purposiveness, and consciousness in things; it invigorates human morale; it projects and supports morality; it makes the movement of history intelligible; it provides a possible explanation for the mystical experience; it gives hope and direction to life.

Yet this, be it recalled, is not an authoritative or even a recommended envisagement. It is presented only as a specimen to be considered, dissected, learned from, improved upon.

Judaism has never looked sympathetically on the notion that one man can save another's soul. It has no doctrine of vicarious salvation. What is true of man's moral pilgrimage is equally true of his intellectual guest. A man may assist his fellows, but no one can find God or fashion a conception of Him for anyone else. Each man in this respect must redeem himself. He must venture the peril and heartbreak but also the glory and deliverance of finding God in his own way, after his own spirit.

IV

This discussion of the common-sense foundations of religious belief would not be complete without reference to one additional reason for faith, relevant only to Jews. I refer to the fact that with faith a Jew is thoroughly at home in his Jewishness, without it always something of a stranger.

The Jew without religious belief, whether he is without it because he has simply neglected to cultivate it or because he is honestly incapable of it, is in a sorry case—as a human being, in the first instance, but more specifically as a Jew. He will read and revere Scripture but disavow its key thesis. He may observe rituals but be out of harmony with their point. He is unfortunate. Yet, given his intellectual constitution and the requirements of integrity, he may have no choice save to accept his disabilities and get along with them as best he can.

But for the Jew capable of belief, Jewishness supplies an additional and final argument on its behalf. The act of faith completed, he is thereafter and forever basically at peace, not only with God but also with Israel and Torah.